Hi, I'm China

Institute for Planets
The China Society on Tibetan Plateau

China Pictorial Press · Beijing

图书在版编目（CIP）数据

这里是中国：英文 / 星球研究所，中国青藏高原研究会著 . — 北京：中国画报出版社，2025.9
ISBN 978-7-5146-2126-6

Ⅰ . ①这… Ⅱ . ①星…②中… Ⅲ . ①地理 – 中国 – 普及读物 – 英文 Ⅳ . ① K92-49

中国版本图书馆 CIP 数据核字 (2022) 第 113666 号

审图号：GS 京〔2022〕188 号

这里是中国（英文）
Hi, I'm China

星球研究所　中国青藏高原研究会　著

出 版 人：方允仲
责任编辑：刘晓雪
助理编辑：牛语晨
特约编辑：李　穆　鄢林敢　王　岚　杨舒钠
英文编辑：王子木　牛语晨
英文翻译：付一鸣
英文润色：〔英〕詹妮弗·陈
英文审稿：刘海乐
英文定稿：王国振
英文专业词汇审定：韩昭庆
封面设计：王建东　吕丽梅
内文排版：吕丽梅　郭廷欢
责任印制：焦　洋
出版发行：中国画报出版社　中信出版集团
地　　址：中国北京市海淀区车公庄西路33号　邮编：100048
发 行 部：010-88417418 010-68414683（传真）
总编室兼传真：010-88417359　版权部：010-88417359
开　　本：16开（787mm×1092mm）
印　　张：37.5
字　　数：450千字
版　　次：2025年9月第1版　2025年9月第1次印刷
印　　刷：北京汇瑞嘉合文化发展有限公司
书　　号：ISBN 978-7-5146-2126-6
定　　价：298.00元

**Rediscover
the
Beauty
of
China's
Geography**

Special thanks to

All the photographers who contributed their great works to this book!

What Is China?
523

References
570

Glossary in *Pinyin* and English
585

Foreword
China Needs the Popularization of Quality Geographical Sciences

As a geographical researcher, I eagerly anticipate works that seek to popularize the geographical sciences, but at the same time I hold these works to very exacting standards. In this context, the release of the book *Hi, I'm China* is unquestionably gratifying.

Hi, I'm China was co-authored by the Institute for Planets, an organization that promotes the popularization of geographical sciences, and the research team who took part in China's second scientific expedition to Qingzang Gaoyuan (Qinghai-Xizang Plateau). This is the first popular science book jointly produced by both organizations. The first chapter of the book, "Where Does China Come From?" is a direct outcome of this collaboration.

Since 1949, the Chinese Academy of Sciences (CAS) has been committed to the exploration and research on Qingzang Gaoyuan. Back in the 1970s, the CAS established a scientific expedition team to Qingzang Gaoyuan, initiating the first comprehensive scientific survey of the plateau. In fact, I was lucky enough to participate in this program as a student. The first scientific expedition lasted for over 20 years. Through the efforts of this program, we established a systematic understanding of Qingzang Gaoyuan. On August 19, 2017, the second scientific expedition to Qingzang Gaoyuan was launched as a national strategic mission.

In 2018, on the first anniversary of the launch of the second scientific expedition, a report was prepared to highlight the achievements of the first phase of this second scientific expedition. The cooperation with the Institute for Planets led to the publication of the article entitled *Where Does China Come From?* which was an effort to popularize the field of geographical science. The article not only summarizes how the emergence of Qingzang Gaoyuan, due to continental plate collisions, influenced on China's geography, but also expands on the chain reaction that resulted from the Qingzang Gaoyuan uplift. As soon as the article was published online, it went viral on various social media platforms including WeChat Moments. After reading the article, many people began to realize the importance of the Qingzang Gaoyuan in Chinese geography.

It is fascinating to explore China from a geographical perspective. The vast land of China is dotted with a great diversity of landscapes with many types of landforms including glaciers, lakes, rivers, oceans, loess, and karst. In addition, an extensive range of human activity has helped to form China's landscape and soil. Different groups of people have lived and procreated on this land over a multitude of historical periods, leading to the eventual emergence of the Chinese civilization. All of these elements are part of today's China. Excellent work to popularize geographical sciences helps to strengthen and put in perspective the Chinese people's love and pride for the physical land of their country—its beautiful rivers, mountains and terrain. Furthermore, such work helps more people to understand the interaction between the environment and mankind and it arouses their sense of responsibility for contemporary and future generations. This is a meaningful and valuable undertaking.

As a popular science work, this book is based on theoretical scientific knowledge and empirical facts. Authors of such a work are required to read scientific research publications extensively. They then draw upon their own experience and incorporate relevant evidence from a wealth of academic sources, which they then condense and simplify to facilitate the general reader's understanding. Such a work can only pass the test of time and become valuable if the underlying work is solid.

Moreover, the popularization of scientific knowledge is not simply a matter of enumerating or transferring scientific knowledge. It needs to be in touch with the daily life of the people, and it requires creativity to impart this knowledge in an interesting manner. Otherwise, the popularization of scientific knowledge will devolve into science news or merely old-fashioned lecturing, making the scientific knowledge inaccessible to a general readership.

The Institute for Planets has an excellent popularization of scientific knowledge team. Each article they write takes from about twenty days to one or two months to finish, ensuring each article is thoroughly prepared and well-polished. It is commendable that the works of popular science are prepared to the same rigorous standards as academic writings. Therefore, the Research Team of China's Second Scientific Expedition on Qingzang Gaoyuan began collaborating with the Institute for Planets right from its inception.

The popularization of geographical science is both a science and an art. Here, the meaning of art is twofold:

Firstly, geography has an intrinsic aesthetic nature. The beauty of the environment and the surrounding landscapes call for careful and close observation. General readers are often first attracted by beautiful images and photos. They then become eager to visit the places captured in the photos or even develop a desire to learn about the formation of the beautiful scenery they see in the pictures. The Institute for Planets has unquestionably excelled in this regard, producing articles accompanied by a wealth of beautiful photos and maps. This effectively captures the reader's attention, and they then follow the team's work and develop an interest in reading the scientific articles produced.

Secondly, there is an imaginative perspective. "Science is not a heartless pursuit of objective information," said American paleontologist Stephen Jay Gould. "It... is a creative human activity, its geniuses acting more as artists than as information processors...." Whether it be science or popular science, both endeavors require a rich imagination equal to that of an artist. This requires making connections between old and new ideas, as well as integrating different disciplines. Only in this way can we brainstorm ideas and produce works that are interesting and eventually attractive for a large readership. In this regard, the Institute for Planets is undoubtedly a leading light in terms of popularizing geographical science in China. Its articles generally feature information from multiple disciplines, and they are coherently linked, a task which obviously requires some imagination. Furthermore, effective use is made of devices like metaphors or schematic diagrams to make clear esoteric ideas or theories for a general readership.

Of course, there are certain requirements for effective writing of a book about geographical science for a general audience. This is especially true when it comes to the scientific understanding of China's geography. Because China was relatively late to the field of science popularization, it lacks truly effective vehicles to spread science to the general public. We need authors of popular science who have a professional background and knowledge of the humanities and mass media. We must keep up our creative efforts. All sorts of problems are bound to appear in the pursuit of this process, but ideals are what drive and motivate us to continue on our quest.

The efforts to popularize science and scientific research require collaboration that can produce wonderful work, especially in the field of geographical science. *Hi, I'm China* is a good example of that endeavour. It is my sincere hope that more and better works that can effectively popularize the worlds of science and geography will be created so that more people can learn about and become even more fascinated by China and its geography.

Yao Tandong

Member of the Chinese Academy of Sciences
Chairman of the China Society on Tibetan Plateau
Chief Scientist of the Second Tibetan Plateau Scientific Expedition and Research

August 7, 2019

Foreword
An Achievable Ideal

I have a dream that:

> *One day, I will travel to all the snow mountains of China.*
> *One day, I will travel to all the rivers of China.*
> *One day, I will travel to all the cities of China.*
> *...*

I don't just want to see them; I want to learn about them. I want to put everything I witness into words so that more people may fall in love with all of China's most beautiful places. When I tell others about my dream, many say that it's impossible to achieve considering China's vastness.

Indeed, China is truly vast, but isn't it also true that anything, regardless of how large and complex, is comprised of countless smaller pieces? Isn't China, as vast as it is, comprised of different smaller areas?

Geography offers us an excellent perspective on such questions.

In terms of China's landform types, mountains account for 33%, plateaus 26%, basins 19%, hills 10%, and plains 12%.

In terms of administrative divisions, the country is divided into 38,602 township-level administrative zones, divided out between 2,843 county-level administrative regions which are nested in 333 prefectural-level administrative regions. Finally, all these smaller units are housed within 34 provincial-level administrative regions.[1]

---

1 Source: "Statistical Table of Administrative Divisions of the People's Republic of China (as of December 31, 2022)" issued by the Ministry of Civil Affairs.

In terms of land use, forests account for 253 million hectares, grasslands 219 million hectares, and arable land 133 million hectares. The land occupied by cities, villages, factories and mining encompasses 31 million hectares in total. Added to that are the 3.66 million hectares of land used for transportation. Of the 3.66 million hectares of land can be found 130,000 kilometers of railways, 4.84 million kilometers of highways, and one million bridges and so on.[2]

My journey may not take me to every corner of China, but I can learn about all aspects of the country through study of its distinct geographical units. I simply need to analyze the geographical units one by one as I write my articles. Of course, it is impossible for me to complete this grand project alone in my lifetime. Thus, a group of explorers has set out to try to fulfill this dream together.

In this way, this lofty dream has become a shared mission.

Guided by this ideal, our aim is not to hastily prepare articles that cater to the moment. Rather, we seek something more profound. Our aim is to produce excellent works that are systematically prepared and inherently valuable. These are the types of articles that stand the test of time. Our tireless work will continue as we explore day and night, imparting our knowledge of China to more people and conveying the power and wonder of exploration.

Ultimately, these efforts will result in an encyclopedia of Chinese geography. It is a massive undertaking, but one that gives us incalculable joy.

Now, we finally present to you *Hi, I'm China*, a book project that represents the preliminary fruits of this encyclopedic effort which has taken three years to compile. It is an aggregate of the essence of the China-

---

2 The above data are from the National Bureau of Statistics, New Edition of Chinese Physical Geography, and the 2016 China Bulletin on Land Resources.

themed articles produced by the Institute for Planets.

In terms of chapter arrangement, the book is divided according to the three-step topography of China.

The book has a three-tiered division which reflects the Three-Level Terrain Ladder that forms the general pattern of Chinese topography. It also reflects the gradual shift from wilderness to metropolis as the book progresses from the First to the Third Terrain Ladder. We hope that this structure allows readers to experience the interaction between the Chinese people and the land of China.

In order to provide the best reading experience possible, our cartographers and designers have spent over 1,000 hours creating maps for each article. This process included painstaking selection, optimization, and finalizing of all photographic works. The effort involved photographers working tirelessly to select photos and sometimes even making special trips to take new photos. The book presents 365 images produced by 191 photographers.

It must be stated clearly that this book is but a first step. It serves as a prelude for us to "read China in its entirety." Although it does not cover every single mountain, river, or region in China, this book does provide an overview of an ambitious program with a vast scope, and we hope it builds anticipation for future works. As it is our first book, it will inevitably contain more than a few flaws. Therefore, readers' criticisms and suggestions will be greatly appreciated. We will improve the text in subsequent versions.

In conclusion, I hope that one day we can learn about all aspects of China and make this impossible ideal a reality. Here, "we" means all of us, including you, our dear readers.

Geng Huajun

Director of the Institute for Planets

July 15, 2019

^ The topography of China and its surrounding regions/Photo by 123RF

Where Does China Come From?

Where does China come from?
Where is China going?

These questions could be answered through a whole range of perspectives, but the geological perspective is perhaps the most unique.

Similar to the origin of the universe itself—the Big Bang—the current geographical pattern of China is largely the result of a major plate collision.

This collision created Qingzang Gaoyuan (Qinghai-Xizang Plateau), the highest and youngest plateau on Earth today, and it has affected and will continue to affect the landforms, climate, water systems and life in China for countless generations.

As a human being, "Where do I come from?" and "Where am I going?" are the questions most of us are intensely curious about.

As a Chinese person, "Where does China come from?" and "Where is China going?" are questions that fascinate me.

Light can be thrown on these questions if we approach them from a number of different viewpoints. Geologists arguably can provide one of the most extraordinary responses because they view the question from a planetary perspective. The answer to the question of origin does not lie in affluent metropolises that dominate China's economy but in Qingzang Gaoyuan, a frigid upland that is one of the most unique geographical features on this planet.

Our current understanding of Qingzang Gaoyuan only began to form around 40 years ago. At that time, China was embroiled in the anarchy caused by the "cultural revolution" (1966-1976). A group of scientists armed with modest equipment traveled to Qingzang Gaoyuan to carry out China's first comprehensive scientific expedition to the plateau. This ambitious mission involved trekking to every part of the plateau including its most remote, extreme corners.

The Second Scientific Expedition on Qingzang Gaoyuan was launched as a national strategic mission in 2017, more than 40 years after the initial expedition. Thousands of scientific researchers have participated in this research, which is a project that is scheduled to last more than 10 years. This is one of the most prestigious initiatives undertaken in the geoscience community anywhere in the world.

Thanks to the scientific research like this, we can formulate answers to questions like "Where does China come from?" and "Where is China going?"

What sorts of answers will we find?

> **The topographic map of Qingzang Gaoyuan**

Qingzang Gaoyuan, which has an average altitude of over 4,000 meters, is the highest plateau in the world and is hailed as the "Roof of the World." It stretches from the Pamirs in the west, to Hengduan Shan (Hengduan Mountains) in the east, the southern edge of the Himalayas in the south, and to the north side of Kunlun Shan (Kunlun Mountains)-Altun Shan (Altun Mountains)-Qilian Shan (Qilian Mountains) in the north. It is approximately 3,000 kilometers wide from east to west and 300-1,500 kilometers from north to south, most of which is located in China. The specific range used in this map is based on research by Zhang Guoqing et al. (2015).

1 Massive Collision

The current geographical features of China are closely associated with a massive plate collision—like the Big Bang which is regarded as the origin of the universe. About 65 million years ago[1], the Indian Plate col-

^ The Himalayas/Photo by Shang Rui

Qowowuyag Feng
(Cho Qyu)
8,201m

lided with the Eurasian Plate at relatively fast speed, causing a massive impact, resulting a super-large scale surface uplift, which has been lasting to nowadays. Thus, Qingzang Gaoyuan, the tallest and youngest plateau on Earth today, was born. Qingzang Gaoyuan has an average elevation of over 4,000 meters, and the thickness of the crust underneath can reach up to 80 kilometers. Because of its peculiar environment and massive amounts of glacial ice, it is also called the "third pole," in addition to the south and north poles of Earth.

Chogori Feng
(Chogori Peak)
8,611m

1 The experts are still debating the question of when the Indian Plate and the Eurasian Plate collided. Our book uses the view of Academician Ding Lin of the Chinese Academy of Sciences.

⌄ Karakorum Shan (Karakoram Range)/Photo by Wen Junhao

North slope of Qomolangma Feng/Photo by Li Jian

Yunnan Red-Earth Fairyland/Photo by Yong Zhou
Located on Yunnan-Guizhou Gaoyuan (Yunnan-Guizhou Plateau), Yunnan Red-earth Fairyland is on the second terrain ladder of China.

Namjagbarwa Feng (Nanga Bawa Peak)/Photo by Zhang Qiang
Located at the eastern tip of the Himalayas, Namjagbarwa Feng belongs to the First Terrain Ladder.

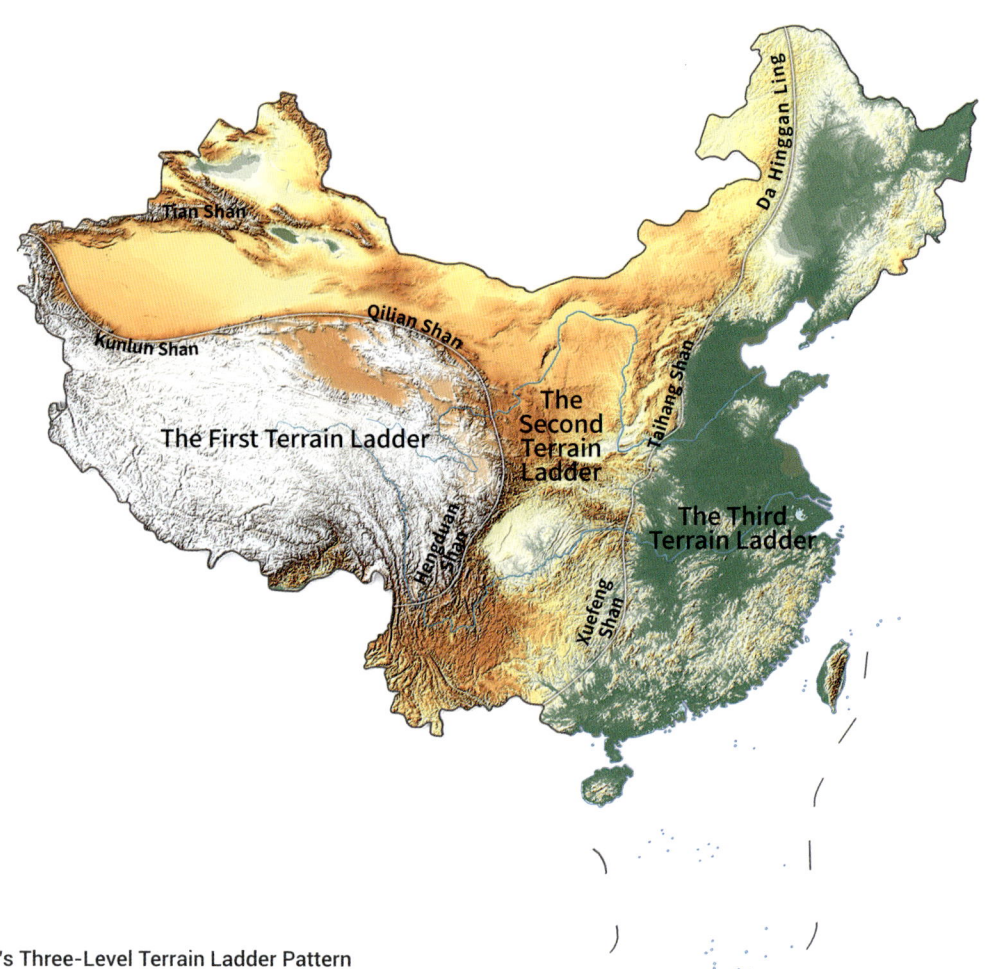

^ China's Three-Level Terrain Ladder Pattern

v Huabei Pingyuan (North China Plain)/Photo by Chen Junjie
Huabei Pingyuan belongs to the Third Terrain Ladder.

Numerous gigantic mountains on Qingzang Gaoyuan rose one after another, due to the surface uplift. The Himalayas and Kunlun Shan (Kunlun Mountains)-Altun Shan (Altun Mountains)-Qilian Shan (Qilian Mountains) are located in the south and north, respectively; Gangdisê Shan (Kailas Range), Nyainqêntanglha Shan (Nianchingtanggula Mountains), and Tanggula (Dangla) Shan (Tanggula Mountains) are situated in the hinterland; the Hendu Kosh-Karakorum Shan (Karakoram Mountains), and Hengduan Shan (Hengduan Mountains) are situated in the west and east. The land is home to 14 peaks that reach more than 8,000 meters in height, as well as many peaks that are over 7,000 meters in elevation. In addition, there are countless peaks between 5,000 to 6,000 meters tall. Therefore, this massive collision can easily be regarded as the most critical orogenic event in the past 200 million years.

Qomolangma Feng (Mount Qomolangma), towering 8,848.86 meters above sea level, is the world's highest peak. Qogir Feng (Chogori Peak), at an elevation of 8,611 meters, is the world's second-highest peak. Shisha Pangma, the world's 14th highest mountain at 8,027 meters above sea level, is entirely located within the borders of China. Other famous towering mountains form the pillars in western China, including Namjagbarwa Feng (Namche Barwa Peak) in Nyingchi, Xizang; Kangrinboqê Feng (Mount Kailash) in Ngari, Xizang; Moirig Xueshan (the Kawagarbo) in Yunnan; Muztagata Shan (Muztagh Ata) in Xinjiang; Konggar Shan (Mount Gongga) in Garzê, Sichuan; and Yangmaiyong Shan (Mount Yangmaiyong) in Yading Scenic Area, Daocheng County, Sichuan.

However, the massive collision has not finished releasing its mighty force. The great collision that gave birth to Qingzang Gaoyuan diffused its force into the surrounding regions. Other high-altitude places were also squeezed and uplifted, including Huangtu Gaoyuan (Loess Plateau), Yunnan-Guizhou Gaoyuan (Yunnan-Guizhou Plateau), and Nei Mongol Gaoyuan (Inner Mongolia Plateau).

All of China's four major plateaus were greatly affected by the massive collision. A prominent three-level terrain ladder emerged, forming the landscape of China as a result. Qingzang Gaoyuan has the highest altitude, making it the First Terrain Ladder. Nei Mongol Gaoyuan, Huangtu Gaoyuan and Yunnan-Guizhou Gaoyuan, each with an altitude of 1,000 to 2,000 meters, constitute the Second Terrain Ladder; the regions east of Da Hinggan Ling (the Greater Hinggan Mountains), Taihang Shan (the Taihang Mountains) and Xuefeng Shan (the Xuefeng Mountains) are generally below 500 meters above sea level and belong to the Third Terrain Ladder. The geographical pattern of China has thus been formed.

The differences in the three terrain ladders add great diversity to China's geomorphologic landscape. Countless gorgeous mountains and rivers have been formed on these three terrain ladders. One could argue that without the massive collision forming China's landscape, China would be very different from its present appearance. Especially as it would lack the diversified geomorphologic landscapes caused by the differences in the three terrain ladders.

However, the impact of the massive collision on China goes beyond geomorphology. Scientists have discovered that a super "fan" has emerged over Qingzang Gaoyuan as the greatest product of this massive collision. The presence of this "fan" could eventually disrupt the planetary wind system[1] that is predominant in China.

---

1 A planetary system of winds, also known as a planetary wind belt, is a general term for the prevailing wind belts on a global scale without considering adjustments for terrain, including land and sea.

2 The Plateau "Air Fan"

If the existing terrain was not a factor, the atmospheric winds close to the surface of the earth would flow in a regular pattern. This is the planetary wind system.

In the subtropical zone near latitude 30° north, air currents controlled by the planetary wind system constantly sink from a high altitude down to the ground. As the temperature increases, water vapor is less likely to condense, making it difficult for rainfall to form. As a result, a vast arid zone appears near latitude 30° north, extending from North Africa to West Asia. Without some sort of anomaly interfering with this pattern, southern China, which is also located near latitude 30° north, would be much drier than it actually is.

But an "anomaly" did interfere. Qingzang Gaoyuan, with an average altitude of over 4,000 meters, is subject to more solar radiation than the surrounding plains. In summer, the solar energy absorbed by the surface of the plateau heats the air above the ground. It is equivalent to putting a gigantic solar-powered electric blanket in the atmosphere 4,000 meters above sea level. As the atmosphere gets warmer, the air pressure on the ground decreases, and the plateau "sucks" in the surrounding air for replenishment. This leads to a huge "exhaust fan." As a result, the South Asian monsoon and the East Asian monsoon are strongly enhanced by the "sucking effect" of Qingzang Gaoyuan, and can go deep into the Eurasian Continent.

The South Asian monsoon roars northwards from the Indian Ocean, and a great deal of moisture carried by the monsoon permeates the mountains. The air current enters from canyons to form turbulent water vapor channels or gathers at the southern edge of the Himalayas to form heavy rainfall. Mêdog, Zayü and other places in southern Xizang therefore enjoy abundant rainfall.

The East Asian monsoon, which originates in the Pacific Ocean, is greatly increased in strength. It reaches the hinterland of China from the ocean to completely transform the impact of the planetary wind system in southern China. The abundant water vapor dispels the typical drought conditions found at the latitude 30° north, giving a rise to a region with frequent rainfalls—the Jiangnan region. These anomalies would have not existed without the huge "exhaust fan" of Qingzang Gaoyuan.

However, nature always seeks to create balance. After creating a rainy Jiangnan region, Qingzang Gaoyuan blocks the northward advance of water vapor from the Indian Ocean. The dry inland areas of northwestern China became even more arid, where deserts have emerged on a large scale.

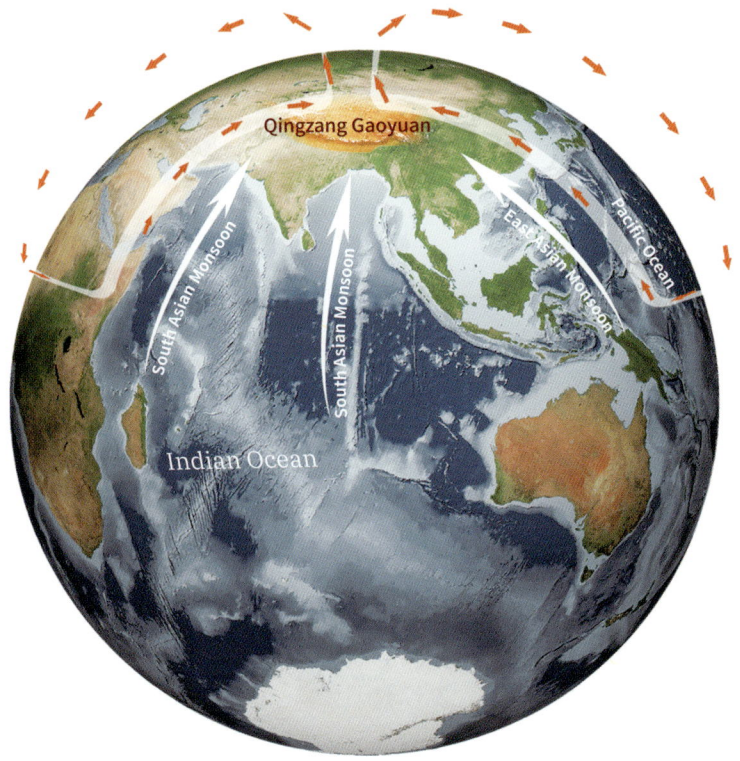

^ The influence of Qingzang Gaoyuan on the Asian Monsoon

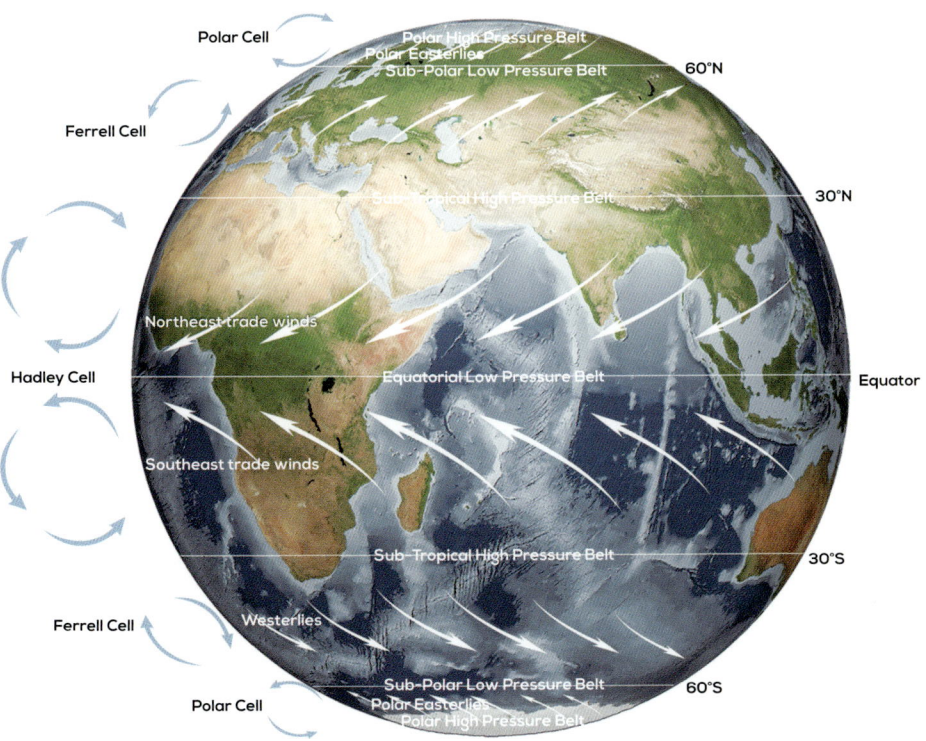

^ Planetary wind system

Moreover, the violent westerly winter wind was also blocked by Qingzang Gaoyuan, causing it to veer off course. It stirred up the sand and dust in the northwest desert and advanced eastwards along the northern edge of Qingzang Gaoyuan. Dust particles settled in the region to the west of Taihang Shan and to the north of Qin Ling (Qinling Mountains), forming Huangtu Gaoyuan, which is up to 400 meters thick.

These shifts all resulted in the rainy Jiangnan region, vast arid deserts in northwest China, and Qingzang Gaoyuan with an alpine climate. China has thus seen the formation of three major natural regions: the Eastern Monsoon Region, the Northwestern Arid and Semi-arid Region, and the Qingzang Alpine Region.

The plateau's "exhaust fan" has reshaped China's climate. Moreover, a "super water tower" has formed on the plateau, changing China's river system.

‹ A sea of clouds in southeast Xizang/Photo by Li Heng

⌵ Dinghu Feng (Dinghu Peak), Zhejiang/Photo by Ma Yuhan
This photo was taken at the Xiandu Scenic Area, Jinyun County, Zhejiang. Dinghu Feng is situated in southeastern China, which has a humid climate. The mountains are shrouded in mist due to the abundant water vapor.

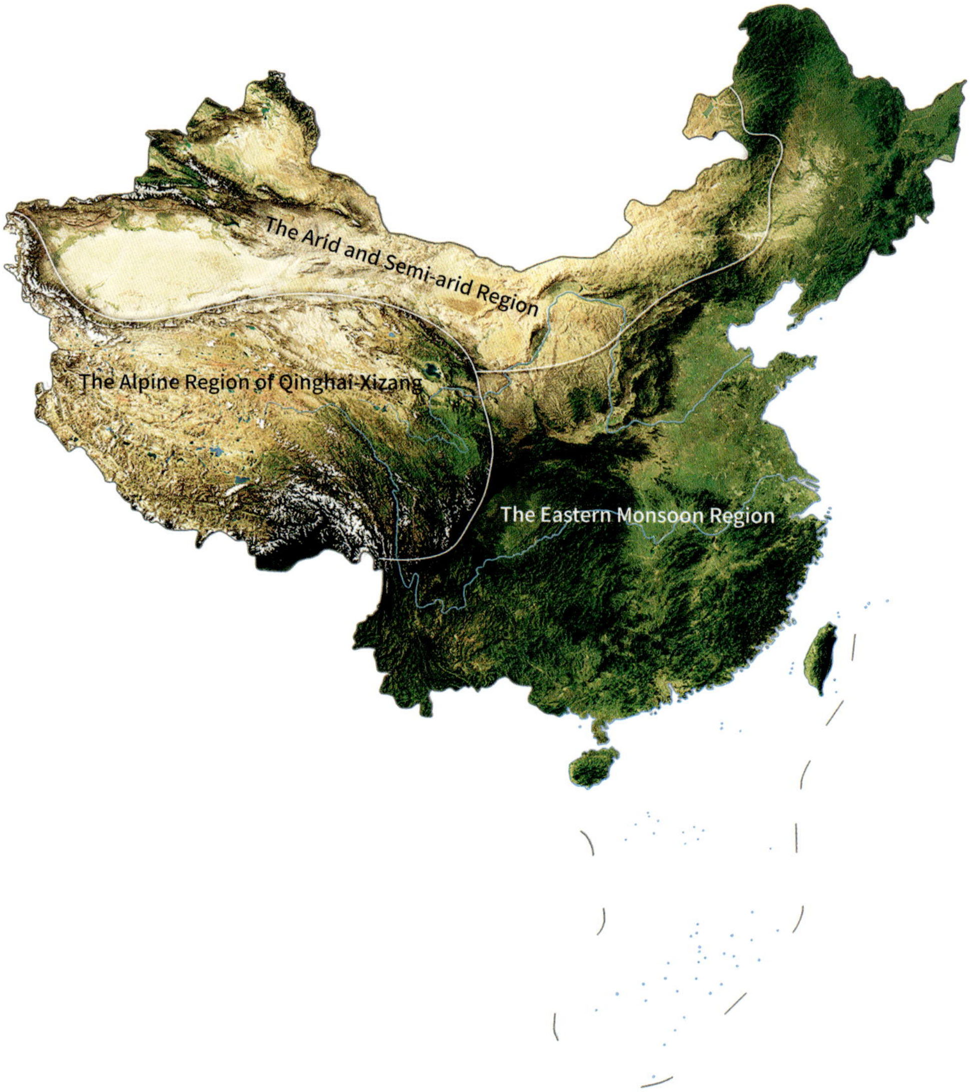

^ China's three major natural regions

> Taklimakan Shamo (Taklamakan Desert)/Photo by Zhao Laiqing

This photo shows Taklimakan Shamo and a desert poplar grove. Taklimakan Shamo is located in the hinterland of Tarim Pendi (Tarim Basin). Due to its significant distance from the sea and the impact of Qingzang Gaoyuan on the general circulation of atmosphere, the climate there is extremely arid, with an annual precipitation generally below 50mm. The exceptionally dry climate results in extremely low vegetation coverage, with most hills in the region being barren and deserted. Trees such as the desert poplar are mostly distributed on the edge of the desert and areas near rivers.

Glaciers in southeast Xizang/Photo by Cao Tie

3 "Super Water Tower"

As altitude increases, the water vapor in the atmosphere above Qingzang Gaoyuan condenses, forming heavy snowfalls. This snowfall accumulates over time to form glaciers hundreds of meters thick, looking like the insurmountable ice wall. These glaciers range from a few kilometers to dozens of kilometers in length. Some glaciers resemble dragons cascading down the valley, and some stretch out endlessly like tree branches.

How many glaciers are there on Qingzang Gaoyuan? The answer is more than 40,000. Altogether, the glaciers span about 44,000 square kilometers, much larger than the island of Taiwan. It accounts for over 80% of China's glaciers. At the same time, it is also the world's largest glaciation center among similar areas at the same latitude.

Qingzang Gaoyuan features the largest number of plateau lakes which are located at some of the highest al-

titudes on Earth. There are over 1,000 lakes with an area of over one square kilometer, accounting for about 50% of the total area of all the lakes in China. In addition, lakes on Qingzang Gaoyuan are incredibly diverse. In terms of size, the lakes range from pearl-like small mountain lakes to China's largest lake—Qinghai Hu (Qinghai Lake). In terms of formation, there are tectonic lakes, glacial erosion lakes, barrier lakes, etc. In terms of water quality, there are freshwater lakes, saltwater lakes, and salt lakes.

With so many glaciers and lakes, in addition to groundwater and surface rivers, Qingzang Gaoyuan has become a "super water tower" that rises over 4,000 meters above sea level. When the "water tower" opens its gates, water surges forth in great torrents, laying the foundation for the formation of the river systems in China and even Asia at large.

In northwestern China, Shiyang He (Shiyang River), Hei He (Heihe River), and Shule He (Shule River) flow towards Hexi Zoulang (Hexi Corridor), while Tarim He (Tarim River) empties into Tarim Pendi (Tarim Basin). Each of these rivers nourishes many oases. In eastern China, Huang He (Yellow River) and Chang Jiang (Yangtze River) roar down the three terrain ladders, nurturing the Chinese civilization.

⌄ The Bayi Glacier/Photo by Wu Wei

As a flat-topped glacier, the Bayi Glacier is located in the middle section of the north side of Qilian Shan.

Qinghai Hu/Photo by Qiu Menghan
Qinghai Hu is China's largest lake with an area of 4,435.69 square kilometers, which is equivalent to two thirds of Shanghai's land area. The picture shows a part of Qinghai Hu.

In southwestern China, Lancang Jiang (Lancang River), Nu Jiang (Nujiang River), Dulong Jiang (Dulong River), Yarlung Zangbo Jiang (Yarlung Zangbo River), Langqên Zangbo (Xiangquan He, Xiangquan River), Sênggê Zangbo (Shiquan He, Shiquan River) and Mabja Zangbo (Kongque He, Kongque River) flow out of the country, becoming water sources of many civilizations in Asia.

The "super water tower" has given birth to super rivers. These rivers account for 44% of China's hydropower reserves, forming one of the world's regions with the most hydroelectric reserves. These powerful water currents cut through mountains, forming splendid landscapes such as the Three Parallel Rivers and "big bend."

China's terrain, climate, and river systems had taken shape. It was time for the emergence of life. However, how would alpine regions like Qingzang Gaoyuan affect life?

Chabyer Caka (Zabuye Salt Lake)/Photo by Lu Yuchun
Chabyer Caka, which is located in Zhongba County, Xigazê Prefecture, Xizang Autonomous Region, boasts rich salt resources.

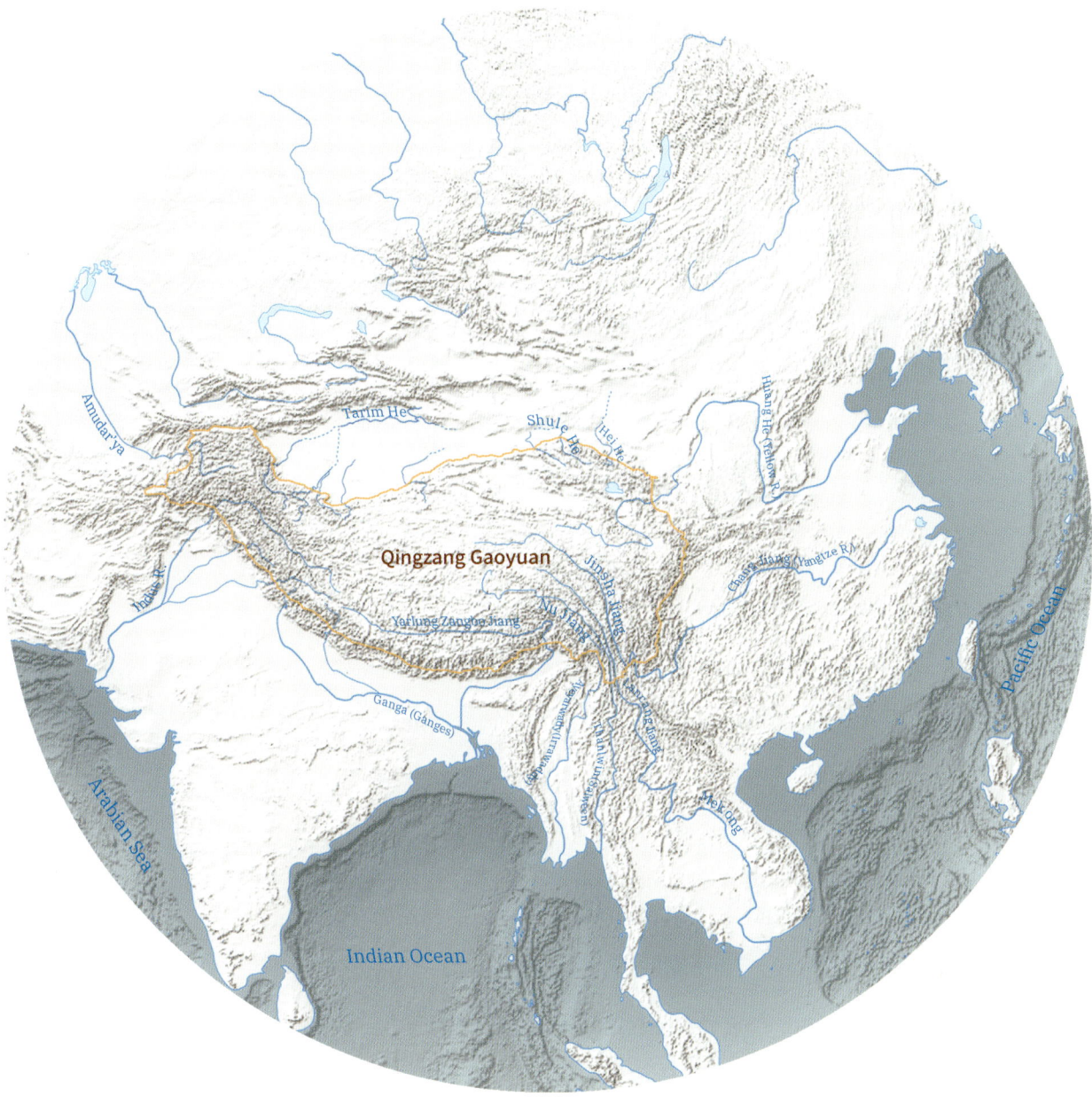

⌃ Main rivers originating from Qingzang Gaoyuan

Qingzang Gaoyuan, which has an average altitude of over 4,000 meters, is the source of legions of rivers. These rivers flow to all directions, laying the groundwork for river system patterns in most parts of Asia. Important rivers in Asia such as Huang He (the Yellow Rriver), Chang Jiang, the Ganges, the Mekong River, the Indus, the Salween, and the Irrawaddy River originate from Qingzang Gaoyuan. Therefore, Qingzang Gaoyuan is also known as the "Asian Water Tower."

⌃ Huang He/Photo by Xu Zhaochao

Huang He forms five S-shaped meanders at the junction of Shanxi and Shaanxi.

4 Ark of Life

In Zanda Pendi (Zanda Basin) in Ngari, Xizang, the earth pillars, ravines and gullies crisscross, forming an arid and barren wasteland.

On August 7th, 2010, scientists excavated several fossils here. The fossils belong to what is called the *Panthera blytheae*, the oldest "big cat" in the world. Later, in-depth research revealed an amazing fact: the Pantherinae animals originated in Qingzang Gaoyuan. They left the plateau for East Asia and South Asia, where they evolved into *Panthera palaeosinensis*—an early Pleistocene species from northern China—and the mainland clouded leopard. Later, they arrived in the Americas and evolved into the jaguar. These felines also arrived in Africa, evolving into the African lion and the leopard.

Since that excavation, more fossils have been discovered in Zanda Pendi, including thousands of other vertebrate fossil specimens. Scientists have discovered that in addition to Pantherinae, many of the Arctic animals also originated in Qingzang Gaoyuan, rather than the Arctic, as people previously thought.

During the slow uplift of Qingzang Gaoyuan, animals on the plateau evolved to adapt to the frigid environment in several ways, such as growing thick fur. 2.58 million years ago, the Quaternary Ice Age began and last to nowadays, making a previously warm Arctic a frigid region. However, the animals on Qingzang Gaoyuan had long been accustomed to the freezing environment. Animals including Arctic foxes and woolly rhinoceros spread from Qingzang Gaoyuan to the Arctic, where they eventually settled.

It can be said that the migration and evolution of animals originating in Qingzang Gaoyuan laid the groundwork for the biodiversity found inside and outside of our "Third Pole."

On the vast Qingzang Gaoyuan today, the numerous steep mountains are home to 40% of China's vascular plants and 43% of terrestrial vertebrates, making it the cornerstone of China's biodiversity. These include the snow leopard, a sister species of Panthera blytheae, as well as many species indigenous to Qingzang Gaoyuan, such as the Tibetan fox, Tibetan wild donkey, Tibetan antelope, and wild yak.

In such a unique environment, the people living on Qingzang Gaoyuan have created a unique culture and practices of spiritual worship, which are woven into the greater Chinese civilization.

Tibetan antelopes in a duel/Photo by Zhang Qiang

The photo was taken in Hoh Xil.

Snow leopard/Photo by Ci Ding (Wild China Film)

The photo was taken in Qinghai. Note: There are two snow leopards in the photo.

∧ The origin and spread of woolly rhinoceros
Image courtesy of Deng Tao's team of Institute of Vertebrate Paleontology, Chinese Academy of Sciences (2012).

› Restored skull of the Panthera blytheae/by Mauricio Antong, Zeng Zhijie

⌄ Creatures in Zanda Pendi/by Julie Selan
This artist's rendition recreates a scene of creatures living in Zanda Pendi 5.3 million to 2.6 million years ago.

Nam Co (Lake Nam)/Photo by Li Heng

Nam Co was previously the largest lake in Xizang. In recent years, as glacial runoff and rainfall in the Qinghai-Xizang area increased, Siling Co (Siling Lake), which was previously the second largest lake in Xizang, has grown significantly in size, replacing Nam Co as the largest lake in Xizang. In the photo, we can see Nyainqêntanglha Shan (Nyenchen Tanglha Mountains) and its main peak Nyainqêntanglha Feng (Tanglha Peak) in the distance, which are actually located to the southwest of Nam Co. In the foreground is the famous Heavenly Gate in the Shape of a Sacred Elephant.

5 Future

The massive collision which created a vast landscape called China influenced its landforms, climate, river systems, and lifeforms, among other things. This impact is still ongoing.

The Indian Plate continues its advance northwards at a speed of 44-50 millimeters per year, making the interior of the plateau and its surroundings a zone of high seismic activity. Many of the devastating earthquakes that have occurred in recent years, such as the Wenchuan earthquake in 2008, the Ya'an earthquake, the Yushu earthquake, and the Jiuzhaigou earthquake were mostly a result of this movement.

The plateau's "exhaust fan" is pulling in the monsoons, resulting in heavy rainfall in southern Gansu, Sichuan, and Yunnan. Floods and mudslides are common. Moreover, as the glaciers are melting and the lakes are expanding, Qingzang Gaoyuan is becoming warmer and more humid. Under the influence of the changes to this "super water tower," the runoff of major rivers will grow or decline. These trends could even undermine the survival and development of the neighboring 3 billion people.

How will Qingzang Gaoyuan affect our lives? What should we do?

To answer these questions, the researchers who participated in the second scientific expedition to Qingzang Gaoyuan have set off to study the plateau once again. They have been climbing snow-capped mountains and crossing major lakes for many days and even months. Thanks to the tireless pursuit of scientific knowledge, China can continue to progress and evolve.

1

The First Terrain Ladder

1.1 Hoh Xil:
China's Greatest Wilderness
049

1.2 Ngari:
The Civilization of the Wilderness
083

1.3 Hengduan Shan:
A Mountain Range with the Most Breathtaking Scenery in China
113

1.4 Jiuzhaigou:
Destruction and Creation
139

1.5 Siguniang Shan:
A Song of Ice and Rock
163

Wilderness areas provide a home for wild animals and plants, and they have become scarce in China. Of the wilderness areas that still exist, one of the most famous is Hoh Xil on Qingzang Gaoyuan. It is host to a great diversity of animals which includes the Tibetan antelope as well as many different bird species and an abundance of vegetation. It is reputed to be the greatest remaining wilderness in China. We must do everything we can to preserve the greatness of this wilderness by keeping it wild.

1.1 Hoh Xil:
China's Greatest Wilderness

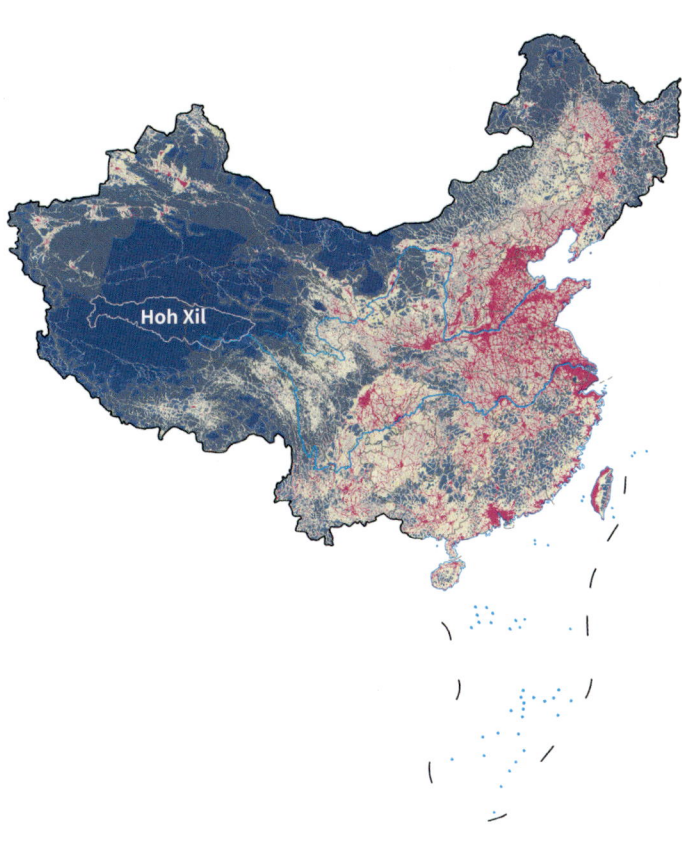

︿ Human footprints in China

Human impact on the environment is measured by using multiple indicators such as urban construction, land use, road distribution, and night lights. The redder the color, the greater the impact. Hoh Xil and its surrounding areas are measured as the least affected by human activities in China, according to the 2009 statistics of the Wildlife Conservation Society.

‹ Tibetan antelope/Photo by Wu Gang

A male Tibetan antelope forages in the Hoh Xil region of Qinghai. The mountain in the distance is Hoh Xil Shan (Hoh Xil Mountain).

The human population has increased since 60,000 or 40,000 years ago, villages and towns sprung up one after another. Since around 10,000 years' animal husbandry and continuous farming, farmland and livestock spread all over China's landscape. For the last hundred years, modern industry has been rapidly advancing, extending roads and railways that reach every corner of the country.

However, this great human civilization was created at the expense of China's wilderness.

Currently, 70% to 80% of plant species in China are on the verge of extinction, and 40% of mammal species are endangered. The South China tiger, which used to be a famous species in China, may have completely disappeared from the wild long ago. Since around 7,000 years ago, Asian elephants were forced to retreat step by step from northern China to the south. Now, their sole habitat within China is limited to only a few places in Yunnan.

Few habitats remain for wild animals and plants, and wilderness areas have become extremely rare in China. The most famous of the remaining wilderness areas is Hoh Xil on Qingzang Gaoyuan.

However, Hoh Xil is renowned in China not for its natural beauty but because of its dark, appalling past. Poachers with machine guns used to hunt Tibetan antelopes, brutally peeling off their skins. Gyisang Soinam Dagyi, a nature conservation worker, sacrificed his life during an anti-poaching operation. Stories such as these have mainly formed people's impressions of Hoh Xil over the past 20 years.

Fortunately, the poaching of the Tibetan antelope in Hoh Xil completely ended in 2009, and Hoh Xil earned its place on the World Heritage List in 2017. Now that its dark history is past, it is time to learn more about its beauty as it shines underneath the sunlight.

Because Hoh Xil has not only Tibetan antelopes but also various kinds of birds, beasts, and plants. It is renowned as the greatest wilderness in China.

Ever since *Home Sapiens* first arrived to the area, China's landscapes have been transformed through human activity.

> The topographic map and geographical scope of Hoh Xil

Geographically speaking, Hoh Xil is a vast region, including Hoh Xil Shan and the surrounding planation surface of the plateau, with a total area of about 250,000 square kilometers. For most people, however, "Hol Xil" refers to the Hoh Xil National Nature Reserve. The nature reserve is located in Qinghai, between Kunlun Shan and Hoh Xil Shan, bounded by the Qinghai-Xizang Highway to the east, with an area of about 45,000 square kilometers. In 2017, Qinghai Hoh Xil was inscribed onto the list of World Heritage sites. The border of the new World Heritage site extends beyond the original nature reserve, spanning from the Qinghai-Xizang Highway in the east to Tongtian He (Tongtian River) in the west. The total area of its core area plus buffer zones is approximately 60,000 square kilometers.

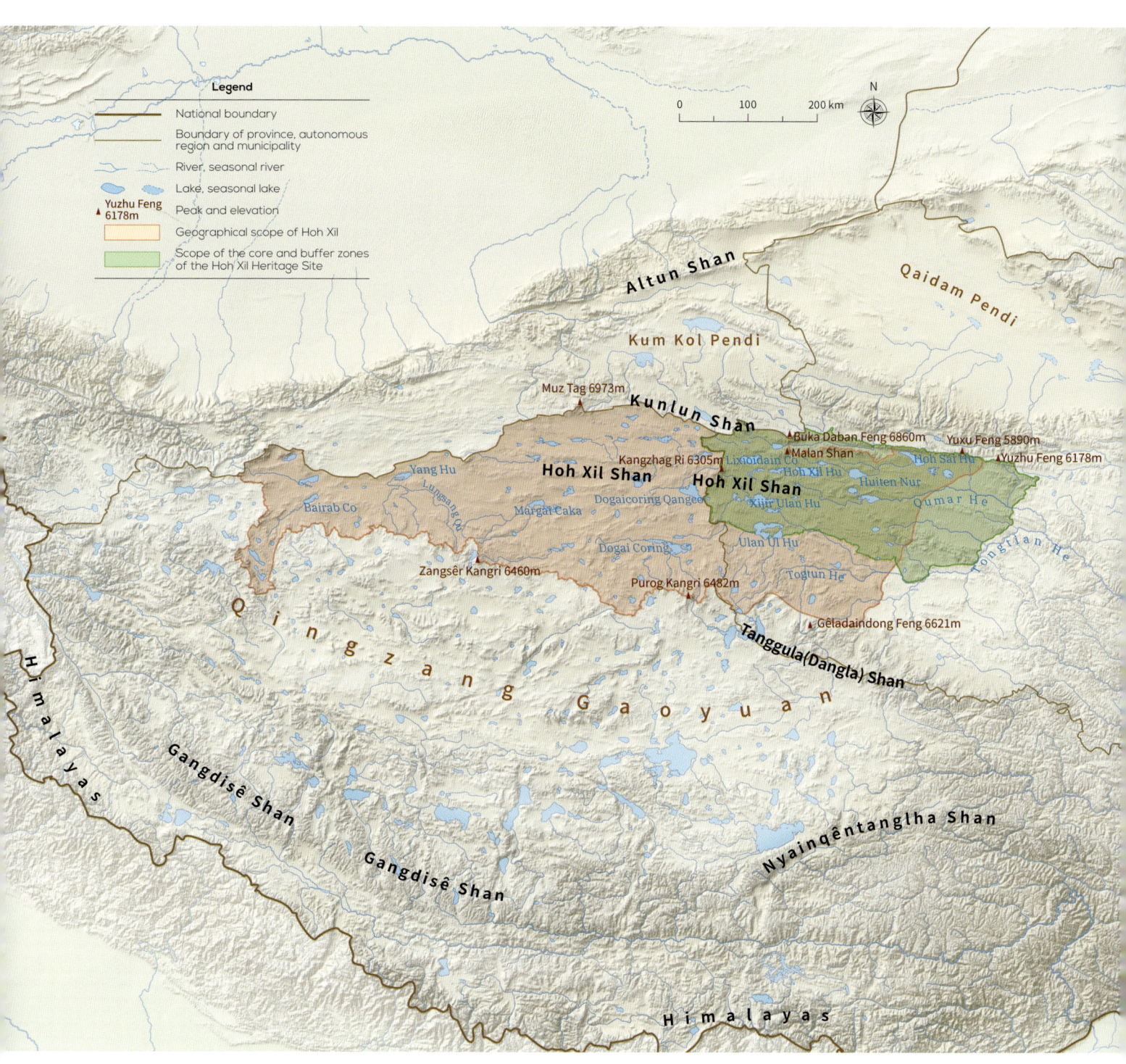

1 The Birth

Around 300 million years ago, the area encompassing Hoh Xil's location today was an ocean. Subsequent plate movements sealed off the ocean and pushed up a vast piece of land. About 65 million years ago, the Indian Plate and the Eurasian Plate began a rapid and powerful collision, and Qingzang Gaoyuan started its. Lava gushed out from the ground, forming numerous volcanic remnants. This also heated the groundwater, creating the world's highest hot spring cluster at an altitude of 5,000 meters.

During this time, Tanggula (Dangla) Shan, now with an average elevation of 5,600-5,700 meters, rose in the south. The eastern section of Kunlun Shan, now with multiple peaks that reach 6,000 meters, rose in the north while Hoh Xil Shan (Hoh Xil Mountain), Fenghuo Shan (Fenghuo Mountain), and Ulan Ul Shan (Ulan Ula Mountain) emerged in the center.

These mountains extend in a parallel line from west to east. They are connected by wide sedimentary basins that exist between them. Numerous peaks and ridges are interspersed amid the basins. Looking over this area today, we see the results of a dramatic plate collision, from which a vast wilderness area, Hoh Xil, was born.

Hoh Xil stretches across Qinghai, Xizang, and Xinjiang, with a total area of about 250,000 square kilometers, equivalent to the total size of the United Kingdom. Even if we only calculate the area of the core region and buffer zones of this World Heritage site, it still covers a remarkable 60,000 square kilometers, which is 1.5 times the area of Switzerland.

However, considering mankind's strong desire to transform nature, the vastness of Hoh Xil alone was unable to keep human development at bay. For this reason, it needs to develop more "skills" to protect itself and survive as a wilderness.

▲ **Baixiang Shan (Baixiang Mountain)/Photo by Qingmu**
Baixiang (White Elephant) Shan is a result of volcanic activity in Hoh Xil, named after its elephant-like shape. It has lava tubes inside.

▼ **Malan Shan (Malan Mountain)/Photo by Buchung**
Malan Shan of Hoh Xil Shan. Its main peak rises 6,016 meters above sea level.

2 "Skills" of the Wilderness

The primary "survival skill" is the imposition of frigid temperatures.

The Hoh Xil region has an average elevation of 5,000 meters, which is a relatively higher area on Qingzang Gaoyuan. By contrast, the elevation of the Lhasa urban area is only over 3,600 meters, and that of the Xining urban area is even less than 2,500 meters. The high altitude has created a cold world. The annual average temperature in Hoh Xil is between minus 10 degrees Celsius and minus 4.1 degrees Celsius, and the lowest temperature recorded is an extremely frigid minus 46.2 degrees Celsius.

The cold weather causes Hoh Xil to remain in its natural state—a frozen field. Permafrost covers more than 90% of its land area, with a permafrost layer that is 80-120 meters thick.

Huge glaciers have been formed in the high mountain areas above the altitude of 5,500 meters. Buka Daban Feng (Buka Daban Peak), Muz Tag (Muztagata Peak), Purog Kangri, and Gêladaindong Feng (Gêladaindong Peak) have the most dynamic glaciers. Many glacial tongues pour down for dozens of kilometers from the tops of the mountains. These tall ice bodies are even more impressive up close. Walking among them, you feel like an ant facing a huge wall of ice.

As the glaciers erode the mountains on such a massive scale, they also produce a large number of deposits. After repeated freezing and thawing in an extremely cold environment, these deposits have been broken down into sand and gravel of various granulations. Together with other materials such as sands and soils from the surface, forming many continuous alpine dunes.

Next, Hoh Xil's second "survival skill" in wildlife preservation has been the formation of wetlands such as lakes and marshes.

Water from melted ice and snow from the high mountains continuously flows down into Hoh Xil Pendi (Hoh Xil Basin). The terrain in the basin is flat and has poor drainage. The permafrost prevents the water from penetrating into the ground. Therefore, the water accumulates in lakes. In Hoh Xil, there are seven large lakes with an area of more than 200 square kilometers. There are numerous bodies of water with a surface area of over one square kilometer each, and they cover a total of 3,825 square kilometers, which is nearly 600 times larger than the famous Xi Hu (West Lake) in western Hangzhou, Zhejiang. There are also more than 7,000 lakes densely distributed in areas that measure less than one square kilometer in size.

Glaciers on the south side of Buka Daban Feng (Bukadaban Peak)/Photo by Buchung

This picture shows the glaciers on the south side of Buka Daban Feng, of which the largest and longest one in the middle of the photo is unique. Its tail is wider, resembling a human foot. Thus, it is named the Foot Glacier.

Glaciers and alpine dunes/Photo by Buchung
In Hoh Xil, many small alpine dunes are often found at the end of the glaciers and on the shore of the lakes.

The lakes are of different sizes, with straight or crooked lakeshores. The depth and degree of mineralization of their waters also varies, causing the lakes to have many different colors, such as light blue, blue-green, and indigo. The famous Yang Hu (Sun Lake) gathers its glacial waters from Buka Daban Feng, Malan Shan (Malan Mountain), and Weixue Shan (Weixue Mountain). It is 43 meters deep, and the water is crystal clear. Its spacious, zigzagging shore is like a seacoast. In the evening, the surface reflects the twilight and the continuous snowy peaks, creating a dreamlike ambiance. The center of Xijir Ulan Hu (Xijir Ulan Lake) is blue-green. On its west side, the color of the water becomes darker as it goes from near to far, while on the east side, the color is indigo blue. Painted by the refraction of sunlight from the salt lake, the clouds over the lake area are also dyed blue-green. The sky perfectly integrates with the water, creating a fantastic infinite vista.

In addition to the lakes, there are many wetlands. Even with modern means of transportation, entering and traveling through Hoh Xil is not easy.

In order to remain a wilderness, the third "survival skill" of Hoh Xil has been the inaccessibility and remoteness of its location—the hinterland of Qingzang Gaoyuan.

Most of the rivers that originate here belong to endorheic water systems centered around lakes. Only a few river systems flow out of the Hoh Xil area, either through Kunlun Shan to the arid Qaidam Pendi (Qaidam Basin) in the north; or into Chang Jiang or Huang He, becoming the source of each of these mighty rivers. The endorheic rivers tend to have a relatively small water volume and limited erosive force, unlike the rivers on the edge of Qingzang Gaoyuan which cut through the terrain and can generate low-altitude river valleys. For example, the Lhasa Hegu (Lhasa River Valley) and the Huangshui Hegu (Huangshui River Valley)—Huang Shui (Huangshui River) is a tributary of the upper reaches of Huang He—are in many ways ideal for humans to live. The Hoh Xil area, on the other hand, has not been severely eroded by rivers. Its terrain is flat, with an altitude difference of only 300 to 600 meters. It is the most intact, inaccessible plateau platform on "the Roof of the World."

With these three "survival skills"—in frigid temperatures, water saturated lands, and inaccessible landscapes as an intact plateau—the Hoh Xil area remains mostly unaffected by human activities.

So, the stage is ready. Who will be the protagonists on this high plateau platform?

˄ **Lixioidain Co (Lexie Wudan Lake)/Photo by Buchung**
The lake in the picture is Lixioidain Co, and Buka Daban Feng can be seen in the distance.

˅ **Qumar He (Chumar River)/Photo by Liu Supei**
Qumar He, the northernmost of the three sources of Chang Jiang, originates from Hoh Xil Shan.

3 Everything Grows

First come the cushion plants, the pioneer of plateau life. Among them, *Thylacospermum caespitosum* flourishes the most in this environment. Once rooted and sprouted, it will spread into a huge circle with a diameter of up to two meters. Its leaves are mixed with sand and fine soil, which can absorb moisture and help keep it warm. Even if the ambient temperature drops below zero, the plant's internal temperature can maintain itself at one to two degrees Celsius. It can also promote the decomposition of dead leaves, accumulating organic matter and improving soil conditions. This is not only conducive to its own growth but also lays a foundation for the migration of other plants. *Saussurea japonica, Leontopodium leontopodioides, Lagotis glauca, Bistorta macrophylla*, and other plants have flourished here with the help of the stabilized, superior internal environments created by cushion plants.

In Hoh Xil all these cushion plants must live within a 100-day growth cycle. They must complete their entire lifecycle—germination, growth, flowering, and seeding—in just two or three months.

In June, the land remains barren. But one month later, almost overnight, countless flowers and grasses suddenly sprout from the soil and start to bloom; in August, the seeds of the plants mature and fall off, floating in the wind under the blue sky of Hoh Xil. During this time, even if there is sudden snowfall, many plants will still bloom and bear fruit tenaciously.

1	3
	4
2	5

1 *Meconopsis horridula*/Photo by Zhao Xinlu

Meconopsis horridula is an annual herb. The whole plant is covered with yellow-brown or light-yellow thorns. It grows in alpine meadows, rock crevices, or rocky shores at an altitude of 4,200 to 5,400 meters. It is resistant to drought and barren conditions.

2 *Thylacospermum caespitosum*/Photo by Zhao Xinlu

Thylacospermum caespitosum is a perennial cushion-like herb. Its above-ground part is usually spherical. It mostly grows in alpine swamps, rocky shores, and rock crevices at an altitude of 4,300 to 4,600 meters. It is a key species of pioneer plants in the Hoh Xil area.

3 *Phyllolobium heydei*/Photo by Qin Hui

Phyllolobium heydei belongs to the *Phyllolobium* genus of the Fabaceae family, which grows mostly in high mountains and on gravel at an altitude of 4,500 to 5,300 meters.

4 *Astragalus mongholicus*/Photo by Zhao Xinlu

Astragalus mongholicus is a perennial herb. In Hoh Xil, its growing season is extremely short. It blooms in the snow like many flowering plants here.

5 *Leontopodium nanum*/Photo by Qin Hui

Leontopodium nanum is a perennial herb that grows on grasslands, in gravel, and around salt lakes on high mountains at an altitude of 3,500 to 5,000 meters. It often grows together in mats to form a vast expanse.

Luxuriant plants can make Hoh Xil vibrant with life, but the real protagonists on this stage are the animals. As this area is practically inaccessible to humans, the animals can live and breed freely here on the plateau.

The petite pika—with a body length of only slightly more than 10 centimeters—likes the plateau meadows in Hoh Xil the most. Especially in places where the turf is cracked into blocks due to dryness because they can easily dig out complex caves to avoid natural predators. It's just like the old Chinese saying: "A crafty rabbit has three burrows." The abundant resources and perfect habitat in the wild plateau meadows allow them to reproduce in large quantities.

Black-lipped pikas playing in the snow/Photo by Pei Jingde

By contrast, its cousin the plateau rabbit, which also belongs to the Lagomorpha order, is less fortunate. Hoh Xil lacks bushes for plateau rabbits to hide. With a body just as long as that of a domestic cat, they are far fewer in population than the abundant pikas. Another common burrowing animal here is the Himalayan marmot, which is especially known for its plumpness and roundness. Marmots feed on tender grasses within 500 meters of their burrows. Being very alert, they often stand up to keep watch and hide immediately into their holes whenever danger is approaching.

The horned lark is a small songbird with a body length of only about 15 centimeters, and it likes to build nests on the ground. This bird rarely flies long distances. Instead, it picks up grass seeds and catches insects on the ground for food. The white-rumped snowfinch, which is of similar size, also feeds on grass seeds and insects. It likes to gather in small groups in the pikas' colonies and is always ready to use abandoned pika burrows for its nest. The black-necked crane, a kind of large wading bird, migrates from afar and pecks on plants and fish in the shallow waters of Hoh Xil. It has a black and white body and has a dark red spot on the top of its head. Being extraordinarily elegant, groups of black-necked cranes can compose some of the most beautiful scenery in Hoh Xil.

1	2
3	
4	

1 Black-lipped pika/Photo by Fan Shangzhen

The black-lipped pika, also known as the plateau pika, has dark-brown upper and lower lips. Its body color is brownish yellow or sandy tan. It inhabits alpine grasslands and meadows with an altitude of 3,200 to 5,200 meters.

2 Plateau rabbit/Photo by Qin Hui

The plateau rabbit has long and fluffy body hair that ranges from gray-yellow to a brownish-yellow in color. Its ear tips have a darker color. It lives in the rocks, shrubs, and forest margins of the alpine grasslands and plateau meadows at an altitude of 2,700 to 5,200 meters.

3 Himalayan marmot/Photo by Zhang Qiang

The Himalayan marmot has a stout body with short, thick limbs. Its front paws are well-developed and suitable for digging soil. It lives mostly in alpine grasslands and meadows with an altitude of 3,300 to 5,200 meters. The marmots in this picture are standing at the entrance of their burrow while looking around vigilantly for danger.

4 White-rumped snowfinch/Photo by Zhang Qiang

The white-rumped snowfinch is a bird belonging to the snowfinch group of the Ploceidae family, a species that is endemic to China. The adult bird is lighter in color than other snowbirds, with dense spots on the upper back, large white spots on the waist, and black eyes. It mainly inhabits high mountains, grasslands, and deserts at an altitude of 3,000 to 4,500 meters. It likes to nest in wall holes, abandoned rat holes, or on the ground.

Black-necked crane/Picture from Hoh Xil Management Office
The black-necked crane is the most recent new species of crane discovered in the world, and it is an animal under national first-class protection in China. Its head, throat, and entire neck are black, with only small white patches under and behind the eyes, while the exposed eyes and the top of the head are red. It usually breeds on Qingzang Gaoyuan and spends winters in southwestern China, Bhutan, and India.

Ungulates—some of the largest animals in Hoh Xil.

The white-lipped deer, a species endemic to Qingzang Gaoyuan, is big and robust. The males have antlers stretching up to a meter in length, splitting into multiple prongs at their tips.

Male argali are known for the spirally curved horns of the males, while the females' horns are much shorter with very little curvature.

Blue sheep mostly live in mountainous areas, especially in very rugged terrain.

2
1	3

1 Argali/Photo by Fan Shangzhen

The argali is also known as the bighorn sheep. Both males and females have horns. The horns of the males are thick and curved in a 360° spiral, while a female's horns are much smaller and only slightly curved. The argali on the left in the picture is male and the one on the right is female.

2 White-lipped deer/Photo by Zhang Qiang

The white-lipped deer, a species endemic to Qingzang Gaoyuan, is under national first-class protection in China. As its name suggests, its upper lip and nose tip are white. The color of its body is light yellow, gray-brown, or dark brown, and the change of its coat color is related to gender, season, and distribution area.

3 Blue sheep/Photo by Qin Hui

The blue sheep has a low, sturdy body and strong limbs that are well suited for walking on rocky areas. Both male and female blue sheep have horns. Males have relatively large and thick horns, while females have much smaller ones.

1 Running Tibetan gazelles/Picture from Hoh Xil Management Office

The Tibetan gazelle, a species endemic to Qingzang Gaoyuan, is under national second-class protection in China. This species of gazelle is small and features slender limbs. Its hips usually have striking heart-shaped white spots with brownish-yellow edges.

2 Tibetan wild donkey/Photo by Zhang Qiang

The Tibetan wild donkey, a species endemic to Qingzang Gaoyuan, is under national first-class protection in China. As the largest species of wild donkey, it features bright brown fur, a strong body, and powerful limbs. It excels at running.

3 Wild yak/Photo by Buchung

The wild yak, a species endemic to Qingzang Gaoyuan, is under national first-class protection in China. The wild yak is the ancestor of the domestic yak. Compared with the domestic yak, the wild yak is extraordinarily large, about twice the size of the domestic yak, and boasts stronger limbs. The back of the neck of the wild yak is most notable for its large protrusion. The picture shows a running wild yak, stirring up the dust with its hooves.

The Tibetan gazelle, with its two eye-catching white spots on its buttocks, runs exceptionally fast and is quite slim. The vast wilderness surrounded by snow-capped mountains provides an ideal habitat for these animals.

The Tibetan wild donkey, which is tall and fit, likes to live together in groups. Its coat color is different shades of reddish-brown, while the lower parts of the body and limbs are bright white, making it very easy to identify. It excels at running and is incredibly competitive. While it is running, it's tail flutters in the wind, and the dust it raises is left in trails far behind. It seems so proud of itself as if no other animal on the plateau could compete with it in looks or motion.

The wild yak is noted for its huge size and is considered the most intimidating animal in Hoh Xil. There is a large protrusion on the back of its neck, and its long hair drops to its feet. A wild yak that lives alone is more prone to attack. When it is attacking, its eyes will be wide with rage, the horns pointing forward, the tail erected high, and it will rush toward you with the force of a landslide and the power of a tidal wave.

A herd of Tibetan antelopes near Zonag Hu (Zonag Lake)/Photo by Pei Jingde
Zonag Hu is the main breeding ground for Tibetan antelopes. Every summer, a great number of Tibetan antelopes migrate from the surrounding areas to the shore of the lake to bear their young.

The most graceful animal in Hoh Xil, however, is none other than the Tibetan antelope.

Today, the population of Tibetan antelopes in Hoh Xil has grown to 60,000.

Adult male Tibetan antelopes have dark faces and horns up to 60 to 70 centimeters in length. The horns are shiny black. They reach upwards in almost perfectly vertical lines from the top of the head, and the horns are notably eye-catching against snow-capped mountains in the background. The Tibetan antelope is called "the elf of the snowy lands," a name that is well deserved.

Male Tibetan antelopes often get into fierce fights during the mating season. Even if one defeats its opponent, it does not mean that it automatically gains the favor of a female. It still needs to use all its strength to chase the female until it succeeds in mating. Once they conceive, females soon leave their mates, starting the last great migration of ungulates in China. They traverse valleys, cross railway lines, and finally reach the shores of the dreamlike Zonag Hu (Zonag Lake).

Thousands of female Tibetan antelopes gather on the lakeshore of Zonag Hu to give birth to their babies and then lead their fawns back to their winter habitat. After the completion of this great journey, a new cycle will begin again.

> Tibetan antelope/Photo by Buchung

The Tibetan antelope, or chiru, scientific name *Pantholops hodgsonii*, belongs to the *Pantholops* genus of the Bovidae family in the order Artiodactyla. It is a species endemic to Qingzang Gaoyuan under national first-class protection in China. The hair of the Tibetan antelope is thin, short, and dense. The back and sides of its body are dark-brown or black. Its muzzle is wide, and both sides of the nasal cavity are bulging and hemispherical. Male Tibetan antelopes have straight and slender horns. They often fight for mates and the horns on their heads are the main "weapons." The upper picture on the right page shows a Tibetan antelope fawn. The middle right picture on the right page shows two male Tibetan antelopes fighting. The lower right and left pictures on the right page both show a pair of male and female Tibetan antelopes.

The population of predators in Hoh Xil is also expanding, just like the recovering antelopes.

Large birds of prey, such as saker falcons and big buzzards, fly downwards from the sky. The Tibetan fox, known for its large and square face, and the Pallas's cat, which resembles a domestic cat, hunt from the ground, preying on small animals such as pikas, plateau rabbits, marmots, and horned larks. Larger lynxes also target baby blue sheep and Tibetan antelopes.

The wolf is the ultimate hunter in Hoh Xil. They often cooperate to hunt prey as big as adult Tibetan wild donkeys.

Although the brown bear is larger, it is not as agile as the wolf and doesn't coordinate its hunt as a group. It mainly feeds on plant rhizomes and small animals such as pikas and marmots.

The bearded vulture, named after a small cluster of black feathers that create "beards" at corner of its beak, is placed at the lowest end of the predator spectrum. It does not prey directly on animals. Instead, it hovers in the air as it searches for animal carcasses on the ground. When it finds one, it will not immediately dive down to feed. Instead, it will scout the area to confirm that there is no danger before swarming to its meal. They can devour the carcass of a huge animal, turning it into just a skeleton in less than an hour.

1	5
2	6
3	7
4	

1 Upland buzzard/Photo by Zhang Qiang

The upland buzzard, a national second-class protected animal in China, is a resident bird of Hoh Xil that mainly feeds on rodents.

2 Himalayan vulture/Photo by Buchung

The Himalayan vulture, scientific name *Gyps himalayensis*, belongs to the Accipitridae family of the order Accipitriformes, and it mainly lives in high mountains and river valleys at an altitude of 2,500 to 4,500 meters.

3 Bearded vulture/Photo by Zhang Qiang

The bearded vulture is a resident bird under national first-class protection in China. It likes to pick up the bones of small or larger prey, throws them on the rocks to break them open, then it eats the marrow inside.

4 Saker falcon/Photo by Buchung

The saker falcon, a national second-class protected animal in China, is a resident bird of Hoh Xil. The saker falcon can grow up to 50 centimeters in length. The color of its plumage is lighter than that of other falcon species.

5 Wolf cubs/Photo by Zhang Qiang

The wolf often lives in groups, preying mainly on the ungulates as well as small animals such as hares and marmots. The picture shows two wolf cubs.

6 A Tibetan fox after a successful hunt/Photo by Buchung

The Tibetan fox is a species endemic to Qingzang Gaoyuan. It feeds on rodents, lagomorphs, and ground-dwelling birds.

7 Tibetan brown bear/Photo by Buchung

The Tibetan brown bear is a geographical subspecies of the brown bear. It is endemic to Qingzang Gaoyuan and is under national second-class protection in China. The picture shows a female bear and her cub.

4 Let Wilderness Always Be Wild

From small animals such as pikas, plateau rabbits, and horned larks, ungulates such as Tibetan antelopes, Tibetan gazelles, and Tibetan wild donkeys, to predators such as falcons, lynxes, and wolves, wild animals are already masters of this wilderness.

This is Hoh Xil, China's greatest wilderness.

What we must do is to preserve the greatness of this wilderness by letting it always stay wild.

Tibetan antelope/Photo by Qin Hui
The photo taken near Zonag Hu shows a female Tibetan antelope standing alone in the wild.

Both the ancient Zhang Zhung and Guge kingdoms have been lost to history. Nevertheless, Ngari still retains its unique charm today. It is the best place for stargazing in China and boasts unique flora and fauna and very hospitable people.

Ngari is in the wilderness, yet it is both wild and civilized.

1.2 Ngari:
The Civilization of the Wilderness

Where is Ngari?

As a prefecture under the jurisdiction of Xizang Autonomous Region, Ngari is located in the far western part of China. For most people in China, it seems too far away to visit. Even for those in Xizang, Ngari is still a very remote area. The linear distance between Shiquanhe Town, Gar County—where the administrative office of Ngari is located—and Lhasa, is 1,100 kilometers. That is farther than the distance between Beijing and Harbin.

In addition to its remoteness, Ngari also has the highest average elevation in Xizang, so it is also known as the "Roof of the Roof of the World." The surprisingly high altitude results in a harsh living environment and makes Ngari a sparsely populated place. It has a total area of 345,000 square kilometers, which is larger in total area than the combined area of three provinces on the eastern coast of China: Jiangsu, Zhejiang, and Fujian. The population of Ngari is just more than 100,000 people. It is one of the most sparsely populated areas in the world.

There is a local saying in Ngari:

> *The land here is so barren, the path to it is so high up, only the dearest of friends and the greatest of enemies, will pay us a visit...*

However, this barren land has unusually gorgeous scenery, and it has given birth to splendid and mysterious ancient civilizations. Some of the important rituals in Xizang's culture and religion today are closely related to those ancient civilizations. The demise of these ancient cultures has caused many archaeologists and religious scholars to diligently explore the region. This local heritage can be compared with Dunhuang for its profound cultural legacies.

Scholars believe that in order to understand Xizang civilization, one must first understand Ngari.

What qualities does Ngari have? Why is it so important for Xizang?

To understand, we must start with the three main elements of Ngari and their inherent power to change everything.

The Himalayas and Gangdisê Shan/Photo by Sun Yan

In the distance are the Himalayas and its main peak in Ngari Naimona'nyi (Mount Namu Na'ni). In the vicinity there are Gangdisê Shan and the main peak Kangrinboqê Feng (the Kangrinpoche).

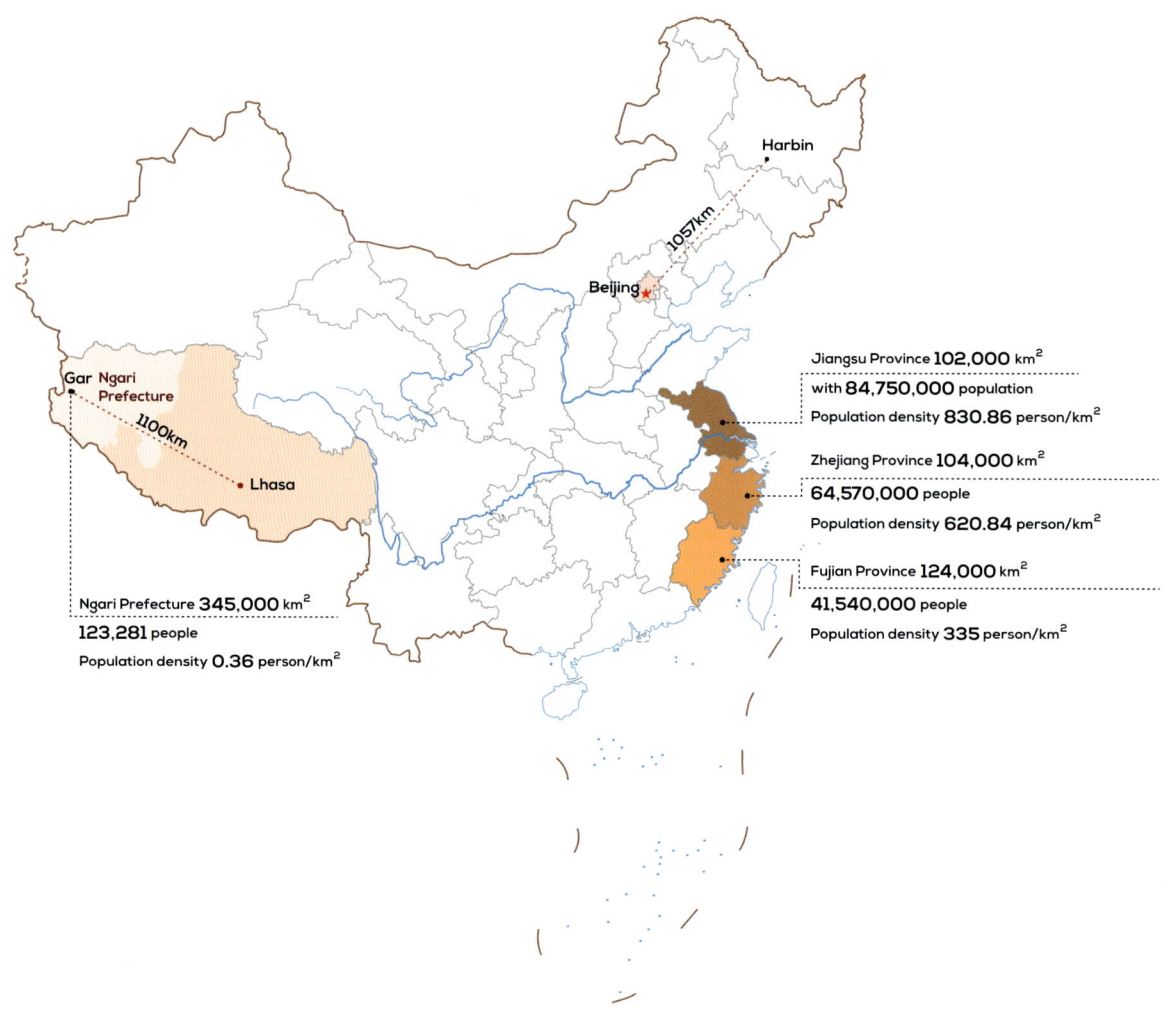

∧ A comparison of Ngari's location and population density with the southeast coastal provinces.

Population data are based on the Seventh National Census, which was released by the National Bureau of Statistics.

> ### The topographic map of Ngari

Ngari is in the northwestern part of Qingzang Gaoyuan, with an average elevation of more than 4,500 meters and is the highest area in Xizang. There are countless mountains in Ngari. The main mountain ranges include the Himalayas, Gangdisê Shan, Karakorum Shan, and Kunlun Shan. Most of the mountain ranges extend from northwest to southeast, and there are many secondary mountains between these main ranges. Famous peaks include Naimona'nyi (Mount Namu Na'ni) and Kangrinboqê Feng.

1 Let There Be Mountains

Due to continuous plate tectonic movement during hundreds of millions of years, the Ngari region uplifted constantly. Ranges of orogenic mountain belts uplifted and converged in the west of Qingzang Gaoyuan, such as Kunlun Shan, Karakorum Shan (Karakorum Mountains), Gangdisê Shan, and the Himalayas.

The primary element that constitutes Ngari are mountains.

Kunlun Shan rises in the north of Ngari and the Himalayas in the south. Karakorum Shan extends from northwest to southeast and is separated into two columns within the territory of Ngari. One column extends eastward and gradually enters the hinterland of the plateau; the other extends southeast and connects with Gangdisê Shan. These large mountains are not far from each other. Gangdisê Shan and the Himalayas are only 70 to 80 kilometers apart at their nearest point. Seen from afar, these two columns of mountains seem to stand together in parallel. Many sub-level mountain ranges are derived from these large mountain ranges. Various connections exist between the countless peaks. Among them, Ayila Ri'gyü (Ayila Rigyu Mountains), a branch of the Himalayas, looks painted because it contains minerals with varied colors, hence its nickname "Five-color Mountain."

^ Xiagangjiang Feng (Xiagangjiang Peak)/Photo by Ding Liang

Xiagangjiang Feng of Gangdisê Shan in Gêrzê County, Ngari, is 6,822 meters above sea level.

v Gangciren Feng (Gangciren Peak) viewed from the Kongque Hegu (Kongque River Valley)/Photo by Sun Yan

Gangciren Feng belongs to the Kurrance Mountains, a part of the Himalayas. Villages and towns in the Kongque Hegu nestle in the arms of snow-capped peaks of the Himalayas and Gangdisê Shan.

^ The north side of Kangrinboqê Feng/Photo by Zhang Qiang
< An aerial view of Kangrinboqê Feng/Photo by Xiang Wenjun

Many peaks tower among these high mountains, the most famous of which is Kangrinboqê Feng (Kangrinpoche), the main peak of Gangdisê Shan, with an elevation of 6,656 meters. An impressive feature of this peak is the diversity of its terrain. The south side is relatively soft-sloped, and the huge rock grooves found there form an impressive cross pattern in the middle; the north side is steep as if it had been chopped off by an axe. If you look down from the air, what stands out is not the peak's roundness or steepness. Your eye will naturally be attracted to the S-shaped ridge that was formed by glacial erosion, easily the peak's most prominent feature. The ridge bends and extends downward, as sharp as a blade.

2 Let There Be Water

The dense and strikingly high mountains are the cradle of Ngari's second important element, water.

Across thousands of years, snowfall (precipitation) has accumulated into many glaciers in the mountains. The densest expanses of glaciers are found around Naimona'nyi, Kangrinboqê Feng, Lunggar Shan (Mount Lunggar), and the northern part of Ngari. With constantly melting glaciers, surface precipitation and under-ground water, Ngari has nurtured many river systems.

The river systems that are less erosive cannot enter the ocean, often disappearing inland or converging into lakes and remaining a part of Ngari's internal system of rivers. These internal river systems occupy nearly 3/4 of Ngari's total area. They converge into lakes, large and small, on the plateau's surface. Among the many lakes, there are more than 100 lakes that have a surface area greater than one square kilometer each. In total, there is more than 6,000 square kilometers of lake-covered surface. Lakes are covering the surface of Ngari in dense distribution.

Hidden amongst the peaks of Gangdisê Shan and Zhari Namco is the largest lake in Ngari. It covers an area of more than 1,000 square kilometers, and thus it is the third largest lake in Xizang.

The famous Mapam Yumco (Lake Manasarovar) and La'nga Co (Lake Rakshastal) are sandwiched between Gangdisê Shan and the Himalayas. The freshwater runoff from the surrounding mountains mostly flows to Mapam Yumco. It covers an area of more than 400 square kilometers and is the largest freshwater lake in any region of comparable altitude in the world. The water of the lake is clear and quiet, and the vegetation of the surrounding grassland grows luxuriantly, forming a high-quality natural pasture.

▲ Glaciers and a glacial lake/Photo by Xiang Wenjun

The glacier on the left of this picture is the North Gongdaciren Glacier in the Himalayas, and the meltwater from the glacier on the right converges at its foot to form a glacial lake.

▼ Kunggyii Co (Kuuga Lake)/Photo by Jiang Xi

Naimona'nyi and its reflection in the lake at sunrise.

Located in the immediate vicinity, La'nga Co is just the opposite. Lacking a freshwater supply, the salinity of the water in this lake continues to increase, making it bitter and undrinkable. The extremely barren lakeshore only has sparse vegetation.

However, the small Kunggyii Co (Lake Kuuga) to the north of Mapam Yumco is amazingly beautiful. At sunrise, the snow-capped mountains and the lake make for a pristine mountain vista, especially when seen in the golden morning glow of the rising sun.

Even more impressive is Bangong Co (Lake Palgon). The undulating mountains connect behind the lake, thus forming an extremely spectacular scene. Bangong Co is long and narrow, straddling the border between China and the Kashmir region. There are very different water sources for the eastern and western sections of the lake. As a result, the eastern section in China is mainly comprised of freshwater, while the

western part extending to the Kashmir region gradually turns into a saltwater lake.

Other lakes also have their unique characteristics. For example, Gyaring Co (the Gyaring Lake) has a tortuous shoreline, and Lungmu Co is shaped like a gourd.

‹ **Mapam Yumco/Photo by Jiang Xi**
Kangrinboqê Feng in the distance and a flock of sheep in the foreground form a beautiful picture together with Mapam Yumco.

› **Gyaring Co/Photo by Sun Yan**
The peninsula that runs deep into the lake has a coastline that twists and turns.

Compared with the internal river systems, the external river systems are forceful and powerful. They cut into the surface of the plateau, making their way forward and converging into larger rivers, which finally flow into the ocean. The four major rivers that originate from the area around Kangrinboqê Feng are all external river systems, namely Sênggê Zangbo, Langqên Zangbo, Mabja Zangbo, and Damqog Zangbo (Maquan He, Maquan River).

Sênggê Zangbo is called Shiquan He in Chinese and is renamed the Indus River after flowing into Kashmir. It originates from the northern slope of Gangdisê Shan, which is approximately 5,500 meters above sea level. With its current flowing nonstop amidst the mountains, the width of the river valley gradually expands from 3,000 to about 10,000 meters, while the elevation decreases gradually. When it arrives at Shiquanhe Town, the altitude has dropped to about 4,200 meters.

The erosive cutting force of Mabja Zangbo is even stronger. It enters Nepal through Burang County, Xizang Autonomous Region, and then flows into the Ganga (Ganges) before merging into the sea. Its source in the Himalayas is located at an altitude of 5,400 meters. At Burang Town, Burang County, the river valley's altitude has dropped to less than 3,900 meters.

Among the three rivers, Langqên Zangbo boasts the most powerful erosive force. It comprises the upper reaches of the Sutlej, the largest tributary of the Indus River. It originates in Gangdisê Shan, where its source is close to 5,500 meters above sea level. After it reaches Shibuqi in Zanda County, the river valley is only 2,800 meters above sea level. The altitude difference is more than 2,700 meters, which bestows on this river the distinction of having a first-class cutting force.

The internal river systems create dense lakes, while the external river systems carve deep valleys. The influence of the two kinds of river systems has produced very different effects on the environment. The areas within the internal river systems that have a weak erosive ability maintain a higher altitude, where it is difficult for humans to survive. Thus the "Northern Highland," Qiangtang, was born.

The river valleys carved by the external river systems have much lower altitudes and create a relatively suitable environment for humans to inhabit and thrive.

By the time the valleys formed, our human ancestors began to create a civilization. Before the rise of ancient civilizations, however, humans still needed Ngari's third most important element to shape their lives.

< **Langqên Zangbo/Photo by Kabu**
Langqên Zangbo meanders and diverges in the valley, forming a zigzagging flow. The floodplain, the river island, and the water are all connected to the meandering river.

Shiquan He (Shiquan River)/Photo by Gao Cheng
The meandering river nourishes the grass in the wetlands, which paints the ground with different colors.

3 Let There Be Earth

About 5 million years ago, Xiangquanhe Pendi (Xiangquan River Basin) between Ayila Ri'gyü and the Himalayas was still a large lake. At that time, a large amount of silt and other materials brought by the surrounding rivers were deposited on the bottom, forming a sedimentary layer up to 800 meters thick.

Finally, we arrive at Ngari's third important element, earth.

After that, the uplift forming mountains on both sides accelerated, blocking water vapor from entering. The area that had been a great lake turned into a rain shadow, a region that is hot, dry and with little rainfall. The lake gradually dried up, exposing the earth below. Thus was Zanda Pendi formed.

The flowing waters from Langqên Zangbo and the short summer rains in the area constantly scour the thick soil layers. This continuously cuts into the sediments of the lake basin that originally formed a flat plateau. The soil on the surface was drenched and fragmented, forming a unique landform—Tu Lin, that is, "sediment pillars."

The earth pillars formations can reach hundreds of meters in height. They may swarm together in clusters or stand upright as individuals. They may rise step by step or spiral up like a rotating staircase, reaching up in snowy peaks or towering majestically as a huge wall formed by nature. Countless earth pillars, earth towers, earth walls, and earth castles are gathered together, creating a super earth pillars which stretches 175 kilometers from northwest to southeast and 45 kilometers in width, covering an area of about 2,400 square kilometers. From the constant drenching and fragmenting, this unique land feature was born. It is the Zanda Earth pillars.

The mountains have given birth to well-developed river systems, the water has created low-lying river valleys, and the earth has formed magnificent earth pillars. All three of these important elements of Ngari are in place. Based on this unique environment, what kind of civilization would the local ancestors create here?

> The Zanda Earth Pillars/Photo by Zhang Qiang

4 And There Were Wilderness and Civilization

Ten to twenty thousand years ago, humans had already made their mark on Ngari. They made stone tools and portrayed their daily life on rocks.

In the 4th century BC, local ancestors established a powerful tribal alliance. Their influence covered most of today's Xizang, and they were known as the Zhang Zhung Kingdom. Living in a territory that centered around the Xiangquan Hegu (Xiangquan River Valley), which had the most favorable environment in the vicinity, they grazed and hunted on the plateau and established farmland in the valley. They created golden masks and introduced luxurious brocades from Zhongyuan (Central Plain). The king of Zhang Zhung accumulated a huge amount of wealth and mobilized a tremendous amount of manpower to build a large capital city.

However, there was a lack of wood for construction due to the sparseness of trees on the plateau, so the Zhang Zhung people turned their eyes to the earth pillars with its dense soils. They created cave dwellings with complex structures in the earth pillars such as "caves within caves" or "houses within houses," and residences with "three rooms and one hall" or residences with "four rooms and one hall." These cave dwellings were complemented with other buildings and served as residences, palaces, and temples. They worshiped a mythical bird called the Golden Winged Roc, which is also called Qiongniao (literally, "Jade Bird") in Chinese. Even the layout of the capital city resembled a bird, hence the name "Silver Roc City."

The capital city built in the earth pillars had excellent defensive advantages. The wealth of the king of Zhang Zhung was housed inside. The younger sister of Songtsen Gampo—king of the Tubo Kingdom (an ancient empire built on today's Qinghai-Xizang Plateau from the 7th to 9th century, whose rule extended far beyond the current Xizang Autonomous Region to present Qinghai, Gansu, and Sichuan Provinces, etc.) —married the king of Zhang Zhung. On their wedding day, the princess sang:

> *I get married with the king of the Silver Roc City. Seen from the outside, it is only cliffs, but when viewed from the inside, it is made of gold and precious stones.*
>
> —Jin Shubo, *Coming from Zhang Zhung* (altered)

The king dominated secular life, and their god dominated the spiritual world. The local religion Yungdrung

1 Ngari rock painting/Photo by Kabu

This rock painting, a record of the daily activities of the ancestors of Ngari, Xizang, was photographed in Rutog County, Ngari. There are many similar rock paintings in Ngari.

2 3 The Golden Mask and the Silk Fabric/Photos by Jin Shubo

The Golden Mask and the piece of Silk Fabric were unearthed from the Gurujiamu Cemetery in Gar County, Ngari, Xizang. This silk piece has the patterns of Chinese characters "王" and "侯" and is the earliest silk fabric ever discovered on Qingzang Gaoyuan.

Bon originated in Gangdisê Shan. The believers engraved patterns and texts on the stones for ceremonies of blessing. Prototypes of the Mani Stones and Mani Piles that are all over Xizang today were born from this practice. They gave the Yungdrung symbol[1] a sacred meaning, and it was constantly used in religious rituals.

They worshiped sacred mountains and holy lakes, especially Kangrinboqê Feng, which was highly respected due to its huge cross-like groove that resembled the symbol of Yungdrung. The Yungdrung Bon carries the origin of the Zhang Zhung civilization. The religious sect spread eastward along Damqog Zangbo from its origin at Kangrinboqê Feng on the upper reaches of the Yarlung Zangbo Jiang, and its influence was seen all over Xizang.

The Zhang Zhung Kingdom lasted for about 1,000 years. In the 7th century AD, the wife of the king of Zhang Zhung—the sister of Songtsan Gampo—eventually threw in with the Tubo army to overthrow the ancient kingdom. The glory of the Zhang Zhung Kingdom eventually ended, but the glory of Ngari persisted.

In the middle of the 9th century, Tubo aristocrats attacked each other endlessly. Buddhism introduced from India had entered into a fierce conflict with the local religion Yungdrung Bon, and the Tubo Kingdom (618-842) fell apart. Prince Kyide Nyimagon fled to Zhang Zhung, his hometown, to establish a separatist regime, and changed the name

---

1 The symbol of Yongzhong ("卍" or "卐") appeared in ancient cultures all over the world. In the early days, both rotating directions contained the same meaning. In the Han culture, it is called the "symbol of the Wan character," and its pronunciation was confirmed during the reign of Empress Wu Zetian during the Tang Dynasty (618-907).

< **The Ruins of Silver Roc City/Photo by Kabu**

This picture shows an aerial view of the Ruins of Silver Roc City in Qulong Village, Zanda County, Ngari Prefecture, Xizang Autonomous Region. The mountain in the middle is like the roc's body and the mountains on both sides are like the roc's two wings. The Tibetan name of Silver Roc City means "roc silver castle." Therefore, Silver Roc City is also translated as "Qionglong Silver City" in Chinese. Silver Roc City's exact location is still controversial, and another highly likely site for its location is in Kaerdong, Gar County.

Zhang Zhung to Ngari, meaning "territory." This was the moment when the name "Ngari" appeared first in an official text.

Kyide Nyimagon granted his sons fiefdoms, and one of them ruled what is today's Ngari region. That area was named the Guge Kingdom.

The fertile land of the Xiangquan Hegu, the Shiquan Hegu (Shiquan River Valley) and the Kongque Hegu (Kongque River Valley) had been intensively cultivated by that time. The king personally directed the construction of canals to irrigate countless fertile fields. Additionally, the salt lakes of Qiangtang provided inexhaustible sources of salt for locals, the mountains were rich in gold, and the grasslands offered tremendous amounts of cashmere. The Guge Kingdom took advantage of these resources as the basis to develop trade with neighboring kingdoms and established a "Silk Road" on the plateau.

The wealthy Guge royal family paid gold to Indian monks and invited them to hold the largest dharma assembly in the Xizang region. Buddhism began to spread at an unprecedented rate in Ngari. Construction projects in the earth pillars peaked again, with many temples and Buddhist grottoes built all over. The Guge royal family invested huge amounts of wealth on murals inside the temples. In terms of art style, those murals blended the open, exaggerated painting styles of South Asia and Persia, forming unique aesthetical features. Short-sleeved and tight-fitting dresses, full breasts, slender waists, slanted crotches, and exposed navels of female gods were featured to reveal the beauty of the human body.

⌄ Guge Murals/Photo by Cabu

The Murals were photographed in the Red Palace at the ruins of Aliguge King City. The colors are vivid and bright, and the painting style is bold.

› A pilgrim/Photo by Tang Qiao

With Kangrinboqê Feng in the distance, a pious pilgrim is putting her hands together and kowtowing in worship.

The Buddhism of Guge absorbed many elements of the Yungdrung Bon, eventually replacing it and becoming the dominant religion in the kingdom. Kangrinboqê Feng, which features a unique shape and serves as the source of several major rivers, has been venerated as the "center of the world" by both Buddhism and the Yungdrung Bon. Pilgrims came from all over the world to worship the peak every year.

Perhaps the most eye-catching accomplishment was the construction of the capital city of the Guge Kingdom, which was built on the hillside among the earth pillars and peaks. A total of 445 houses, 879 caves, 58 watchtowers, and 28 pagodas were all stacked on top of the earth pillars. With a relative difference in elevation of

> Ruins of Guge Capital City/Photo by Mao Feng

The Ruins of Guge Capital City are located on a mountain on the south bank of Langqên Zangbo in Zanda County, Ngari Prefecture, Xizang Autonomous Region, which is about 18 kilometers away from the county seat of Zanda. It was once the center of the Guge Kingdom established by the descendants of the Tubo royal family. In the middle of the 17th century, it was destroyed by Ladakh invaders and only the ruins remain.

175 meters, the capital city on its high ground featured steep terrain. Atop the mountain was the imperial palace. From the foot of the mountain to the palace there was only a single, unobstructed man-made un-derpass which was surrounded by cliffs. It was one of the most insurmountable fortresses in the era of cold weapons.

However, the splendid Guge Kingdom was later destroyed by Ladakh, and the millennium-old fortress was gradually abandoned, leaving only ruined walls and numerous mysteries.

5 Today's Ngari

Both the Zhang Zhung and Guge Kingdoms are gone.

Today, Ngari still maintains its unique charm. It has China's most impressive starry nighttime sky, the most unique flora and fauna and rustic and hospitable residents.

Ngari is in the wilderness, yet it is both wild and civilized.

> A pilgrim/Photo by Jiang Xi

At the Koga Temple in Burang County, Ngari Prefecture, the photographer ran into a young girl who might have come from Nepal. Her smile was as bright as the sun. Ngari opens its arms to pilgrims from all over the world.

There is a land that exists in southwestern China. This land is a world of mountains, a kingdom of mountains. It is a place so inseparable from mountains that even its Chinese name—Hengduan—sounds like it holds a grudge against the mountains. It is Hengduan Shan.

Hengduan Shan covers an area of about 360,000 square kilometers, 98% of which are mountainous. Deep in this mountain area, there are countless well-recognized tourist destinations such as Jiuzhaigou, Huanglong, Ruoergai, Xamgyi'nyilha, Daocheng Yading, Dali and Lijiang.

1.3 Hengduan Shan:

A Mountain Range with the Most Breathtaking Scenery in China

Of all the different types of natural landscapes, Chinese people always prefer mountains. There is a verse in *Shijing (Classic of Poetry, or The Book of Songs)* likening men of virtue to lofty mountains and deeds of uprightness to the road to enlightenment. A high mountain rising above the ground is reason enough for all living beings to look up in wonder.

When there are thousands of mountains in one place, what would that effect be like?

A place exactly like this can be found in southwestern China. It is a world of mountains, a kingdom of mountains. It is a place so inseparable from its mountainous nature that even its Chinese name—Hengduan—sounds like it holds a grudge against the mountains. It is Hengduan Shan.

Hengduan Shan covers an area of approximately 360,000 square kilometers, and 98% of it is covered by mountain ranges. Extremely high mountains, those above 5,000 meters, and high mountains, which are between 3,500 and 5,000 meters, account for 73% of the total area. Konggar Shan, Moirig Xueshan (Meili Snow Mountain), Siguniang Shan (Mount Siguniang), Yulong Xueshan (Yulong Snow Mountain), Que'er Shan (Que'er Mountain), Gê'nyên (Genieshen Mountain), Yangmaiyong, and Xuebao Ding are all included in the group of famous mountains that are gathered in this area.

Amidst the mountains, there are countless well-known places of interest. Famous tourist attractions include Jiuzhaigou, Huanglong, Zoigê, Xamgyi'nyilha, Daocheng Yading, Dali, and Lijiang, just to name a few.

The three highways running through the area—National Highways 318, 317, and 214—have become China's most famous sight-seeing routes. As the highways pass through any of the breathtaking spots in Hengduan Shan, top scenic resorts in eastern China may be overshadowed by comparison.

Why does Hengduan Shan have so much beautiful scenery?

> **The topographical map of Hengduan Shan**

Hengduan Shan refers to a series of mountain ranges running north-south in the southeast of Qingzang Gaoyuan. From west to east, they are Baxoila Ling (Shubola Mountains)-Gaoligong Shan (Gaoligong Mountains), Taniantaweng Shan (Taniantaweng Mountains)-Nu Shan (Nushan Mountains), Ningjing Shan (Mangkam Shan, Ningjing Mountains)-Yun Ling (Yunling Mountains), Shaluli Shan (Shaluli Mountains), Daxue Shan (Daxue Mountains), Qionglai Shan (Qionglai Mountains), and Min Shan (Minshan Mountains).This group is also known as the "Seven Ranges of Hengduan." Running between the mountains are Nu Jiang, Lancang Jiang, Jinsha Jiang (Jinsha River), Yalong Jiang (Yalong River), Dadu He (Dadu River), Min Jiang (Minjiang River), and their tributaries. Regarding the specific boundary area of Hengduan Shan, especially its north and south borders, there are many disputes among scholars. This article is mainly based on Li Bingyuan's "Discussion on the Scope of Hengduan Shan," which defines Hengduan Shan as the area that consists of peaks over 4,000 meters above sea level and the deep valleys in between.

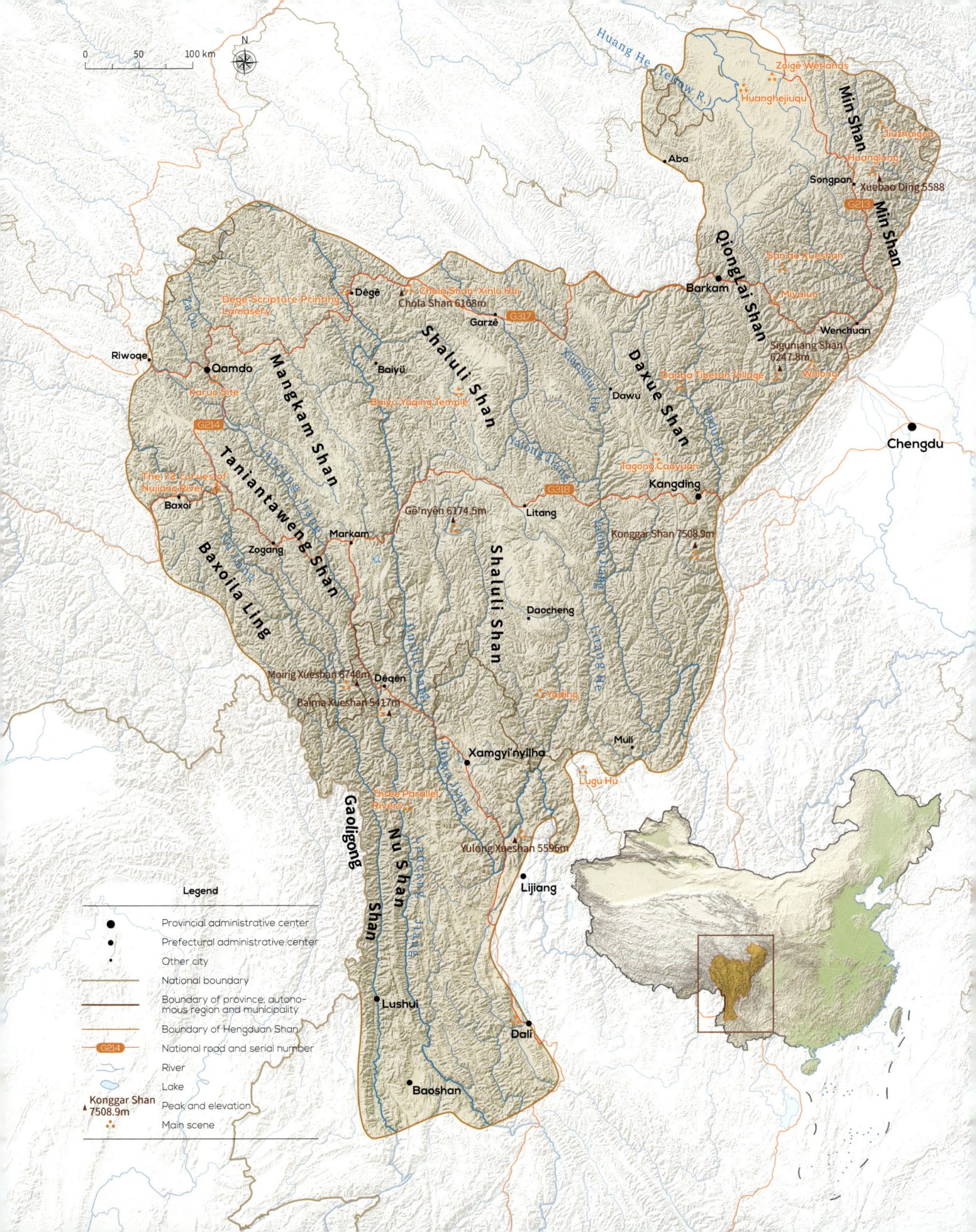

West slope of Konggar Shan/Photo by Nanka
The photo was taken at the Zimei Pass. From here you can obtain fantastic views of the western slope of Konggar Shan.

1 The Formation of Mountains

About 65 million years ago, the Indian Plate violently collided with the Asia-Europe Plate as it traveled from south to north. The resulting uplift created Qingzang Gaoyuan, and the resulting pressure was released to the east and west. At the east end, it encountered strong resistance from the Yangtze Plate. During this "close combat," the land compressed and shrank, forming huge folds and faults.

These folds were the early form of today's Hengduan Shan. They are roughly divided into seven columns that extend from north to south, including Baxoila Ling (Shubola Mountain)-Gaoligong Shan (Gaoligong Mountains), Taniantaweng Shan (Taniantawong Mountains)-Nu Shan (Nushan Mountains), Ningjing Shan (Mangkam Shan, or Ningjing Mountains)-Yun Ling (Yunling Mountains), Shaluli Shan (Shaluli Mountains), Daxue Shan (Daxue Mountains), Qionglai Shan (Qionglai Mountains), and Min Shan (Minshan Mountains). These mountains are generally referred to as the "Seven Ranges of Hengduan."

The average distance between the main ridges of these mountains is only about 100 kilometers. They form close mountain chains and are connected to each other.

Take Shaluli Shan in the center of the Seven Ranges as an example. It is the widest of the Seven Ranges of Hengduan. Viewed from above, Shaluli Shan looks like the array of a mighty army composed of numerous snowy peaks. The famous Que'er Shan, Genie Shan (Genie Mountain), Haizi Shan (Haizi Mountain), Yulong Xueshan, and Haba Xueshan (Haba Snow Mountain) are among this army of mountains.

∧ Miancimu Feng (Mianzimu)/Photo by Wang Jianfeng

Miancimu Feng is located on the south side of Moirigkawagarbo (Kawagebo Peak), at an elevation of 6,054 meters.

∨ Xianuoduoji (Chana Dorje)/Photo by Jiang Tao

Xianuoduoji, one of the "Three Sacred Mountains in Daocheng," stands 5,951.3 meters above sea level.

Daxue Shan, which is to the east of Shaluli Shan, has many peaks reaching over 6,000 meters above sea level, and it is the highest mountain among the Seven Ranges of Hengduan. Its highest peak, Konggar Shan, stands 7,508.9 meters above sea level and is the tallest of all the peaks of Hengduan Shan.

As the altitude increases, it supports the formation of huge glaciers on the high mountains. Today, as glaciers around the world continue to disappear, there are still 1,961 glaciers in Hengduan Shan. Together, the glaciers cover a total area of more than 1,300 square kilometers, which is 200 times the size of Xi Hu. Among them the most well-known include the Hailuogou Glacier, the Yanzigou Glacier, the Mingyong Glacier, the Que'er Mountain Glacier, and the Yulong Snow Mountain Glacier.

With so many glaciers continuously eroding the mountains, together with the effects of gravity and constant weathering, the peaks have been shaped into extremely sharp and eye-catching structures. Many of today's famous peaks were formed in this way, including Konggar Shan, Siguniang Shan, MoirigXueshan, Yulong Xueshan, YalaXueshan, Yang Maiyong, and Xianuoduoji.

Even the lesser known "supporting actors" are equally brilliant, such as Miancimu Feng, one of the 13 peaks of Moirig Xueshan; Pomiao Feng (Pomiao Peak)—which is nearby the glorious Yaomei Feng (Yaomei Peak), the main peak of Siguniang Shan, and the spectacular Tu'er Shan (Tu'er Mountain).

Hengduan Shan is not only outstanding for its shape, but it is also the best place among the major mountain ranges in China to view reflections of snow-capped mountains. Among these mountains, the glaciers have made numerous glacial cirques and eroded depressions, which gather water to form thousands of mountain lakes.

Although these lakes are not large, their appearance creates a harmony with the surrounding mountains.

For example, Bajiaopeng Haizi (Bajiaopeng Lake) and Yangmantai Haizi (Yangmantai Lake) in Siguniang Shan, as well as Lengga Co (Lengga Lake) and Lisuo Hai (Lisuohai Lake) in Konggar Shan, can create perfect reflections of the extremely tall mountains on their surfaces. The shapes of the mountains are echoed by their duplicates on the water, creating a dreamlike vista in which reality and fiction coexist.

‹ Reflection of Yaomei Feng/Photo by Yang Sutie

The reflection of the north side of Yaomei Feng. The photo was taken at Yangmantai Haizi.

⌄ Reflection of Konggar Shan/Photo by Yin Guiyuan

The reflection of the west side of Konggar Shan. The photo was taken at Lengga Co.

2 Managing Water

If the area merely consisted of countless snowy peaks, then the scenery of Hengduan Shan would be no different from that of the hinterland of Qingzang Gaoyuan; the only difference would be the concentration of scenic spots in the area. However, due to the power of flowing water and the role it plays, this is not the case.

Moisture from the South Asian monsoon arriving from the Indian Ocean and moisture from the East Asian monsoon arriving from the Pacific Ocean are both intercepted by Hengduan Shan. With the clouds and mists that evaporate in the mountains, precipitation increases on the ground. Combined with effects of runoff water and groundwater, a vast ancient lake located in the northwestern of Hengduan Shan did not dry up after the source stream of Huang He connected to it about 30 thousand years ago. This lake gradually became shallow and nourished plants, finally turned into a vast expanse of swamps—the famous Zoigê Wetland. The Wetland continues to provide non-stop water sources to Huang He.

In mountainous areas with many carbonate rocks, flowing water dissolves the carbonate minerals in the

︿ **Huanglong/Photo by Qiu Menghan**

Huanglong is in Songpan County, Aba Tibetan and Qiang Autonomous Prefecture in Sichuan. Its typical landscape feature is the travertine terraces.

﹀ **Zoigê/Photo by Jiang Xi**

The photo was taken near Zoigê County. Surrounded by mountains, the central part is low and flat with wide valleys, poor drainage, numerous lakes, and meandering rivers.

rocks, creating deposits that form travertine along the way. The travertine can take the shape of stacks, like terraces. In this way, the Baishui Terrace in Xamgyi'nyilha, Yunnan, was born. The most striking examples of this are Huanglong and Jiuzhaigou, whose travertine landscapes spread across several valleys and have gained fame near and far. Due to the different microbial communities that grow on the surface, travertine displays different colors, which, coupled with the colorful surrounding plants, can make for a very splendid, colorful world.

A greater volume of water flows along the valleys between the Seven Ranges of Hengduan, gradually forming six major rivers: Nu Jiang, Lancang Jiang, Jinsha Jiang (Jinsha River), Yalong Jiang (Yalong River), Dadu He (Dadu River), and Min Jiang (Minjiang River), and they are generally referred to as the "Six Rivers of Hengduan."

Among them, Nu Jiang flows between Baxoila Ling-Gaoligong Shan, and Tani-an-taweng Shan (Taniantaweng Mountains)-Nu Shan. From Chavalong in Chayu County, Xizang, to Liuku, the capital of the Lisu Autonomous Prefecture, Nujiang, Yunnan, about 300 kilometers of the river course is sandwiched between mountains from 4,000 to 5,000 meters above sea level. The difference in elevation between the valley bottom and the mountaintops can reach 2,000 to 3,000 meters. This is the Nu Jiang Grand Canyon. The narrowest part of the riverbed in the canyon is only a few dozen meters wide. The turbulent river roars through, shaking the valley with its powerful sound, giving Nu Jiang, which means "angry river" in Chinese, its name.

The difference in elevation between the valley of Lancang Jiang, which faces Nu Jiang across the Taniantaweng Shan and Nu Shan, and the mountaintops along its banks is much greater. Lancang Jiang Grand Canyon in Deqin County, Yunnan has an elevation of approximately 2,000 meters. On its eastern side, Zhalaqueni Feng (Zhalaqueni Peak) stands 5,460 meters above sea level, and on its western side, the highest peak in Yunnan, Moirigkawagarbo (Kawagebo Peak), is 6,740 meters above sea level. The maximum difference is found along Lancang Jiang, which surpasses 4,700 meters. With high mountains, deep valleys, steep rocky walls, and turbulent river waters, Lancang Jiang seems extremely dangerous.

The terrain that extends along the north-south line of Hengduan Shan forces the rivers to flow southward along the mountains. After flowing outside of China's territory, Nu Jiang turns into an important river in Myanmar, known as the Thanlwin (Salween), and Lancang Jiang becomes known as the Mekong River.

⌃ Nu Jiang/Photo by Li Heng
The picture shows the big bend of Nu Jiang in Exi Township, Luolong County, Changdu.

⌄ Lancang Jiang/Photo by Du Pengfei
The picture shows the Yanjing section of Lancang Jiang.

The First Curve of Chang Jiang/Photo by Cui Yongjiang

The First Curve of Chang Jiang is located between Shigu Town, Lijiang, which is in the northwest of Yunnan, and Shasongbi Village in the south of Xamgyi'nyilha. At present academics believe the curve was an abrupt bend of the riverbed formed due to river piracy. But there still are disagreements about this hypothesis.

Two of the Six Rivers of Hengduan have already "surrendered" to Hengduan Shan's terrain by flowing to the south. Would the other four rivers also "resign themselves" to the same fate?

If this were the case, China's rivers patterns would have undergone major changes. Chang Jiang, called the "mother river" by Chinese people, would not be as large as it is today.

However, Jinsha Jiang, which has the greatest water volume of the Six Rivers of Hengduan has turned things around.

From its very beginning in Hengduan Shan, Jinsha Jiang has been held hostage by the mountains. It runs parallel to Nu Jiang and Lancang Jiang to the south, separated by two mountains in the middle. At the narrowest point, the three rivers and two mountains are only about 70 kilometers away. This is the famous "Three Parallel Rivers."

Some scholars believe that about 17,000 years ago, the mountains near Shigu Town, Lijiang, Yunnan were cut through by the northward-flowing ancient Chang Jiang. The southward-flowing ancient Jinsha Jiang was connected to Chang Jiang. Thus, Jinsha Jiang became part of Chang Jiang, and rid itself of Hengduan Shan's control, turned northward, and formed a unique Ω-shaped turn, that is, the First Curve of Chang Jiang.

After that, the length of Chang Jiang expanded and the momentum became more majestic, making Chang Jiang similar to today's scale. It rushes and surges through the 12-kilometer-long Tiger Leaping Gorge without fear of being hindered by the obstacles presented by various boulders, with the resulting sound of the roaring water echoing for miles. Along the way, it also embraces three more of the Six Rivers of Hengduan: Yalong Jiang, Min Jiang, and Dadu He.

Thus, the pattern of seven ranges and six rivers in the area of Hengduan Shan has taken shape.

1	2	3
4	5	6

1 Nu Jiang/Photo by Aaron Liu

The photo was taken next to National Highway 318 in Bangda Town, Basu County, Changdu.

2 Lancang Jiang/Photo by Hu Shu

The photo was taken along Lancang Jiang in Yanjing Township, Mangkang County, Changdu, Xizang.

3 Jinsha Jiang/Photo by Du Pengfei

The Tiger Leaping Gorge section of Jinsha Jiang.

4 Yalong Jiang/Photo by Wen Junhao

The photo shows the Bayirong Township section of Yalong Jiang.

5 Dadu He/Photo by Xia Junmin

The photo was taken from an airplane, and the viewpoint is from the north looking south. The village beneath is Kairao.

6 Min Jiang/Photo by Wei Wei

The Wenchuan section of Min Jiang. The area in the valley is the urban area of Wenchuan County.

3 Cutting off the East-West Traffic

In the seven ranges and six rivers of Hengduan, high mountains and deep valleys run parallel to each other. This is the most spectacular mountain-valley area on Earth due to the incredible density of canyons and rivers. The north-to-south running high mountain chains and the turbulent rivers are difficult to cross, forming a natural barrier that cuts off the traffic from the East to the West.

In 1863, General Shi Dakai of the Taiping Heavenly Kingdom intended to lead his troops across Dadu He into Hengduan Shan. However, the entire army was blocked by the flood. They had no way to cross the river, and finally were defeated by the chasing Qing army.

In 1935, the Red Army crossed Dadu He and captured the Luding Bridge after a tenacious battle. After several months, they climbed over Erlang Shan (Erlang Mountain) and Jiajin Shan (Jiajin Mountain), and then they passed through the swampy wetlands of Hongyuan and Zoigê. They were able to get out of Hengduan Shan, but only after they paid a heavy price.

However, these great obstacles to human travel also help to maintain the integrity of the relatively pristine ecological environment here.

This is a region with one of the richest naturally occurring vertical belts in the world, ranging from mountain forests to alpine shrubs, then to the alpine deserts and to the belt below the snow line. Maple forests, birch forests, hemlock forests, spruce forests, cypress forests, rhododendron forests, and various meadows all have their place at various altitudes.

‹ **Vegetation of Hengduan Shan/Photo by Qin Jie**
The photo was taken at Jianziwan Shan (Jianziwan Mountain) on National Highway 318, and the viewpoint is from the west looking east. The towering snow mountain in the picture is Konggar Shan.

The abundance of animal species here is even more impressive.

In 1869, the French missionary Armand David discovered giant pandas in Hengduan Shan. This adorable creature quickly aroused the curiosity of the world, and many zoologists and hunters came to China specifically to find them. Even today this curiosity has remained.

In 1890, Westerners captured the Yunnan snub-nosed monkey in Hengduan Shan. They live in the dark coniferous alpine forest at an altitude of over 3,000 meters, and they are one of the few primates that inhabit the highest places in the world.

New species are still being discovered. In 2017, Chinese scientists confirmed the existence of another new species, the Skywalker hoolock gibbon, which was found in Hengduan Shan. It is the only anthropoid named by Chinese scientists. Its current population in China is less than 200.

Other types of animals are equally eye-catching, such as the red panda, the white-lipped deer, the rock sheep, the Tibetan fox, the yellow weasel, and the black woodpecker.

1 2 3

1 Giant panda/Photo by Zhou Mengqi
A giant panda is baring its fangs and showing its claws high in a tree.

2 Skywalker hoolock gibbon/Photo by Kyle Obermann
The Skywalker hoolock gibbon is a typical arboreal primate. It usually inhabits mid-mountain humid evergreen broadleaf forests, monsoon evergreen broadleaf forests, and mountain rain forests.

3 White-lipped deer/Photo by Zhang Qiang
The white-lipped deer is under national first-class protection in China. It mainly lives in the alpine grasslands of Qingzang Gaoyuan. The picture was taken in Daofu County, Ganzi Prefecture, Sichuan.

Yunnan snub-nosed monkey/Photo by Hu Qiusheng
The Yunnan snub-nosed monkey, a species endemic to China, is distributed at the junction of the three provinces of Sichuan, Yunnan, and Xizang. The picture shows a mother and her child.

Hengduan Shan cuts off east-west traffic, but at the same time it opens a channel for north-south communication.

About 6,000 years ago, some of the ancient people living in Huanghe Pendi (Yellow River Basin) continued to move south along the valley of Hengduan Shan. In the subsequent evolutionary process, several ethnic minorities, including the Tibetans and the Yi people, gradually emerged in this region. Sociologist Fei Xiaotong calls this north-south passage the "Zang-Yi Corridor."

After that, Tibetans built monasteries, held grand Buddhist events, and constructed sturdy Diaofang (a kind of local household that also functions as a defensive structure) at the foot of the snow-capped mountains. The Bai people beneath Cang Shan (Cangshan Mountain) built exquisite cities and prayed for blessings beneath towering pagodas. The Naxi people looked at Yulong Xueshan in the distance and built magnificent Tusi (chieftain) fortresses. The Dulong people, who were in a comparatively weaker position at that time, started the tradition facial tattoos on women, in order to scare away outside intruders.

1	
2	3

1 Yulong Xueshan viewed from Lijiang Old Town/Photo by Liu Zhuming

In the distance is the Yulong Xueshan; not far away lies Shizi Shan (Lion Rock) on the left and Xiangshan Shan (Elephant Mountain) on the right.

2 Dege Sutra Printing House/Photo by Jiang Xi

Dege Sutra Printing House is in Dege County, Ganzi Prefecture, Sichuan. It is the most important Buddhist sutra printing house in Tibetan-inhabited areas. Its engraving and printing skills were included in the UNESCO Representative List of the Intangible Cultural Heritage of Humanity in 2009.

3 Dulong Facial Tattoos/Photo by Shen Yunyao

Historically, there are many reasons why Dulong women have the tradition of applying facial tattoos. Preventing outsiders from looting was just one of them.

4 Traffic Once Blocked Has Turned Smooth

The Hengduan Shan area has dense mountains, crisscrossing rivers, numerous species, and diverse ethnic groups. However, the dangers of travelling the high mountains prevent the outside world from understanding this rich area. Hengduan Shan, with its densely packed natural and cultural landscapes, is the latest recognized large mountain range in our collective consciousness. It was not until the second half of the 19th century, due to surveys conducted by groups of Western explorers, that the mysterious veil of Hengduan Shan started to be lifted. The mention of its name in the historical record came even later. At some point between 1900 to 1901, the Chinese geographer Zou Daijun (1854-1908) of the late Qing Dynasty (1616-1911) mentioned it for the first time in a geography lecture:

> *The plateau between Altai Shan (Altai Mountains) and the Himalayas... has large sandy stone mountains, the south of which is Min Shan, Xue Ling (Xueling Mountain) and Yun Ling. All these mountain ranges extend from north to south. They are named Hengduan Shan.*
>
> —Lecture Notes of Chinese Geography of the Imperial University of Peking

Today, the once nearly hopeless traffic situation in Hengduan Shan has greatly improved. Roads have been built to cross the mountains and valleys. An increasing number of people are starting to enter this mountainous area, looking up at the snow-capped peaks or looking down at the streams.

When we admire the treasure of the Hengduan Shan let us also protect this mountain range with the most breathtaking scenery in China.

Daxue Shan / Photo by Jiang Xi
The highest peak in the distance is Konggar Shan.

If we learn the history of Jiuzhaigou's formation, we will come to understand that to "cultivate" a landscape to a level matching Jiuzhaigou's beauty, incredible ordeals and disasters must take place. For mother nature, the damage caused by an earthquake is insignificant because all injuries to the land can be healed and the destruction mended.

1.4 Jiuzhaigou:
Destruction and Creation

At 21:19 on August 8, 2017, a magnitude-7 earthquake struck Jiuzhaigou, a famous tourist attraction in China.

The natural, colorful dams on the mountain lakes collapsed, instantly draining away the water, and the lakes almost dried up. The once-picturesque Nuorilang Waterfall—which was nearly 300 meters wide and featured magnificent beaded waterfalls—was ruined and reduced to something more akin to a normal slope you would find in any wilderness.

It only took one day to destroy a mountain paradise. The abrupt change caused people to lament its loss. While some might feel lucky that they had enjoyed the scenery of Jiuzhaigou before the earthquake, others might regret that they had not yet taken the opportunity to appreciate its beauty. It seems that the loss of Jiuzhaigo's precious scenery is irreversible.

Has the beauty of Jiuzhaigou been lost forever?

Of course not.

If we know the history of Jiuzhaigou's formation, we will understand that if a landscape wants to "cultivate" itself to the level of Jiuzhaigou's beauty, the "tribulations" it must go through are beyond imagination. Yet for nature, such damage is negligible.

All of the injuries can be healed and the destruction mended.

> The Nuorilang Waterfall/Photo by Lin Rongsheng
> The Nuorilang Waterfall was formed 213,000 to 189,000 years ago. When the earthquake occurred on August 8, 2017, the waterfall collapsed, damaging it severely.

Min Shan/Photo by Ouyang Hong
The picture shows the mountains near Jiuzhaigou. It was taken on a flight from Chengdu to Jiuzhai Huanglong Airport.

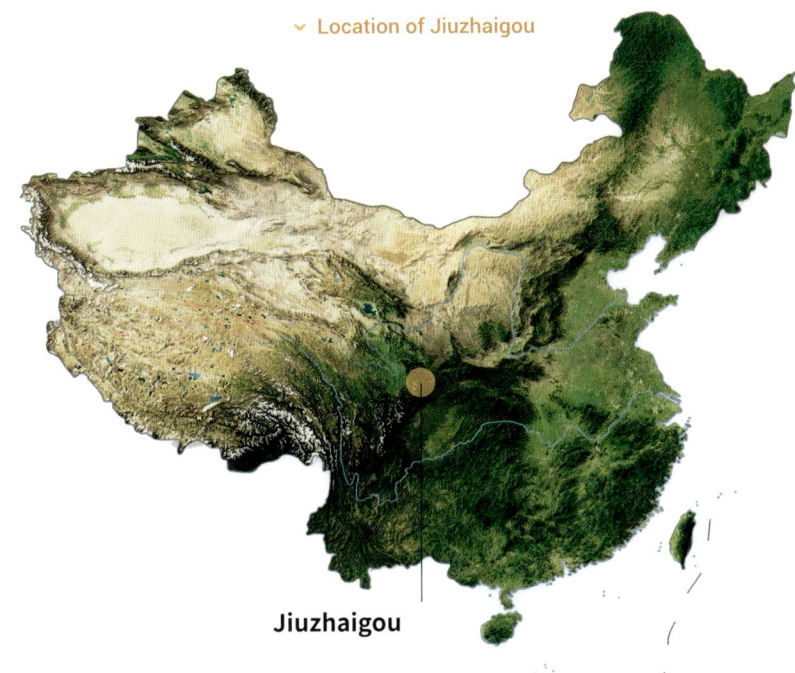

Location of Jiuzhaigou

Jiuzhaigou

1 Jiuzhaigou in Embryo

Jiuzhaigou is located on the eastern edge of Qingzang Gaoyuan in the transition zone from Qingzang Gaoyuan to Sichuan Pendi (Sichuan Basin). Some 400 million years ago, it was still a shallow sea. The seawater was clear and warm, with sunlight directly penetrating down to the bottom of the sea. Many ancient creatures thrived here. Shells and skeletons left from generations of deceased creatures made for an inconspicuous substance that accumulated there over the years. This substance is calcium carbonate.

Calcium carbonate was deposited on the seafloor in the form of carbonate rocks, which reached a total thickness of up to 4,000 meters after hundreds of millions of years. After all this time, it would become the most important material as a basis for the formation of Jiuzhaigou's beautiful scenery.

About 65 million years ago, the Indian Plate and the Eurasian Plate began to collide, and Qingzang Gaoyuan experienced a violent uplift. Around 3.3 million years ago, the eastern edge of Qingzang Gaoyuan had risen to an altitude of about 3,000 meters. A plateau covered with thick layer of carbonate rocks and gentle mountains was born. This was the prototype for Jiuzhaigou's later beauty.

At the same time, the "gods of destruction and creation" came, and the future of Jiuzhaigou's landscape was destined to endless change.

2 The First Destruction and Creation

The first "destroyers" and "creators" were glaciers.

About 2.6 million years ago, as the first ice age appeared and the global temperature dropped sharply, Jiuzhaigou—a mountainous region on a plateau—gave birth to many mountain glaciers. Glaciers have a strong erosive effect on mountains and peaks. The gentle slopes of the mountain peaks were destroyed by the glaciers, and the peaks became steep and rugged. The three most noteworthy peaks are Zhayizhaga Shan (Zhayizhaga Mountain), Dage Shan (Dage Mountain), and Woluosemo Shan (Woluosemo Mountain). Zhayizhaga Shan rises 4,400 meters above sea level. Its peaks are sharp and pierce directly into the sky. Woluosemo Shan's peak is 4,114 meters above sea level, with a majestic posture, which is often covered in mist. The tall, straight, and majestic Dage Shan, made of exposed limestone, stands 4,106 meters above sea level.

The glaciers melted away due to the rise of the global temperature after the first erosion they had done to the mountains. However, a much bigger destruction was bubbling under.

About 700,000 years ago, the second ice age swept across the plateau. This time, the glaciers that formed were larger and the grinding movement was even more violent. The land of the flat plateau was marked with many high, deep, and wide U-shaped gullies. Most of

Before the erosion
The mountain is deeply cut by the river, forming a valley featuring steep slopes along the banks looking like the letter "V"

During the erosion
The glacier and frozen soil erode the mountain

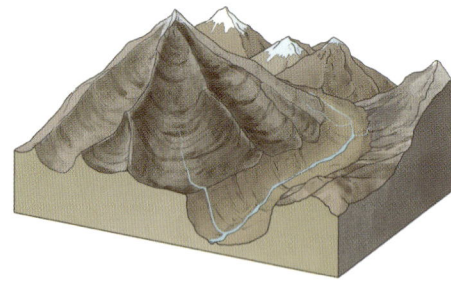

After the erosion
The glacier cut the body of the mountain like a chisel while widening the valley, making it look like the letter "U"

∧ The erosive effect of glaciers

the important gullies we see in the Jiuzhaigou Scenic Area today were formed by glacial erosion during the second ice age. Typical examples include Zechawa Gou (Zechawa Gully), the longest gully in the Jiuzhaigou scenic area which is nearly 32 kilometers long. The rocky mountains on both sides of the gully create steep towers, and at its narrowest point, the gully is only 20 to 30 meters wide. If we look down from the sky, it will seem like we were overlooking the Three Gorges of Chang Jiang from a majestic viewpoint.

⌄ **Woluosemo Shan/Photo by Zhang Linyang**
Wolosemo Shan is 4,114 meters above sea level (other elevation data puts it at 4,136 meters). This photo was taken in Shuzheng Village.

Dage Shan/Photo by Zhang Linyang

Dage Shan is 4,106 meters above sea level (other elevation data places it at 4,200 meters). According to local legends, Dage Shan was a god and Woluosemo Shan was a goddess. The two were a couple of tragic lovers. This photo was taken at Zhenzhu Tan (Pearl Beach).

About 230,000 years ago, when the glaciers retreated, many tarns appeared in the mountains that were originally covered with glacial ice. Take Hei Hu (Black Lake) near Zhayizhaga Shan as an example: Because of its depth, it looks completely dark against the surrounding white snow. In lower gullies, there are many moraine lakes. The most famous one is Chang Hai (Long Lake), the largest lake in Jiuzhaigou. It has a total water volume of 46 million cubic meters during the wet season and is three times the size of Xi Hu. As such a large lake was forming, the water used by ancient lakes downstream was absorbed, causing them to dry up and disappear. It can be said that creation and destruction are always interlinked.

	1
3	2

1 A tarn/Photo by Qian Wei

A tarn in the Jiuzhaigou area. After ancient glaciers eroded and formed cirques, water from melted glaciers gathered in those cirques to form lakes, which are called tarns to describe how they were formed geologically.

2 Chang Hai/Photo by Gong Qiang

The formation of Chang Hai took place between 235,000 and 190,000 years ago. The picture shows a frozen Chang Hai in winter.

3 Distribution of the main landscapes of Jiuzhaigou

3 The Second Destruction and Creation

The land that was eroded by glaciers had become extremely fragile, and a group of "destroyers" and "creators" who were "noisier" than glaciers began to frequently demonstrate their power.

They are collapses, landslides, and mudslides caused by earthquakes and gravity.

About 210,000 years ago, the north and south sides of Nuorilang Shan (Nuorilang Mountain) suffered a severe collapse, and the material from the resulting landslide overlapped sharply, accumulating into a slightly convex, arc-shaped vertical cliff face stretching to the bottom of the valley where the water flows. The widest waterfall in Jiuzhaigou, the Nuorilang Waterfall, was born. The Nuorilang Waterfall is vivid and colorful with the sur-rounding vegetation providing different colors in different seasons. It is unimaginable that such beautiful scenery was born simply due to the collapse of a mountain. Unfortunately, it was later destroyed by an earthquake.

The Shuzheng Waterfall at the lower reaches of the Nuorilang Waterfall was also formed by collapse and landslide.

Jiuzhaigou's landscape, which was once destroyed by glaciers, collapses, and landslides, still hasn't found its final shape.

< Nuorilang Waterfall/Photo by Wei Wei

The Nuorilang Waterfall was formed by the collapse of a mountain, and the accumulation of travertine in the later period made it even more spectacular. This aerial image brings us a rare perspective.

About 160,000 years ago, the third ice age came. The power of the ensuing destruction increased in various ways. Not only did valleys both large and small continue to deepen and widen, but deposits also blocked rivers in many places. These places then accumulated water and formed barrier lakes.

Wuhua Hai (Five-Flower Lake), which is known as the most beautiful lake in Jiuzhaigou, was also formed at that time as mudslides blocked the river. On both banks, mudslide fans can still be seen extending into the lake today. Jianzhu Hai (Arrow Bamboo Lake) in the upper reaches of Wuhua Hai was also formed in the same way.

Lakes formed by early glaciers cannot escape the fate of eventually being blocked and destroyed by falling rocks. However, fate is sometimes strange and never certain. Some lakes, after being destroyed, have become even larger and more beautiful than before. For example, the waters of Xiongmao Hai (Panda Lake) cover an area several times larger than before, and even a sapphire cannot compete with its azure-blue color. However, there are mountains stretching alongside Xiongmao Hai. If those mountains collapse, it is very likely that new barriers could be formed, changing the status quo once again.

⌄ The formation of a barrier lake

The valley is deep, with steep slopes on both sides

Earthquakes, volcanic eruptions and other factors result in mountain collapses and landslides, blocking the river.

The upper reaches of the blocked riverbed are overwhelmed by water, forming a barrier lake. Blockages can be easily eroded and washed away, causing a secondary collapse and further damage.

› Xiongmao Hai/Photo by Li Heng

Xiongmao Hai, a barrier lake, was formed by rocks from mountains that collapsed and blocked the river course from 235,000 to 190,000 years ago. In addition, the accumulation of travertine also helped seal the barrier.

4 The Third Destruction and Creation

Compared with glaciers, collapses, landslides, and mudslides, the other "destroyer" and "creator" is gentler and more silent. It is water.

A large amount of precipitation has destroyed the underground carbonate formations in Jiuzhaigou, creating an extremely powerful groundwater system. Cracks or holes cut out by water can be seen almost everywhere. The water flows in or out along cracks in the carbonate rocks, and the part that flows out to the surface becomes a beautiful river, which connects lakes in series along the valleys.

The current not only provides replenishment for the lakes but also brings an important substance mentioned above—calcium. Water dissolves the calcium in the carbonate rock and deposits it along the way. The resulting sediment is called travertine. Travertine adheres to rocks, lake bottoms, and even trees that fall into the water.

Ten thousand years ago, travertine deposition gradually entered a stable period. Most of the travertine in Jiuzhaigou we see today were formed during this time. Small amounts of travertine built up in layers, becoming increasingly larger and began to demonstrate its power. They have accumulated into dams, cutting rivers into pieces but also creating new scenery. The most typical is Shuzheng Qunhai (Shuzheng Lakes). The embankment of travertine has formed 23 lakes of various sizes in the valley. The lakes are closely connected and cover an area longer than 600 meters. In autumn, the forests are so colorful and create layers that make it impossible to tell whether it is water covered with colorful plants or land covered with jasper-like water.

‹ **Wuhua Hai/Photo by Zhang Kunkun**

Underwater trees are covered by travertine. Here is a fun fact: scale deposits at the bottom of an ordinary household kettle and travertine are made of the same substance. The difference between beauty and ugliness sometimes simply lies in their locations.

Shuzheng Qunhai/Photo by Zeng Yongqian
This picture shows a panoramic view of Shuzheng Qunhai. Collapsing rocks and travertine deposits have divided the Shuzheng Qunhai into many small lakes.

The precipitation of travertine also forms waterfalls. We can take the Jianzhuhai Waterfall as an example. The continuous accumulation of travertine gradually lifts the river course to form the base of the waterfall. The current pours down from the top and is a gorgeous scenery. The Zhenzhutan (Pearl Beach) Waterfall, which has a larger vertical drop, was formed the same way. Even the Nuorilang Waterfall has become more spectacular because of travertine.

The color of travertine also enriches the landscape of Jiuzhaigou to a great extent. Due to different microbial communities growing on the surface, travertine will display different colors, including light yellow, tan, off-white, light gray, and gray-yellow.

These different colors of travertine deposits at the bottom of the lakes as well as the colorful surrounding plants have made for an extremely splendid, picturesque world. The different reflections and absorption of light by travertine, algae, aquatic plants, and deadwood at the bottom of the lakes, coupled with blue sky, white clouds, green grass, and colorful forests, create a world of color that cannot be described with mere words.

Glaciers, collapses, landslides, mudslides, running water, travertine… these "destroyers" and "creators" have worked together to complete the creation of the stunning artwork that is Jiuzhaigou. However, the matter is not quite finished yet.

> Zhenzhutan Waterfall/Photo by Wang Jianfeng

In the opening of the 1986 version of the Chinese TV series *Journey to the West*, the place where the Tang Monk and his apprentices wade with the horse is the Zhenzhutan Waterfall.

v Jianzhuhai Waterfall/Photo by Zhang Kunkun

The Jianzhuhai Waterfall in autumn. The golden trees and the blue lake contrast with each other, and the flowing waterfall makes the picture even more vivid.

5 The Future

Decades ago, humans entered Jiuzhaigou with modern logging tools. During the 12 years from 1968 to 1979, people felled trees at a rate of more than 100,000 cubic meters each year. Many forests disappeared, the soil eroded and disastrous mudslides became more severe. One-third of the lakes in Jiuzhaigou suffered from drought. The large-scale human destruction in the Jiuzhaigou area was

Xiniu Hai (Rhino Lake)/Photo by Zeng Yongqian
In autumn, both banks of the Jiuzhaigou Valley are full of colorful forests. The vegetation and their reflections in the water echo each other, being both true and illusory, forming some of the most charming scenery of Jiuzhaigou.

gradually eliminated after the nature reserve was established in 1978, and the scenic area was listed as a World Heritage Site in 1992.

Jiuzhaigou has experienced 400 million years of growth, destruction and creation. No power can stop it from changing day by day.

Today, even an earthquake surely cannot destroy the beauty of Jiuzhaigou.

In the future, old landscapes may disappear in Jiuzhaigou, but there will also be new ones that emerge. In any case, Jiuzhaigou will remain pure, dreamlike, and colorful.

In recent years, a new group of peaks in Western Sichuan has become a major focus of attention—Siguniang Shan. With its picturesque scenery, it is known as the "Queen of Shushan (Mountains of Sichuan)." Among expert mountaineers and rock climbers, Siguniang Shan is even more famous than Qomolangma Feng. Mountaineers and rock climbers from the West often call it "the Alps of the East" or the "Yosemite of China."

1.5 Siguniang Shan:
A Song of Ice and Rock

The collision and compression of Qingzang Gaoyuan and Sichuan Pendi have formed vast plateaus and continuous mountain ranges in western Sichuan, including Shaluli Shan, Daxue Shan, Qionglai Shan, Min Shan, and Songpan Gaoyuan (Songpan Plateau). We refer to them all together as Chuanxi Gaoyuan (Western Sichuan Plateau).

Here, high mountains and deep valleys adjoin; clear springs and rapid rivers converge. From Jiuzhaigou and Huanglong—with some of the most beautiful waterscapes in the world—to the Wolong Nature Reserve, which is inhabited by China's national treasure, giant pandas; from the pure earthly land of Daocheng Yading, to the majestic Hengduan Shan's highest peak Konggar Shan, many fascinating landscapes are gathered here.

Surrounded by various renowned scenic areas, a "brand new" group of peaks is making a big entrance, becoming the focus of everyone's attention. It is Siguniang Shan. Siguniang Shan has beautiful scenery and is considered the "second peak" in Sichuan, known as the "Queen of Shushan, the Mountains of Sichuan."

In mountaineering and rock-climbing circles, Siguniang Shan is even more famous than Qomolangma Feng. Mountaineers and rock climbers from the West like to call it "the Alps of the East" or the "Yosemite of China"[1]. There are only a handful of people who have successfully reached its top, and they have won praise and gained fans from all over the world. British mountaineer Mick Fowler[2] once said:

> *When I first saw the northwest side of Siguniang Shan from the magazine, I was shocked by this mountain and fell into a long contemplation and ecstasy... The north side of the mountain is the most magnificent route I have ever climbed, and Siguniang Shan is the most charming mountain.*
>
> —Mick Fowler, *On Thin Ice*

---

1 Yosemite refers to the Yosemite National Park located in California in the western United States.
2 Mick Fowler reached the top of Yaomei Feng, the main peak of Siguniang Shan in 2002, and received the highest honor in mountaineering—the Golden Ice Axe Award.

> **Yaomei Feng/Photo by Zhang Shanyou**
> Yaomei Feng, 6,247.8 meters above sea level, the second highest peak in Sichuan next only to Kongga Shan, is dubbed the "Queen of Sichuan Mountains."

1 Misfortune

Siguniang Shan is by no means the second highest peak in Sichuan, contradicting what people commonly believe. Its main peak is 6,247.8 meters above sea level, which doesn't even enter the top five highest peaks. Daxue Shan—where Konggar Shan is located—has many peaks, such as Zhongshan Feng (Zhongshan Peak) at an altitude of 6,886 meters, Aidejia Feng (Aidejia Peak) at an altitude of 6,618 meters, Jiazi Feng (Jiazi Peak) at an altitude of 6,540 meters, and Riwuqie Feng (Riwuqie Peak) at an altitude of 6,376 meters. All these peaks are greater in elevation than Siguniang Shan.

Not only is its height insufficiently noteworthy, but Siguniang Shan's reputation has also suffered from long-term misfortune. It is the most unheeded destination in western Sichuan. It had received a cold-shoulder for thousands of years. When the landscapes in various parts of western Sichuan became famous, it remained unknown and underappreciated.

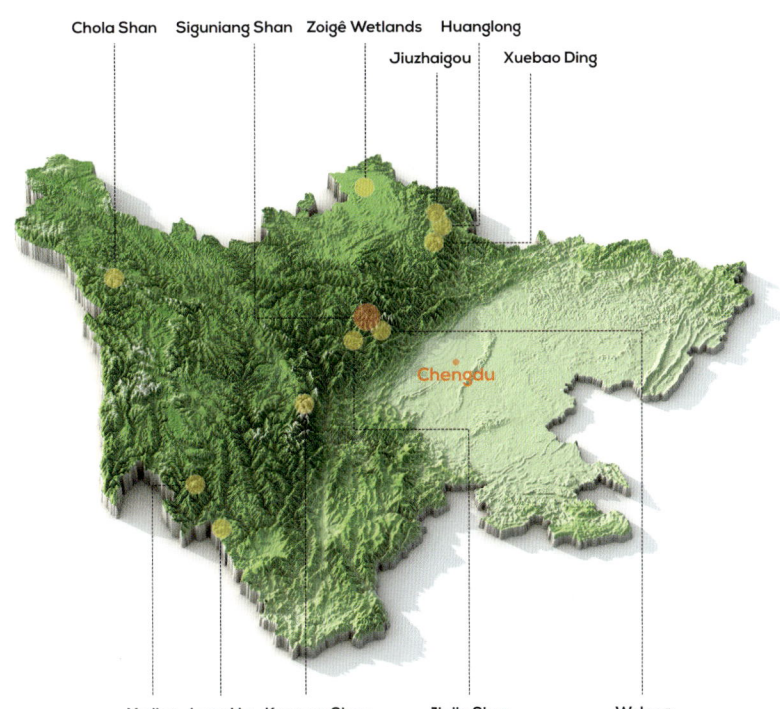

^ The topography of western Sichuan

^ **Yangmaiyong Feng (Yangmaiyong Peak)/Photo by Wen Junhao**

Yangmaiyong Feng, one of the Three Sacred Mountains of Yading, Daocheng, reaches 6,033 meters above sea level.

v **Konggar Shan/Photo by Nanka**

This picture was taken from Yaha Pass. A unique cap-shaped cloud happens to appear above the peak.

The First Misfortune

About 1,200 years ago, Du Fu, the "Sage of Poetry," left us a verse that remains famous through the ages. While looking at the snow-capped mountain range known as Xi Ling (West Range) about 100 kilometers from Chengdu, he wrote:

> *My window frames the snow-crowned Xi Ling,*
> *My door oft says to eastward-going ships "Goodbye."*
>
> —Du Fu, "A Quatrain"

This verse could have been tailored for Siguniang Shan. The straight-line distance between Siguniang Shan and Chengdu City is only 120 kilometers. Looking west from the urban area, its snow-covered peaks are visible all year round.

With this renowned verse, Siguniang Shan seemingly was on the verge of being famous. However, Du Fu did not give a specific location of Xi Ling, and later generations have argued about it. Another mountain that is about 80 kilometers away from Chengdu was later renamed Xiling Xueshan (Xiling Snow Mountain) based on the verse, and it has since become well-known throughout the country.

Siguniang Shan missed fame through the Sage of Poetry. Whether its name is cold or hot just depends on the whim of an instant.

⌄ **A snow-capped mountain viewed from Chengdu/Photo by Yin Pan**
A photo taken on June 5, 2017 shows the western mountains in Pidu District, Chengdu.

The Second Misfortune

In the second half of the 19th century, French missionaries discovered the giant panda and a number of other rare animals in Sichuan. These unique species living in China and the abundant plants and animals in the mountains of western Sichuan aroused a strong interest among Western biologists. Their resulting explorations ranged all over the surrounding area of Siguniang Shan, but the mountain itself did not attract much attention. Instead, the unknown valleys situated close to the mountain's east side became famous. They are known today as the Wolong Nature Reserve, which is renowned for its wild pandas.

Siguniang Shan itself was once again ignored.

The Third Misfortune

In the 1920s, Western explorers' investigations of western Sichuan became more comprehensive, and various peaks began to enter people's awareness.

Konggar Shan, the "King of Shushan," has naturally received the most attention due to its high altitude. Joseph Rock, the famous contributor of *National Geographic* magazine, even mistakenly calculated the elevation of Konggar Shan to be more than 9,000 meters. For a time, its title as "the world's highest mountain" spread all over the world.

Sanshen Shan (Sanshen Mountain) in Yading, Daocheng, although not superior in height, was also recorded by explorers at that time and its fame spread out to the world due to its gentle and beautiful mountain shape.

Siguniang Shan, whose height and shape do not stand out this way, was ignored by the outside world for the third time.

The Fourth Misfortune

In the 1930s, Red Army troops during the Long March entered western Sichuan and crossed many snow-capped mountains in succession, including Jiajin Shan (Jiajin Mountain) to the south of Siguniang Shan and Min Shan (Minshan Mountain) to the north. These mountains in western Sichuan, covered with the footprints of the Red Army, have all been imprinted in people's memories of the revolutionary age and become well-known in China.

> *Glad to see Min Shan covered by snow for miles and miles,*
> *And our warriors who have crossed it break into broad smiles.*
>
> —Mao Zedong, "The Long March"

All the above had nothing to do with Siguniang Shan. Although the nearest meeting place of the Red Army—Dawei—was only 20 kilometers away from Siguniang Shan, it is not on the main route of the Red Army. After the Red Army rejoined forces, they went north to Gansu and Shaanxi, and Siguniang Shan was destined to remain without a place in revolutionary history.

The Fifth Misfortune

In the 1960s, loggers entered Jiuzhaigou with modern equipment. The forest here with its abundant resources allowed them to harvest trees at a rate of 100,000 cubic meters per year. Years of logging finally attracted the attention of the outside world. People realized that protecting the beautiful natural landscapes of Jiuzhaigou is far more important than logging the forest for wealth. Jiuzhaigou seized upon this opportunity to change its fate. It became one of the earliest national nature reserves established in the embryonic stage of modern Chinese people's awareness of the need to protect nature.

At that time, Siguniang Shan was still like a princess being raised in her private boudoir, not yet allowed to know what is happening outside.

It is neither a famous Chinese mountain nor the focus of modern Western explorers. Moreover, it has nothing to do with revolutionary history. But as the saying goes, a great talent takes time to mature. So, in what way will Siguniang Shan be revealed? What is so charming about this mysterious mountain?

Answering this question requires us to start with the two major elements of Siguniang Shan. Taken by themselves, these elements are not particularly outstanding, but when these two elements blend and coexist in symbiosis, miracles occur.

Wuhua Hai in Jiuzhaigou/Photo by Zeng Yongqian
In autumn, the colorful vegetation combines with the reflections in the lake, creating a scene which is colorful and gorgeous.

2 A Song of Ice and Rock

Element One: Ice

Over a million years, Siguniang Shan went through various glacial periods, causing countless mountain glaciers to develop on this high-plateau mountain.

The glaciers cut continuously into the ground, forming many U-shaped valleys packed densely together. Afterward, the glaciers retreated, and rivers formed by meltwater and precipitation continued to shape the land. The U-shaped valley bottoms were continuously eroded by flowing water, forming V-shaped valleys. For example, when one looks up from the bottom of Changping Gou (Changping Gully), the mountains on both sides create a clear V shape.

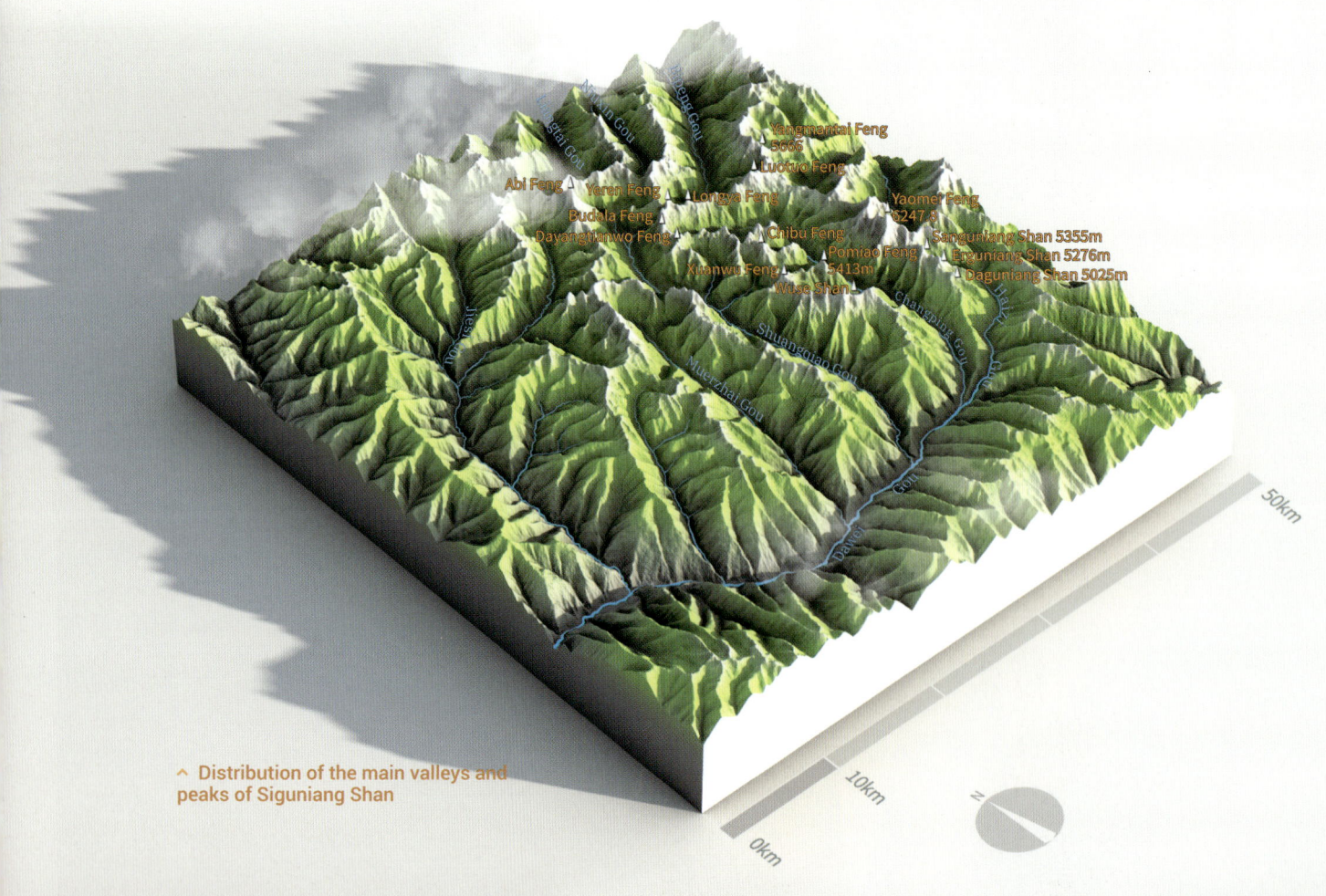

↑ Distribution of the main valleys and peaks of Siguniang Shan

Changping Gou/Photo by Yang Sutie
Changping Gou of Siguniang Shan with its U-shaped valley formed by glacial erosion that gradually turned into a V-shape after being transformed by flowing water. It can be seen from the photo that the V-shape is within the U-shape.

V-shaped valleys tend to be deeper and steeper than U-shaped valleys. The relative height difference between the peaks of the mountains and the bottoms of the valleys can reach from 2,000 to 3,500 meters. Either clouds hover above the mountainside, or fog fills deep valleys.

The valleys have abundant precipitation and hospitable temperatures, forming an important corridor for flora and fauna. Among them, there are 31 national-level protected animals of China, and more than 1,000 species of higher plants, including Blood Pheasant, Himalayan marmots, *Saussurea medusa*, and *Cypripedium tibeticum*. A wide range of species decorates the valleys of Siguniang Shan, making it elegant and unique.

1	
2	3
	4
	5

1 Ginseng Fruit Lawn of Shuangqiao Gou (Shuangqiao Gully)/Photo by Huang Jizhou

A rare Rosaceae plant, *Argentina anserina*, grows in the meadow. The locals call it "Ginseng Fruit." Therefore, the place is called "Ginseng Fruit Lawn."

2 *Saussurea medusa*/Photo by Kenzo Okawa

Saussurea medusa and *Saussurea involucrata* both belong to the genus *Saussurea*, and local people call them "snow lotus." The photo was taken at an altitude of 4,800 meters with Yaomei Feng in the background.

3 Blood Pheasant/Photo by Kenzo Okawa

The scientific name of the Blood Pheasant is *Ithaginis cruentus*. Its large feathers, lower tail feathers, upper tail feathers, feet, side of its head, and the cere of the males have red linings, hence the name blood pheasant.

4 Himalayan marmot/Photo by Kenzo Okawa

A Himalayan marmot seems to be doing some soul-searching in front of this little yellow flower. The photo was taken at an altitude of 4,500 meters.

5 *Cypripedium tibeticum*/Photo by Huang Jizhou

It belongs to the *Cypripedium* genus of the Orchidaceae family. This species mostly grows in deep mountain valleys.

Glaciers not only carve valleys but also dig out many cirques in the mountains at 4,000 to 5,000 meters. When the glaciers melt, the cirques are filled with water, forming tarns, such as Chibu Haizi (Chibu Lake), Pomiao Haizi (Pomiao Lake), and Bai Haizi (Bai Lake). Other types of glacial lakes and moraine lakes are also common. Many different kinds of lakes are dotted everywhere.

In addition to the landforms carved by glaciers, the river systems that developed in the valleys also form spectacular ice waterfalls in winter. In Shuangqiao Gou (Shuangqiao Gully) alone, there are hundreds of these ice waterfalls.

^ The formation of a tarn

> Chibu Haizi/Photo by Kenzo Okawa

Chibu Haizi, located at an altitude of 4,600 meters, is a typical tarn.

Element Two: Rock

The violent uplift of Qingzang Gaoyuan has exposed many rocks on the Earth's surface. One kind of these rocks, granite, is formed underground by magma under high pressure. It is hard in texture and beautiful in color.

Siguniangshan is mainly composed of granites, which contain abundant potassium and sodium. These elements make the clasts weathered from granite slightly acidic. These clasts formed lots of acidic soil, which is conducive to the growth of vegetation, created a variety of special geographic phenomena.

A kind of red algae grows densely on granite rocks in the valleys of Siguniang Shan, forming a large landscape of red stone. Sea buckthorns, which were originally deciduous shrubs, flourish here, absorbing natural resources and growing wildly and turning into tall trees with a height of more than 10 meters.

Too many minerals are dissolved in the water which interferes with fish metabolism and makes it difficult for them to reproduce. There is almost no wild fish in some valleys of Siguniang Shan, and even artificially bred fish cannot survive.

The most important element brought to the area by granite, however, is none other than the granite peaks.

The strong erosive effect of the glaciers, coupled with weathering, has cut away almost all the fragile rock masses on the periphery of the mountains. The rest of the mountain, mainly consisting of granite, towers high and strong in the air. The peaks in the Siguniang Shan area, at an altitude of more than 4,500 meters, are almost all lofty and steep pyramidal peaks, such as Longya Feng (Longya Peak), Yingzui Yan (Eagle Mouth Rock), Yeren Feng (Savage Peak), Chibu Feng (Chibu Peak), Budala Feng (Potala Peak), Yangmantai Feng (Yangmantai Peak), and Luotuo Feng (Camel Peak). They often look like they are floating in a sea of clouds.

˄ **Changping Gou's sea buckthorn forest/Photo by Shi Yaochen**
Unlike many places where sea buckthorn plants are mostly shrubs, sea buckthorn plants in the Siguniang Shan area are typically trees. Through comparing them with the horses in the picture, we have a clear idea of how tall these sea buckthorn plants can grow.

˅ **Red stones at Qiuxi, Bipeng Gou (Bipeng Gully)/Photo by Su Jian**
In the high-altitude areas of southern China, orange-red algae are often found attached to rocks, forming red rock beaches.

The most prominent is Pomiao Feng. Looking up from various angles, people are attracted to its eye-catching appearance. It feels like the mountain can shake hands with white clouds, compete with the blue sky for height, rejoice with autumn leaves, and talk to the white snow in winter.

In addition to the granite peaks, the peaks formed by other metamorphic rocks are equally breathtaking.

Wuse Shan (Five-Color Mountain) located between Changping Gou and Shuangqiao Gou is the most unique. During geological evolution, the original horizontal strata were bended by the mighty compressional stresses, and finally developed into a syncline structure. Due to the strata's different colors, the syncline presented a colorful semi-circular arc, including grayish-white, grayish-yellow, light green, purple-red, and grayish-black. Circle after circle, ring after ring, colors are arranged in a regular pattern of multiple layers, displaying a unique illustration under the sunlight.

There are so many rock peaks in the Siguniang Shan area. Each of them is steep and towering. How majestic they are!

1 2 3

1 Pomiao Feng under white clouds/Photo by Shi Yaochen

2 Pomiao Feng under the cover of green pines/Photo by Mao Feng

3 Pomiao Feng after snowfall/Photo by Mao Feng

Wuse Shan/Photo by Huang Jizhou
Wuse Shan is a fold mountain. The rock formations are compressed, deformed, and bent during geological activities. It is a typical syncline structure.

Symphony of Ice and Rock

A symphony featuring ice and rock is about to begin.

In the 1990s, Japanese photographer Kenzo Okawa visited Siguniang Shan. Seeing the extremely beautiful scenery here, he soon decided to spend his entire life shooting and promoting Siguniang Shan.

Later, more photographers joined him, and the beauty of the "Queen of Shushan" gradually spread to the outside world. The most notable feature of its beauty lies in the reflections of the different shapes of its rock peaks in the lakes shaped by glaciers and rivers.

The lakes in the valleys can reflect entire mountains as well as the sky and clouds. Its scenery can be described as dreamlike and intoxicating.

⌃ **Morning mist of Longzhu Co (Longzhu Lake)/Photo by Gao Jiangfeng**

Longzhu Co is a lake in Shuangqiao Gou. In the early morning, the peaks and their reflections harmonize together, like a dream. The main peaks in the picture are Da Yangtianwo (Large Yangtianwo Mountain) and Xiao Yangtianwo (Small Yangtianwo Mountain).

⌄ **Reflection of the sunset at Siguna Co (Siguna Lake)/Photo by Gao Jiangfeng**

Siguna Co is a lake in Shuangqiao Gou. The main peak in the picture is Abi Feng (Abi Peak).

Tarns at an altitude of over 4,000 meters are even more breathtaking. At such a high altitude, they can cut the 5,000-meter rock peaks in half, only letting the tips of the peaks reflect in the water. The essence of the beauty of these rock peaks lies precisely in the variety of their shapes. In addition, standing at such altitudes creates the illusion that the viewer is sharing the same height as the mountains.

When the mountains are full of ice and snow, the reflections get an upgrade, too.

At this time, the symphony of ice and rock reaches its climax. The whole world has turned into a vision of ice and snow. Even the photo itself seems to be a piece of crystal-clear ice that can easily be crushed and broken.

Yaomei Feng, which is 6,247.8 meters above sea level, has jumped to the front of the beauty competition amongst 5,000-meter rock peaks, transforming itself into a charming, spectacular, pure, and ethereal fairyland.

˄ Reflection of Pomiao Feng/Photo by Kenzo Okawa

˅ Bajiaopeng Haizi/Photo by Yang Sutie
Bajiaopeng Haizi is located on the southern hillside of Haizi Gou (Haizi Gully), where you can photograph the reflection of the south wall of Yaomei Feng.

3 A Climbing Paradise

When reflections of the snow-capped mountains created by ice and rocks were discovered by photographers, mountaineers, rock climbers, and ice climbers, they also noticed the uniqueness of Siguniang Shan.

The rock peaks here are like Yosemite, a famous rock-climbing site in the United States, but Siguniang Shan has a higher elevation and there are more peaks to choose from. It is dubbed a "paradise of rocks." As Mick Fowler said:

> *We are like being in a mixed landscape of Yosemite and Alpine Chamonix, but the momentum here is much more majestic.*
>
> —Mick Fowler, *On Thin Ice*

In 1983, Americans first climbed Pomiao Feng at an altitude of 5,413 meters. After that, rock climbing in the area became increasingly popular, and rock climbers from various countries rushed to visit and complete their first ascents in Luotuo Feng, Niuxin Shan (Mount Niuxin), and Budala Feng. The most eye-catching Pomiao Feng, as of 2014, had nine climbing routes opened.

The most popular four peaks for mountaineers line up from north to south: Yaomei Feng, Sanguniang Shan, Erguniang Shan (Mount Erguniang), and Diguniang Shan (Mount Diguniang). Among them, Daguniang Shan, Erguniang Shan, and Sanguniang Shan are not difficult to climb, so they are suitable for beginning mountaineers.

The real challenge lies in Yaomei Feng. It is steep and towering with a ridge like a blade, and its three walls are a perfectly difficult combination of ice and rock. Among them, the northwest wall is a nearly vertical granite slope, and the ice and snow in the ditches are extremely unstable. On the south wall, there are glaciers. As the glaciers break, they create many deep cracks. The rock is also severely weathered and easy to break. The east wall has the most glaciers of the three sides. In addition to the inconvenient transportation to the foot of the valley, it is extremely difficult to approach.

1 | 2

1 Climbing Yangmantai (Yangmantai Mountain)/Photo by Azuo
The climbers are making a difficult endeavor.

2 Shuangqiao Gou ice wall/Photo by Azuo
Many waterfalls in Shuangqiao Gou are iced in winter, creating a winter wonderland for ice climbing.

Climbing Xuanwu Erfeng (Second Xuanwu Peak)/Photo by Azuo
This picture was taken while climbing Xuanwu Erfeng. On the right side of the picture, there are climbers on top of the mountain.

Siguniang Shan/Photo by Wang He

Yaomei Feng of Siguniang Shan, Sanguniang Shan (Mount Sanguniang), Erguniang Shan (Mount Erguniang), and Daguniang Shan (Mount Daguniang), from left to right, have an elevation of 6,247.8 meters, 5,355 meters, 5,276 meters, and 5,025 meters, respectively.

However, all of this did not stop climbers from coming. Instead, it attracted many of the most excellent climbers from around the world. Since the Japanese team successfully climbed to the top from the southeast ridge in 1981, 12 teams have completed the ascent of Yaomei Feng. Almost all these climbing achievements have become classic cases for study in the mountaineering community.

Among them, the most famous is undoubtedly the extremely difficult northwest wall climb completed by British mountaineer Mick Fowler in 2002, for which he received the Golden Ice Axe Award in that same year. The Chinese's first ascent came a little later, completed by Ma Yihua and others in 2004. However, what most inspires the Chinese is the "Soul of Freedom" route successfully pioneered by Zhou Peng and Yan Dongdong on the south wall of Yaomei Feng. It can be said that this climb ignited the interest in Chinese Alpine climbing[1]. Interestingly, in 2011, a French mountaineering team named their climbing route "You are so beautiful" after successfully challenging the north wall again.

---

1 Alpine climbing is a climbing technique referring to one person or a small group of two to three people climbing in a high mountain environment, advancing with light equipment and at a fast travel speed.

˄ **The northwest wall of Yaomei Feng/Photo by Yang Sutie**

The northwest wall of Yaomei Feng is a steep granite wall, which is extremely difficult to climb.

˅ **The south wall of Yaomei Feng/Photo Kyle Obermann**

The south wall of Yaomei Feng is the most common showing wall. A "human face" image can be vaguely imagined in the combination of rocks on the wall.

Yes,
Siguniang Shan,
you are so beautiful!

The east wall of Yaomei Feng/Photo by Huang Jizhou

If you look at Yaomei Feng in the distance from Chengdu, this is what you see.

2

The Second Terrain Ladder

2.1 Ili:
A Corner of the Far West of China
199

2.2 Lop Nur:
The Rise and Fall of Loulan during Five Thousand Years
225

2.3 Gansu:
The More Diverse, the More Beautiful
246

2.4 Xi'an:
Rich and Affluent for a Thousand Years
281

2.5 Chengdu:
Three Thousand Years of Vibrant Traditional Lifestyles
311

2.6 Fanjing Shan:
A Paradise in the Secular World
345

One side of the towering Tian Shan (Mount Tianshan) has a bell-shaped mouth facing west at Ili, forming a super rain collector. In this way, Ili, which is located in an arid region, has some of the most abundant water resources in Xinjiang, and even all of inland Asia, through the help of water vapor collected from the westerlies. It has also become the key place to manage Xiyu (Western Regions).

2.1 Ili:
A Corner of the Far West of China

^ Gedengshan Stele (Gedeng Mountain Stele) bears inscriptions handwritten by Emperor Qianlong in Ili/Photo by Lai Yuning

Xinjiang in southwestern China covers a vast territory today.

Tian Shan lies in the center of Xinjiang. Tarim Pendi and Junggar Pendi (Junggar Basin) separate Xinjiang into two parts, and Kunlun Shan and Altay Shan (Altai Mountains) stand in the north and south, respectively. From mountains, deserts, and grasslands to rivers, lakes, and oases, Xinjiang is unparalleled in richness of its landforms and products.

The exploration of this valuable land by the Chinese people dates back more than 2,000 years. From Zhang Qian in the Western Han Dynasty (206BC-25 AD) to Ban Chao and Ban Yong in the Eastern Han Dynasty (25-220) and then to the famous generals Su Dingfang and Gao Xianzhi in the Tang Dynasty, they all worked hard to manage

Xiyu (Western Regions).

However, even if the Han and Tang dynasties were very powerful and prosperous, small kingdoms such as Xiyu still rebelled again and again in attempts to rid themselves of the central government's rule. During the centuries covering the reign of the Song (960-1279), Yuan (1206-1368), and Ming (1368-1644) dynasties, the central government effectively lost its control of Xiyu.

If this situation had continued to persist over a long time, China would have lost Xiyu forever. At this critical moment, however, a key factor that would strengthen the administration of Xiyu emerged.

It was Ili.

In 1755, Emperor Qianlong of the Qing Dynasty (1616-1911) sent an army into the region of Ili He (Ili River). In the following years, the central government's rule gradually was imposed on the entire Xiyu region. The distant Ili, which had never been taken seriously as a strategic element by previous dynasties, unexpectedly rewrote history, laying the foundation for the current northwest territory of China. The French historian René Grousset wrote at the end of his classic *L'empire des Steppes* (Empire of the Steppes):

> *Ch'ien-lung's annexation of the Ili and Kashgaria marks the fulfillment of the aim pursued since the time of Pan Ch'ao by the Chinese Asian policy of eighteen centuries: the retaliation of the sedentary peoples against the nomads, of agriculture against the steppe.*

It can be said that without the management of Ili by the ambitious Qing Dynasty, there would be no Xinjiang as it is today. Emperor Qianlong, who made this epic achievement, was also quite proud. He clarified the name "Ili" in the official documents as:

> *Plow the enemy's courtyard and sweep the enemy's streets, to unify Xiyu.*

Is remote Ili really that important?

Legend

- ● Provincial administrative center
- ● Prefectural administrative center
- · Other city
- National boundary
- Boundary of province, autonomous region or municipality
- Xinjiang territory in the Qing Dynasty
- River, seasonal river
- Lake, seasonal lake
- ▲ Tomur Feng 7443m Peak and elevation

The hinterland of Eurasia, where Ili is located, is far away from the ocean and the climate is arid. However, the main vein and the branch vein of Tian Shan to the west in Ili. Because water vapor enters the bell mouth on the westerly wind, a lot of precipitation falls on the windward slope. The annual precipitation in the area can reach 600 to 800mm. With the abundant precipitation, the climate in this area is humid and the vegetation is prosperous. Ili has changed its arid appearance and become a famous land with abundant water-rich plants in the hinterland of the Asian continent.

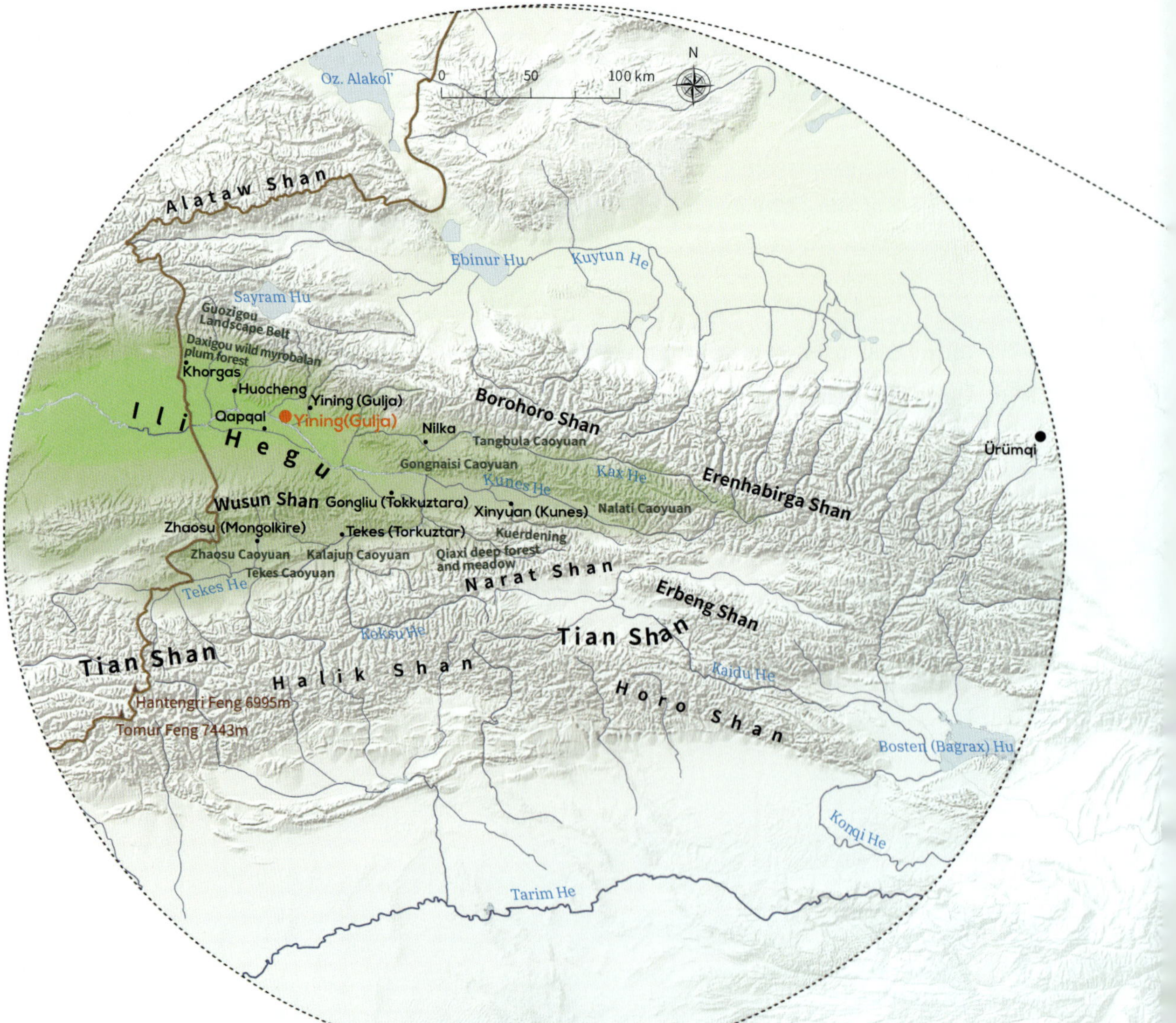

Landforms of the Ili Hegu

1 Super Rain Collector

⌄ **Kabanbayi Feng (Kabanbayi Peak)/Photo by Ma Junhua**
This picture shows Kabanbayi Feng viewed from Kuerdening.

As one can see from the map, Ili is far away. It is on the northwestern border of China, and the straight-line distance between Ili and Beijing is about 2,900 kilometers, which is three times the distance between Beijing and Hulun Buir, which is also famous for its grasslands. The straight-line distance between Ili and Guangzhou, a densely populated and economically developed city in southern China, is as much as 3,700 kilometers, and this also happens to form a diagonal line that runs straight through China's mainland. Ili is located in the west of Xinjiang, unlike today's capital of the Xinjiang Uyghur Autonomous Region, Urumqi, which lies in the heart of the autonomous region.

When we see from the perspective of a complete geographic unit—the entire region of Ili He instead of just the administrative division— certain secrets are revealed.

The region of Ili He is fenced on three sides by the main and branch veins of Tian Shan. Most of these mountains rise over 4,000 meters above sea level. Keguqin Shan (Keguqin Mountain), located on the north side of Ili, is undulating in shape and stretches out over the land. Borohoro Shan (Mount Bolohoro) is even more majestic and vast. On the southeast side of Narat Shan (Narat Mountain), the main peak Kabanbayi Feng (Kabanbayi Peak) is 4,257 meters above sea level and juts abruptly into the sky.

The most precipitous mountain is Haerketawu Shan (Mount Haerketawu) in the south of Ili. Ancient people opened several routes through here to connect the north and south of Tian Shan. The Xiate Ancient Route is one of them. It traverses many passes of Haerketawu Shan, over glaciers and across rapids.

The mountains on the north and south sides merge with Erenhabirga Shan (Yilianhabierga Mountain) on the east side, forming a knot of mountains. Erenhabirga Shan is steep and covered with loose rock formations, so mudslides and landslides often occur. The famous Duku Highway snakes across this steep mountain and is very perilous.

These towering mountains enclose the area from the north, east, and south, forming a mouth that is shaped like the bell of a trumpet, facing west. A "super rain collector" has been created.

The Xiate Ancient Route/Photo by Yang Sihang

This picture was taken in the Xiate Ancient Route, and the snow-capped mountain in the distance is Haerketawu Shan (Mount Haerketawu). Building of the Xiate Ancient Route began during the Western Han Dynasty, with a total length of 120 kilometers. It is believed that the Tang Dynasty monk Xuanzang traveled west along this route to retrieve Buddhist sutras.

The hinterland of Eurasia, where Ili is located, is blocked by Qingzang Gaoyuan in the south, making it difficult for water vapor from the Indian Ocean to arrive here, thus forming a large desert area. To the west of Ili are flat European plains and Eurasian grasslands. The water vapor from the Arctic Ocean, Caspian Sea, Black Sea and ever the Atlantic Ocean which is more than 5,000 kilometers away, can easily travel to Ili.

When the water vapor enters the valley, the super rain collector comes into play. The annual rainfall on the windward slope of the mountains can reach 600 to 800mm, and a large amount of precipitation remains in solid form on the high mountains, forming glaciers. At higher altitudes, glacial meltwater often forms lakes scattered among the mountains. The lake water there is colored a pure cyan blue, looking like a gem.

Many streams develop among the mountains. They rush down the slopes, flow through the forests and grasslands, carve out the canyons, widen the valleys, and finally converge into Ili He, a river with the most abundant waters in Xinjiang. The river turns westward, flowing into the western part of Balkhash Köli (Lake Balkhash) in Kazakhstan. Due to the huge amount of water from Ili He, Balkhash Köli presents an interesting phenomenon: it has fresh water in the west and salty water in the east.

In this way, Ili, which would otherwise be arid, has become one of the regions with the best water resources in Xinjiang and even all of inland Asia, with the help of water vapor from the westerlies.

> Ili He/Photo by Ma Junhua

The annual surface runoff of Ili He in China is 15.87 billion cubic meters, accounting for 70% of the runoff in the entire basin.

Yueliang Hu (Moon Lake)/Photo by Liu Lingbo
Yueliang Hu, also known as Tiantang Hu (Paradise Lake), is located on the Wusun Ancient Route in Tekesi County. It was formed by the accumulation of water from ancient tarns.

Kalajun "Human Body Grassland"/Photo by Du Wenming

The sloping, undulating grassland is located in Kalajun. Under the sun, it looks like the back of a naked lady with the contrast of light and shadow. The locals thus call the grassland "naked island."

2 Abundant Waters and Lush Grasses

With sufficient water vapor, the deep and narrow terrain of the Ili Hegu (Ili River Valley) can form an inversion zone which is cold outside and warm inside, helping the vegetation in this area thrive and become extremely lush.

The famous Schrenk's Spruce (scientific name *Picea schrenkiana*) has a maximum trunk diameter at breast height (DBH) of 2.2 meters, a height of more than 60 meters, and can live for more than 300 years. A forest belt over 1000 kilometers in length is formed by just this species of tree on the northern slope of Tian Shan, which is unique in China.

Thermophilic wild apple, walnut, and apricot trees thrive here. Ili has also become one of the regions with the richest reserves of wild fruit trees in China.

Where trees cannot grow, grasslands spread freely. From alpine meadows to piedmont and forest edge meadows, from undulating, gently sloped grasslands that resemble the curves of a human body to flat valleys and savannas, grasses spread all over the valleys and plains. Some of the densest grassland landscapes in China are formed here, such as Narat Caoyuan (Narat Grassland), Tekesi Caoyuan (Tekesi Grassland), Kalajun Caoyuan (Kalajun Grassland), Zhaosu Caoyuan (Zhaosu Grassland) and so on.

> *Picea schrenkiana*/Photo by Lai Yuning

Picea schrenkiana is mainly distributed in Russia and Xinjiang, China, and is the main species that is found in the local forests. They are vigorous and upright, stretching and towering like a city wall on the mountain.

Ili has long been an area that ancient nomads used for grazing. The Serbs, Wusun, Turks, and the Mongolian Junggar tribes all established powerful grassland regimes centered on Ili.

Tarim Pendi, to the south of Tian Shan, does not have such abundant water vapor conditions. Only small and independent oasis city-states formed on the edge of the basin by relying on melted runoff water from the snow-capped mountains.

The nomadic regimes to the north of Tian Shan could cross the mountains to invade the small oasis city-states in the south. However, a counterattack seemed impossible. Back then, those oasis city-states were often weak and unable to expand northward. As an old saying goes:

> *North can control the south, but the south cannot control the north.*
> – Gong Zizhen, *Classified Compilation of Collected Works of Gong Dingman: Opinions on Setting up a Province in Xiyu*

However, in the Han and Tang dynasties, due to the similarity of the agricultural economy, the focus of the governance of Xiyu was placed on the southern areas of Tian Shan. When the central government was strong, it could also control and pacify the north of Tian Shan. Once it weakened, many years' efforts of the central empire were lost as the nomadic northern regimes invaded the south.

< Xinyuan wild fruit forest/Photo by Li Xueliang

There are many wild fruit forests in the valleys of Tian Shan in the Ili area, including wild apple forests, wild apricot forests, wild walnut forests, wild plum forests, wild cherry forests, and so on.

Horse ranch of Zhaosu Caoyuan/Photo by Lai Yuning

3 The Transformation of Ili

In the Qing Dynasty, Emperor Qianlong, who had a deep understanding of the nomadic peoples, Implemented his vision: To govern Xiyu well, one must first govern Ili well. Therefore, a major transformation of Ili was undertaken.

The first step was to build cities.

The Qing Dynasty built nine cities in the Ili region, with Huiyuan City as the center, forming the largest urban cluster in Xinjiang at that time. The Finnish explorer Carl Mannerheim[1] spoke highly of Huiyuan:

> *Huiyuan is the cleanest and most beautiful Chinese city I have ever seen. The city is well designed, and the straight streets are spacious and beautiful.*
> —Wu Xiaocheng, *Ili in the Eyes of Foreigners a Hundred Years Ago.*

Then they tried to reclaim wastelands for farming.

The climate of Ili Caoyuan (Ili Grassland) is mild and humid, and the soil is fertile, suitable for both animal husbandry and agriculture. Emperor Qianlong did not regard Ili merely as a military center but also put forward an ambitious economic goal, that was, to make Ili's clothing, food, wealth, and tax equal to those of the Zhongyuan.

Driven by this policy, the Northern Xinjiang Reclamation Area developed rapidly. By 1820, there were more than 1.2 million *mu*[2] of farmland.

Ili Caoyuan has fertile soil and vast regions of farmland. It has since become a productive agricultural area, and it continues to be a famous "granary" in Xinjiang to this day.

---

[1] Carl Gustaf Mannerheim (1867-1951) was a Finnish explorer who visited Asia from 1906 to 1908 to gather information for Russia.

[2] One *mu* is 1/15 hectare.

^ The Bell Tower of the Huiyuan Ancient City/Photo by Lai Yuning
Huiyuan is in Huocheng County, Ili. This picture shows the bell tower of the Huiyuan Ancient City.

^ The Ili Hegu covered with blooming flowers/Photo by Lai Yuning
In the flat Ili Hegu, people are growing all kinds of crops, turning it into a fertile farming area.

Finally, the imperial policy was to encourage immigration.

The Qing Dynasty recruited immigrants from all over the country to settle in Ili, including the Erlute Mongols, Manchus, Xibes, Hans, and Uyghurs (Talanqi) from southern Xinjiang. These new immigrants were extremely obedient to the Manchus, and Ili became a unique immigrant society where different ethnic groups lived in harmony. The degree of integration of various ethnic groups was much higher than that of other places, and this still plays a major role in maintaining social stability in Ili today.

Building cities, reclaiming farmland, and encouraging immigration—after long-term development, Xinjiang finally formed a stable administrative region with Ili as its center during the Qing Dynasty. Xinjiang was now truly and firmly integrated into Chinese territory.

During this time, the Ili Hegu was not just the center of transportation for the entire Tian Shan region, but also the heart of Xinjiang. This core status remained until late in the Qing Dynasty when the Russian Empire occupied Chinese territory outside Ili. The status of Ili changed from being the center of Xinjiang to a border area. Xinjiang's political and economic center was forced to move to Dihua (now Urumqi). The Ili era in Xinjiang came to an end.

4 Ili Today

Today's Ili is still a faraway place.

Writer Wang Meng once lived and worked in Ili for over a decade. After returning to Beijing, when recalling his life in Ili, he began his article like this:

In the distant Ili...

Singer Dao Lang, who is famous for singing Xinjiang songs, sings in one of his most famous songs "New Awarguli":

People from afar, may I ask where you are from? Have you ever heard of Awarguli? She took away my heart, went across the Gobi, and lost it in the distant Ili many years ago...

However, this remoteness does not stop people from admiring Ili for its beautiful scenery and rich natural resources.

Transportation is becoming more convenient, and Ili is now more connected to the eastern part of China. Beijing, Shanghai, and Guangzhou all have flights to Ili. Highways and bridges connect Ili to the outside world.

In addition, the Ili region has some of the most unique cities and the best production conditions for high-quality agricultural products in China. It is home to the largest land port in Xinjiang, and it also has economic development zones that offer preferential policies for settled enterprises.

The ambition to build a prosperous Xiyu has been reawakened.

Ili is no longer far away.

Guozigou Bridge/Photo by Lai Yuning

The Guozigou Bridge is a part of the Lianyungang-Horgos Expressway and is a major project connecting the Ili Hegu and northern Xinjiang. The Guozigou Bridge is a double-pylon cable-stayed bridge featuring double-cable planes and steel truss girders, with a total length of 700 meters and a main span of 330 meters. Its two main pylons are 209 meters and 215 meters tall.

Located in the southeastern part of Xinjiang, Lop Nur is in the hinterland of the Eurasian continent. Consisting mainly of deserts, the area is extremely dry. The natural environment is harsh in these barren deserts and can really be called a "death zone." However, this death zone holds a powerful and mysterious attraction. The Beauty of Xiaohe, the "Prince of the Desert." Loulan, Shanshan—these historical figures, ancient cities, and old stories have attracted countless explorers and scientists to come to unravel its mysteries, in the pursuit of which some have even sacrificed their lives.

2.2 Lop Nur:
The Rise and Fall of Loulan during Five Thousand Years

On July 23, 1972, Landsat 1 was launched into space. It scanned the surface of the earth in detail, covering most of the world's landmasses in the following two years. This was the first time in human history that we were able to observe the planet on which we live through such a macroscopic and high-definition perspective, and the secrets of many relatively unknown, mysterious corners were revealed one by one.

An area shaped like a big ear in western China was particularly eye-catching. It is about 60 kilometers long and 30 kilometers wide. It has alternately dark and bright semi-circular and concentric lines and is known as the "Ear of Earth."

People were not aware of what it was or how it was created, only knowing that the place where it was located was called Lop Nur.

Lop Nur, in southeastern Xinjiang, is located deep in the hinterland of the Eurasian continent. It is covered by many deserts, and it is extremely dry. Looking around, almost no grass can be seen, and the natural environment is extremely harsh. It is a veritable "death zone."

However, this death zone holds a great and mysterious attraction.

The Russian geographer and explorer Nikolay Przhevalsky visited the Lop Nur region in 1876. The Swedish explorer Sven Hedin discovered the ruined city of Loulan in 1901. The first Chinese nuclear bomb test was performed successfully at Lop Nur in 1964. Countless explorers and scientists were fascinated by Lop Nur, and some have even lost their lives while unraveling its mysteries.

Moreover, there are countless rumors and pieces of folklore about the area, and it is difficult to tell which tales are true. Therefore, this place has become a popular setting for fantasy novels and works of literature on tomb robbery.

What is it about Lop Nur? Where does its irresistible charm come from?

1 Satellite picture of Lop Nur/Photo by NASA

In the 1960s, Corona program satellites also photographed the "Ear of Earth," but the picture was not clear enough and did not attract much attention. This picture was taken by Landsat 1 on October 3, 1972. The Chinese first came to know of this picture during Chinese geographer Xia Xuncheng's visit to the United States in 1980.

2 An ancient tomb of the Hongshan culture/Photo by Lu Quanguo

This ancient tomb of the Hongshan culture, located in the lower reaches of Konqi He (Kongque River), was robbed at some point in its history.

3 The tomb of Yu Chunshun/Photo by Wen Xinghua

In 1980, Chinese biochemist Peng Jiamu disappeared at Lop Nur. In 1996, Chinese explorer Yu Chunshun got lost here and died of dehydration. Each death evoked a nationwide sensation at the time. This picture shows the tomb of Yu Chunshun in the center of Lop Nur. People passing by will place bottled water in front of the tomb in memory of the explorer.

1 Gathering Water into a Lake

The enclosure created by large mountain ranges such as Tian Shan and Kunlun Shan prevents water vapor from entering the inland region of Xinjiang. In Tarim Pendi (Tarim Basin), in the middle of the mountains, a vast area consisting of deserts and wastelands has been formed. Lop Nur, located at the easternmost fringe of Tarim Pendi, is one of those areas.

However, contrary to common belief, Lop Nur, known today as a "death zone," was once the most humid place in this vast desert area.

The key reason for this is its location in the lowest area of Tarim Pendi. Rivers bred from the surrounding mountains, including Konqi He (Kongque River), Qarqan He (Qarqun River), China's largest inland river Tarim He, and possibly even Shule He originated from Qilian Shan, nurtured Lop Nur.

> **Lop Nur and its surroundings**

Lop Nur is in the eastmost fringe and the lowest section of Tarim Pendi. Once, the rivers in the basin, such as Konqi He, Tarim He, and Qarqan He, all converged at Lop Nur and formed a lake system. Oases were formed around it. Later, due to environmental deterioration and the rapid increase in water use in upstream areas, the downstream rivers were cut off, the lake dried out, and the oases disappeared. Only some ancient ruins remain here today.

Among these ruins, the most famous are the Xiaohe Cemetery and the Ancient City of Loulan.

The Xiaohe Cemetery is in a desert about 60 kilometers south of the lower reaches of Konqi He at Lop Nur, and it is about 150 kilometers northwest of Ruoqiang County. It is a famous cultural site in Lop Nur. In 1934, the Swedish explorer and archaeologist Folke Bergman excavated 12 burial pits here for the first time. From 2002 to 2005, an excavation project, organized by the Xinjiang Cultural Relics and Archaeology Institute, began at the site. Archaeologists unearthed many artifacts and mummies, including a remarkably intact mummy of a young woman, which came to be called the Beauty of Xiaohe (or the Beauty of Loulan).

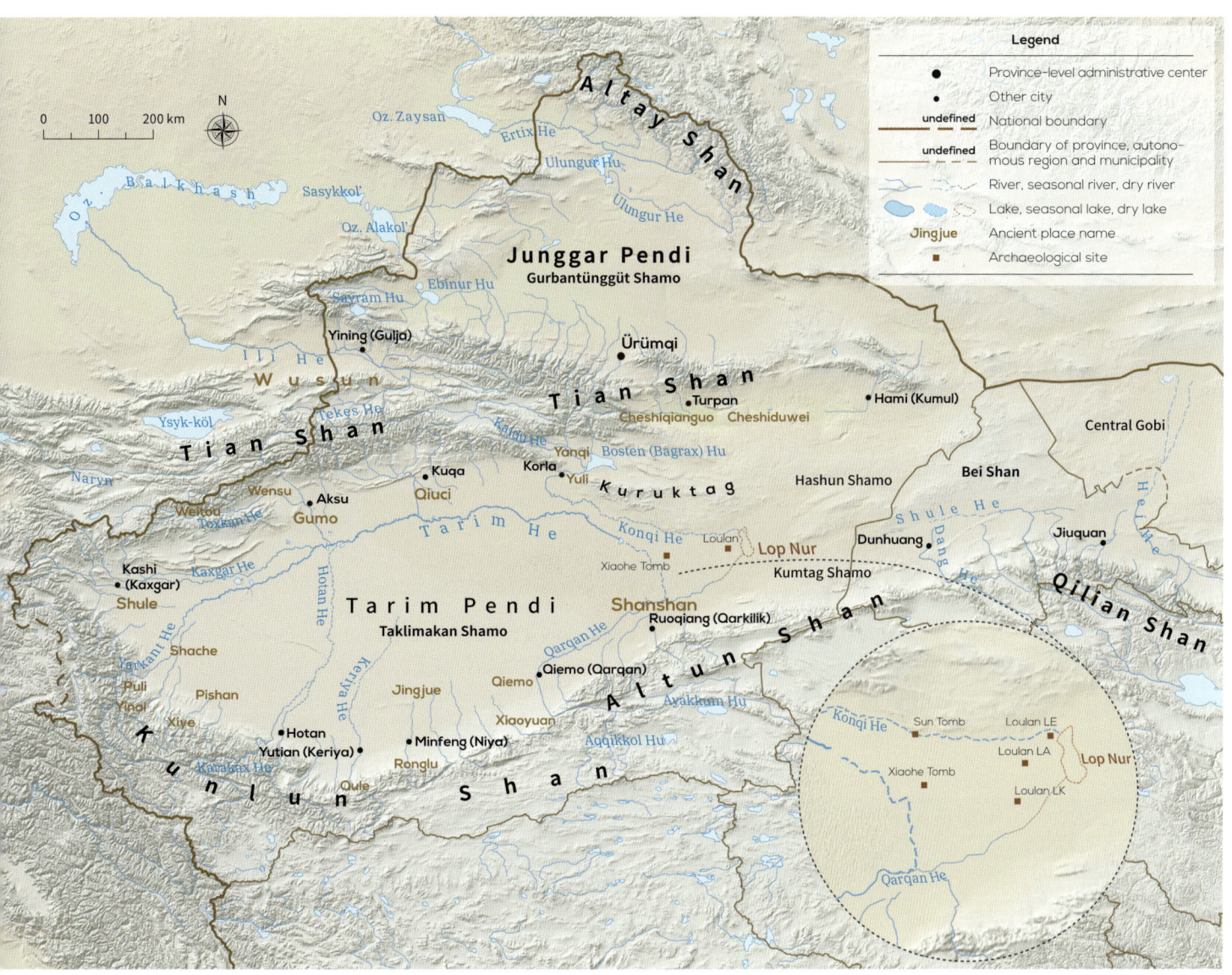

The Ancient City of Loulan was the capital of the Loulan Kingdom, one of the ancient Thirty-six Kingdoms of Xiyu (Western Regions) in China. It is located on the dry delta of the lower reaches of the dried-out Konqi He in the northwest of Lop Nur. The Ruined City of Loulan (site LA, usually thought to be the capital of Loulan) was first discovered accidently by the Swedish explorer Sven Hedin in the early 20th century. Only afterward did it become known to the public. After the discovery, many explorers came here. British archaeologist Aurel Stein made further excavations in 1906 and 1914 around the old lake of Lop Nur and identified many historical sites in the area. He designated these sites with the letter L (for Loulan), followed by a letter of the alphabet (A to T) allocated in chronological order according to when the sites were visited. Since the 1980s, Chinese archaeologists have conducted many investigations and excavations on Loulan. For more than a hundred years, however, there have been many controversies regarding the exact whereabouts of the capital of the Loulan Kingdom, and the status of the LA site as its capital.

Poplar forests along the banks of Tarim He in Shaya County, Xinjiang/Photo by Chen Wei

Tarim He, China's longest inland river, stands as the principal water source of the Tarim Pendi. The river has given birth to the lush oases along its banks, and also fostered vibrant poplar forests.

Daxihaizi Shuiku (Great West Sea Reservoir)/Photo by Zhao Laiqing

Daxihaizi Shuiku is in the lower reaches of Tarim He. The creation of this reservoir was one of the reasons why Lop Nur dried up. It was once much criticized and now it has become a reservoir dedicated to an ecological water supply.

Flowing water scoured the wilderness of Lop Nur, creating long valleys of various widths. The confluence of all these waters eventually formed Lop Nur, a giant lake.

Lop Nur once covered more than 10,000 square kilometers (3,900 sq mi) in Tarim Pendi, and it was more than twice the size of Qinghai Hu, the largest lake in China today. It was the same size as Salar de Uyuni, the world's largest salt flat in Bolivia, which was also born in the wilderness.

Those ancients who were lucky enough to see this extensive salt flat in the west of China might feel very shocked if they saw it today. Chinese historical records *Han Shu (The History of the Han Dynasty)* described the magnificence of Lop Nur:

> *(Lop Nur is) three hundred li (1 li=500 meters) wide. Its water is still and does not increase or decrease in winter and summer.*
> —Han Shu Xiyu Zhuan (The History of the Han Dynasty: Records of Xiyu), Part One

In fact, the confluence of waters formed not only Lop Nur but also a huge lake system that included dozens of large and small lakes such as Kalaheshun Hu (Kalaheshun Lake), Taitema Hu (Taitema Lake), and Chailutekule Hu (Chailutekule Lake). Lop Nur and the neighboring areas, moistened by water, were surrounded by densely distributed rivers and lakes.

With water, life began to prosper.

Both banks of the river, instead of being covered by yellow sand, became vibrant with green plants.

The forest coverage rate in the Lop Nur area was as high as 40%, which is almost twice the forest coverage rate in China today. Some of the beautiful Euphrates poplar *(Populus euphratica)* trees stood alone, some grew in rows, while some cast their reflections in the clear water, forming scenery like that in Jiangnan, the region south of Chang Jiang.

With plentiful water and lush plants, Lop Nur attracted various animals including migratory birds. To this day, 151 species of birds, 17 species of reptiles, 11 species of fish, and 33 species of mammals have been found in the Lop Nur area. Lop Nur is home to the wild Bactrian camel, which is more endangered than the wild giant panda. The wild Bactrian camel population living at Lop Nur accounts for more than 60% of the entire population of the species in the world.

With enough water and abundant flora and fauna, Lop Nur entered into an era of prosperity thanks to the efforts of human settlers.

2 The Ancestors and Loulan

In 3000 BC, one branch of the Europoid people, the Tokharian, began to migrate to the east where there was rich water and flourishing vegetation. They saw the luxuriant oases of Lop Nur and the Populus forests. So, they settled down here.

In 2000 BC, the settlers in Lop Nur had developed the irrigation, copper making, and textile technologies, which implied that they tried to develop their homeland on a large scale. This was the "Bronze Age" of Lop Nur.

Millet from the East and wheat from the West were introduced, and the inhabitants of the region cultivated large areas of farmland around the oases. They raised cattle and sheep, made boots with their leather, and spun their wool for clothes.

1	2	3
	4	

1 A straw basket unearthed at Qawrighul (Gumugou)/Photo by Liu Yusheng

The straw basket unearthed at Qawrighul has clear patterns and a beautiful appearance, and it is very strong and durable. The small basket contained wheat grains (these are some of the earliest wheat grains found in China) and dried millet porridge. Millet originated in northern China and was introduced to Eastern Europe through the Eurasian grasslands. Wheat originated in West Asia and was introduced to Zhongyuan through Xinjiang. Lop Nur is at the intersection of the Eastern and Western civilizations.

2 A felt hat unearthed from the Xiaohe Cemetery/Photo by Liu Yusheng

This felt hat unearthed from the Xiaohe Cemetery is a style that is still fashionable today. More importantly, the quality of its wool plush is very good. Craftspeople could spin fine wool with more than a 70 yarn count, which is even better than many woolen products nowadays.

3 Oxhide boots unearthed from the Xiaohe Cemetery/Photo by Liu Yusheng

The oxhide boots unearthed from the Xiaohe Cemetery are usually made of oxhide or lynx leather.

4 A wood carving unearthed from the Xiaohe Cemetery/Photo by Liu Yusheng

233

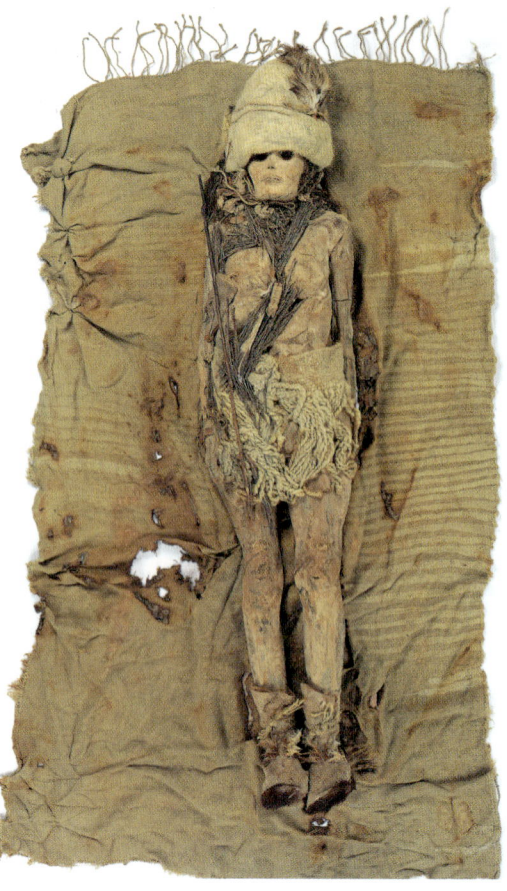

The people of antiquity believed in the immortality of the soul. Protecting the souls of their ancestors was a top priority, and solemn primitive religious ceremonies were held frequently.

Plenty of Euphrates poplar wood provided them with raw materials to produce life-sized wooden human figures and numerous boat-shaped wooden coffins. At the cost of thousands of Euphrates poplar trees, wooden human figures, wooden coffins, and wooden posts were piled up to erect a huge and towering "palace of death" on the ground. This "palace" was divided into five floors, which were made of stacked coffins from different periods. Coupled with the natural accumulation of sand, it was shaped like a sand dune. Their ancestors were buried in boat-shaped coffins that faced toward the sand sea, symbolizing that their souls sailed to the netherworld.

At that time, the Tokharians lived together with the surrounding peoples in the eastern regions, giving birth to beautiful mixed-race children. One of them was especially famous for her beauty. She had white skin and chestnut-colored hair, a high nose and deep-set eyes. She wore a pointed felt hat with bird feathers obliquely inserted in its top. She came to be called the Beauty of Xiaohe, who lived 3,500 to 4,000 years ago. Her mummy was intact and had survived thousands of years without decay. Her long eyelashes stand upright in an attractive manner and are quite impressive.

When the coffin was opened, uncovering the woolen cloth wrapped around the body of the Beauty of Xiaohe, what was revealed was simply amazing. Her slender figure, felt hat, leather boots, waistcoat and various decorations all displayed a great sense of fashion. It is hard to imagine that human beings from a period dating several thousand years earlier would have such a highly developed aesthetic style.

However, whether the life of these ancestors was miserable or happy, their stories abruptly stopped 3,500 years ago, and not a single trace of them was to be found for a long time afterwards.

1 The Xiaohe Cemetery/Photo by Liu Yusheng

The Xiaohe Cemetery is composed of several layers of tombs and other relics stacked on top of each other. The cemetery resembles an elliptical sand dune abruptly rising from a desert. There are many boat-shaped coffins stacked on the sand dune, each marked with an erected wooden post. The male burials were marked with the oar-shaped posts, while the female burials were marked with the phallic posts. The wooden posts are three to five meters tall, reflecting phallicism in the early periods of Lop Nur.

2 3 The Beauty of Xiaohe/Photos by Liu Yusheng

The Beauty of Xiaohe was unearthed in 2003 nearby an ancient river in the southwest of Lop Nur. The coffin, which is in the shape of a boat, was made of Euphrates poplar wood. Her face was covered with a cheese-like substance. When her body was discovered, it amazed the archaeologists at the site.

The first contemporaneous mention of Loulan, in Chinese records, is from 176 BC. A letter from the Chanyu of the Xiongnu to the Emperor Wen of the Han Dynasty, in which the Chanyu boasted of his own exploits and mentioned the name of Loulan[1] by the way:

> *With the blessing of the heaven, the officials and soldiers were very capable, and the horses were strong and powerful, so they had put an end to the Yuezhi, killed all those who resisted, and surrendered the ordinary people. They conquered Loulan, Wusun, Hujie and another 26 states nearby.*
> —*Shiji Xiongnu Liezpuan (Historical Records: The Biography of the Xiongnu)*

> This was the first contemporaneous mention of Loulan in Chinese records. The native name of Loulan was "Kroran," written in Chinese as Loulan (in reconstructed Han Dynasty pronunciation, an approximation of Kroran).

Loulan is a familiar name to the Chinese. The poems about it in later generations are all well-known.

Wang Changling's poem says:

> *Qinghai Hu is densely covered with dark clouds, and the rolling snow-capped mountains are dim.*
> *The ancient frontier fortress and the majestic Yumen Guan (Yumen Pass) are separated by thousands of miles and face each other.*
> *The soldiers guarding the frontiers have gone through hundreds of battles with their armors worn through yet their aspirations immortal.*
> *If they do not defeat the invading enemy they vow not to return to their hometown.*
> —Wang Changling (?-756), "Seven Songs in the Army: The Fourth"

Li Bai's poem says:

> *Snow is still floating in Tian Shan in May, and there are no flowers, only bitter coldness. The flute is blowing the tune of the willows, yet where to find the spring of the willows? Fight with the sound of the golden drum during the day, and sleep with a saddle at night.*
> *I would like to swing my sword, just to defeat Loulan.*
> —Li Bai (701-762), "Six Songs in the Frontier Fortress: The First"

---

1 Loulan was one of the "Thirty-six Kingdoms of Xiyu" recorded in historical records, and it lasted from the 2nd century BCE to the 6th century AD. In 77 BC, Weituqi, the king of Loulan, moved the capital south to Yuni City (now near the county seat of Ruoqiang), and the kingdom was renamed Shanshan. After that, the Shanshan Kingdom successively unified the small tribes in the southeast of Tarim Pendi, such as Xiaowan, Niya, Jingjue, and Qiemo, and became one of the main powers in Xiyu. For the convenience of the readers, we refer to this kingdom as "Loulan" throughout the entire book.

Ruins of the Three Houses of Loulan/Photo by Wen Xinghua

The Three Houses had extremely thick walls, and they are believed to be the place where important files of the Xiyu Changshifu (Government of the Western Regions) were stored.

Stupa at Miran/Photo by Wen Xinghua

The Stupa at Miran was the monastery of the Sangha of the Dharmaguptaka of the Loulan Kingdom. The shape of this stupa is unique. The tower base is square, and its body is cylindrical.

Fifty years after the Chanyu's letter, in 126 BC, the Chinese envoy Zhang Qian wrote some reports on Loulan after returning from there:

> *Loulan and Gushi have city walls and are adjacent to Yan Ze.*
> —Shiji Dayuan Liezhuan (Historical Records: Collected Biographies of Dayuan)

Yan Ze was Lop Nur, and Loulan was the new kingdom established by the descendants of the Beauty of Xiaohe. During the Han Dynasty, imperial soldiers left Yumen Guan, gradually expelling the Xiongnu from Xiyu, and the Silk Road that connected the East to the West was officially opened.

Loulan, which controlled the water source of Lop Nur, was located at the "throat" of Xiyu. The imperial court set up Xiyu Changshifu (Chief Official of Western Region Chief Administration Bureau) in Loulan, officially including the Lop Nur area under its jurisdiction. To ensure the safety of Xiyu and the Silk Road, the central government mobilized hundreds of thousands of people to build the Great Wall of the Han Dynasty, which passed through Lop Nur to reach the westernmost Luntai.

The Loulan Kingdom also expanded its sphere of influence with the help of the central government, gradually occupying the states of Qiemo, Niya, Xiaoyuan, Jingjue, etc. By the mid-Eastern Han Dynasty, the Loulan Kingdom had unified the southeastern part of Tarim Pendi, and Loulan's heyday had arrived.

As a channel for cultural exchanges between the East and the West, Loulan became an "international" metropolis. It integrated Eastern and Western cultures and was very inclusive, just like Hong Kong in the 20th century.

1	
2	3

1 The "China Will Rise When the Five Stars Appear in the East Together" brocade/Photo by Liu Yusheng

The famous "China Will Rise When the Five Stars Appear in the East Together" brocade, which was produced in Sichuan and unearthed at the Niya Ruins, is more than 1,000 years old. It is still gorgeous in color, and the eight Chinese characters on it remain identifiable.

2 Scene of a feast depicted on a mural unearthed in an ancient tomb of Loulan/Photo by Liu Yusheng

Scholars infer that the Loulan tomb with its mural paintings was built by the new immigrants from the Kushan Empire.

3 Coins unearthed along the Ancient Loulan Route/Photo by Liu Yusheng

The picture shows the "Kaiyuan Tongbao" coins of the Tang Dynasty discovered along the Ancient Loulan Route near Lop Nur.

The kingdom accepted Buddhism from India, built huge stupas, borrowed elements from Greek art and added wings to gods and Buddhas to create the famous "winged angels." It introduced the banquet scene of the Greek god of Bacchus into the blissful world of Buddhism, but the wine vessels it produced were based on the shapes from the Kushan Empire. Locals loved the fine brocade from Sichuan, and they also opened their arms in welcome to the bold and exoteric Roman art.

Compared with the Beauty of Xiaohe, the "Desert Prince" obviously had a richer life. The abundant, exquisite, and well-preserved funeral objects found in his tomb were enough for the mummy to become famous worldwide.

The Loulan people, who lived at a place where various cultures met, could not help but reflect on their situation at this crossroads:

> *The land has never failed me, nor has Xumi Shan (Mount Sumeru) and the other mountains. Those who have failed me are ungrateful villains. I am eager to pursue literature, music, and all knowledge between Heaven and Earth, and the world depends on the knowledge.*
>
> —The Kharosthi Script

However, the Loulan people's pursuit of knowledge failed to continue. In the 6th century, the Loulan Kingdom gradually disappeared from history. In 645, the Tang Dynasty monk Xuanzang passed through this region as he was on his way back from his pilgrimage to India, and was surprised to see what little was left of the once prosperous kingdom:

> *The city walls remain untouched, but no one is to be seen here.*
> —Datang Xiyu Ji (Records of the Western Regions of the Great Tang Dynasty).

This work depicts the scenery between Qiemo and Loulan.

What happened to the Loulan Kingdom?

> The "Desert Prince"/Photo by Liu Yusheng

The "Desert Prince" mummy was unearthed from Tomb No. 8 at the Niya Ruins, and he is believed to be the last king of the Jingjue, an independent oasis state. Many fine fabrics were buried with him, and the "China Will Rise When the Five Stars Appear in the East Together" brocade was also unearthed in this tomb.

3 The Water Dries, The People Leave

There are various reasons for the disappearance of Loulan, including enemy invasion, changes in the route of the Silk Road, and even a sudden outbreak of plague. However, the most important reason to consider should be the deterioration of the natural environment.

Ever-increasing human incursions destroyed the already fragile ecosystem, and this led to the deterioration and loss of poplar forests and shrubs. The environment with 40% forest coverage was gone forever. Waters from the upstream regions decreased, rivers dried up, and the lake area shrank, all contributing to the spread of the desert.

At Lop Nur, strong winds raged all year long, bringing dust and sand. With the sudden rainfalls and floods in the surrounding mountains continuing to erode the fragile land surface, many ridges and corridors formed. The kind of landform created through this process is called a yardang. The total area of yardangs at Lop Nur is 3,000 square kilometers, making it the second-largest yardang area in China. Yardangs are like the hulls of thousands of boats or isolated islands of rock in the desert.

▲ Bailongdui Yardangs/Photo by Wang Junbin

Bailongdui Yardangs, located in the northeast of Lop Nur, extend about 80 kilometers from north to south and 20 kilometers from east to west. The soil of Bailongdui is made of gravel, gypsum mud and alkali salt. The color is off-white. In sunlight, the yardangs often take on a silver color similar to scales. Viewed from a distance, Bailongdui Yardangs look like white dragons crouching in the desert, hence the name Bailong—white dragon.

˅ Longcheng Yardangs/Photo by Qian Wei

Longcheng Yardangs, located in the north of Lop Nur, are 6 to 20 meters high. They were formed by wind erosion by air currents which prevail in a certain direction throughout the whole year. They resemble dragons.

The deterioration of the environment immediately triggered a chain reaction. The output of farmland and livestock declined, and the army's rations had to be significantly reduced. In the heyday of the Loulan Kingdom, the daily food supply for an ordinary official was one *dou* (a unit of volume in ancient China, equal to 10 *sheng*) and two *sheng* (a unit of volume in ancient China). Later, it was reduced to six *sheng*. Even so, the superiors kept cutting the rations. As a result, the population began to decrease, and the once-prosperous city was eventually abandoned. Loulan became nothing more than an obscure relic of history.

By the second half of the 20th century, human exploration and the development of Tarim Pendi became more and more vigorous. The construction of dams, which blocked the flow of water feeding into the lake system, helped the formation of farmland and oases. By 1961, the many rivers that used to flow downstream through Lop Nur, including Tarim He, Kongqi He, Qarqan He and other rivers, all dried up. In 1972, the water supply to Lop Nur was cut off, and the lake area completely dried up. In this process, the ever-receding lake water created concentric shorelines. The "big ear" we mentioned above was thus formed.

Now, the Beauty of Xiaohe, the Desert Prince, Loulan—all the historical figures, ancient cities, and tales are gone forever.

In the next millennium, what will Lop Nur create if water refills the region again?

‹ **Dried-out Lop Nur/Photo by Li Xueliang**

In the dried-out Lop Nur area, the soil is full of cracks, like fallen withered yellow leaves scattered all over the ground.

A look at Gansu from a broad perspective reveals that this province in China is not some remote and desolate place famous for its hand-pulled noodles. Rather, Gansu is the most inclusive province with the greatest diversity China has to offer. It is a kaleidoscope of landscapes, plants, as well as customs, cultures, ethnicities, and religions. We discover that the more diverse a place is, the more beautiful it is.

②.3 Gansu:
The More Diverse, the More Beautiful

Snowscape of Qilian Shan/Photo by Qiu Jianjun

Water vapor, intercepted by the towering Qilian Shan, leads to precipitation, giving birth to numerous glaciers. Glacial meltwater and rainfall nourish vast grasslands at the northern foothills of the mountains.

For many people, Gansu is nothing more than a remote western province in China. It has large tracts of arid land, wind, dust, and desolate areas. When seen on a map of China's administrative divisions, Gansu seems to be extending to the west, gradually moving away from the hinterland of the east.

Many people also form their impression of Gansu through travel guides that emphatically introduce how to eat a bowl of authentic Lanzhou beef noodle soup. Local lore attributes its Creation to Ma Baozi, a Lanzhou resident from the Hui ethnic group, in 1915. The history of Lanzhou beef noodle soup can only be traced back a hundred years, but the articles recommending this dish are numerous.

In contrast, there are very few articles that can thoroughly and comprehensively present Gansu to the reader. They may find it difficult to sort out the key facts from the gamut of information and ponder what Gansu is truly like. However, it is easy to find guides that are unreflective and present information without fully considering what this place is like. As far as most people are concerned, Gansu is a remote and desolate province famous for Lanzhou beef noodle soup.

However, according to an assessment done by the Institute for Planets, Gansu is the most diverse and all-embracing province in China. A diversity in natural landscapes and unique flora and fauna can be found here. It is also a hub for various historical relics, cultures, ethnicities, and religions. The more diverse, the more beautiful.

All of this diversity and beauty began with the formation of Gansu's landscape. In terms of geographical divisions, Gansu can be divided into four regions. The formation of each region is an epic symphony of geography and history.

> **Yongtai Fortress/Photo by Cheng Weigang**
The Yongtai Fortress is in Jingtai County, Baiyin, Gansu. The existing city site is comprised of remnants from the Ming Dynasty (1368-1644). It was a fortress built by the Ming rulers to defend against attacks from northern nomadic groups.

1 Huangtu Gaoyuan

Around 1960 BC, disappointed by the corruption of the rulers of the Xia Dynasty (2070-1600 BC), Bu Zhu, who is claimed as an ancestor of the Zhou Dynasty (1046-256 BC), removed his clan from the Zhongyuan to Qingyang, Gansu to live in prosperity. This area was regarded as the land of the Rong and Di ethnic minorities. In *Shiji Zhoubenji* (*Records of the Grand Historian: Annals of Zhou*) it is recorded that:

> *Bu Zhu lost his official position and went to the land of the ethnic minorities of Rong and Di.*

Gansu's first geographical area, Huangtu Gaoyuan of Longdong and Longzhong, appears in historical records.

Back then, Huangtu Gaoyuan included many places such as today's Lanzhou, Dingxi, and Qingyang. Long Shan (Long Mountain) rises in the middle of the plateau, dividing it into the smaller areas of Longdong (east of Long Shan) and Longzhong (middle of Long Shan). Although there are also thousands of gullies formed by running water, most of the area is flat. Coupled with the easy-to-cultivate loess soil that has an average thickness of 50 to 80 meters, this vast area has long been a fertile land. This can be seen in Dongzhi Yuan, a Qingyang loess platform. Even if soil erosion has caused its land area to shrink, its surface area is still as large as 700 square kilometers today. It is known as "the greatest yuan (loess platform) in the world."

In summer, Long Shan, which stands 800 to 2,000 meters above sea level, blocks water vapor from the east, resulting in relatively heavier precipitation. The Huangtu Gaoyuan also changes its natural loess color in summer time and turns into a green surface.

The Zhou clan who migrated here brought advanced agricultural production techniques and used them on this loess land. The clan was able to gradually develop and grow. It first expanded from Qingyang to Qishan (now Qishan County), Shaanxi, and then opened the prelude to King Wu's conquest over King Zhou of the Shang Dynasty (1600-1046 BC) from the Weihe Hegu (Weihe River Valley). In the end, the Zhou tribe established China's last hereditary slavery dynasty, the Zhou Dynasty.

Many dynastic changes have occurred throughout China's history. Regimes in marginal areas conquered those of central areas. The regimes in Gansu had more than one opportunity to do just that.

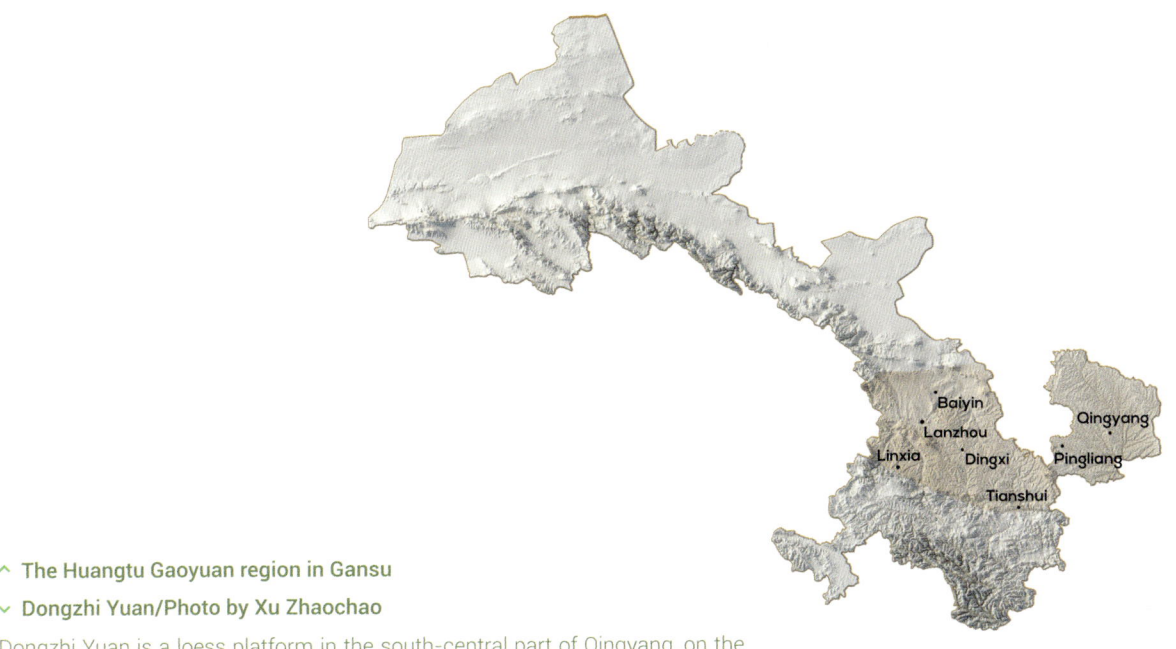

- The Huangtu Gaoyuan region in Gansu
- Dongzhi Yuan/Photo by Xu Zhaochao

Dongzhi Yuan is a loess platform in the south-central part of Qingyang, on the north bank of Jing He (Jinghe River), between Malian He (Malian River) and Pu He (Puhe River). With an area of more than 700 square kilometers, it is the largest loess platform in the region. This picture shows a corner of Dongzhi Yuan.

2 Longnan Shandi (Mountain Region South of Long Mountain)

Ying Feizi, a member of the nobility and the chief of the Ying clan, was a renowned horse breeder. Around 890 BC, King Xiao of the Zhou Dynasty learned of his reputation and put him in charge of breeding and training horses for the Zhou army. King Xiao granted Ying Feizi a small fief at Qin. In modern times, the word "Qin" is usually treated as the other name of Shaanxi Province, however, in Ying Feizi's period, it was a region possibly located in today's Qingshui County, Tianshui, Gansu.

Thus, Gansu's second geographic area, Longnan Shandi, appeared on the map.

Longnan Shandi includes the mountainous areas south of Wei He (Weihe River) and east of Lintan and Tewo, covering Longnan, Tianshui, and part of the Gannan Tibetan Autonomous Prefecture.

Qin Ling from the east and Min Shan from the south converge here. Peaks rise one after another. High mountains and deep valleys bestow spectacular landscapes on the area. Today, there are three national nature reserves, one provincial nature reserve, three national forest parks, and two national wetland parks in this area. If you visit Guan'e Gou (Guan'e Gully) in Dangchang County, Longnan, you will see how the lucid waters and lush hills echo each other to form a picturesque fairyland.

Longnan Shandi has abundant precipitation. In addition to the extremely rich vegetation in the area, this is also where rivers are born. The beautiful Bailong Jiang (Bailong River) flows 450 kilometers through Gansu and has been dubbed the mother river of Longnan. Another important river in Longnan, Xi Han Shui (West Hanshui River), once separated a Qin couple. Their longing was transformed into a famous poem in *Shijing (Classic of Poetry,* or *The Book of Songs)* that has been passed down through the ages:

> *The reeds and rushes are deeply green, and the white dew is turned into hoarfrost.*
> *The man of whom I think, is somewhere across the water.*

‹ **The loess ridges in Dingxi/Photo by Wang Hongbin**
The picture shows the loess ridges with a highway snaking its way across.

These rivers rushed out of the mountains, nourishing lush pastures on both sides of the valley and the flat places of these mountains. The Qin pastures were able to equip a powerful army with high-quality warhorses. Because of the perpetual battles of the Qin people against Xirong, an armed force that was stronger than that of Zhongyuan was gradually formed.

Longnan Shandi is also rich in salt. As the most important economic resource at that time, salt provided Qin with great wealth.

Relying on the favorable conditions of Longnan Shandi, the Qin people gradually expanded their territory over the following 600 years, until they conquered all the other states and unified China by establishing China's first centralized dynasty, the Qin Dynasty (221-206 BC).

∧ Tle region of Longnan Shandi

> A waterfall in Guan'e Gou/Photo by Hu Weidong

Guan'egou National Forest Park is in the suburbs of Dangchang County, Longnan, Gansu. This picture shows a waterfall in the Guan'egou Scenic Area.

3 Hexi Zoulang

The Qin Dynasty established the rule over chunk of China's territory, but the Han Dynasty, which inherited the territory of the Qin Dynasty, faced harassment from the Xiongnu, a powerful nomadic tribe in the northwest. Several emperors chose to wait to accumulate strength until the time when the increasingly powerful Han Dynasty began its attempts to conquer the Xiongnu.

At that time, Emperor Wu of the Han Dynasty learned from captives that the Xiongnu had an irreconcilable enemy in Xiyu (Western Regions)—the Greater Yuezhi. He decided to send warriors to collaborate with the Greater Yuezhi in Xiyu to "cut off the right arm of the Xiongnu."

In 139 BC, Zhang Qian voluntarily served as an envoy to Xiyu. At that time, however, Xiyu seemed to be blocked off from the Han people by a solid wall, and no one knew what it was exactly like. Therefore, Sima Qian, author of *Shiji (Records of the Grand Historian)*, referred to Zhang Qian's feat as "cutting through Xiyu."

Here, the third geographic area of Gansu, Hexi Zoulang, appeared.

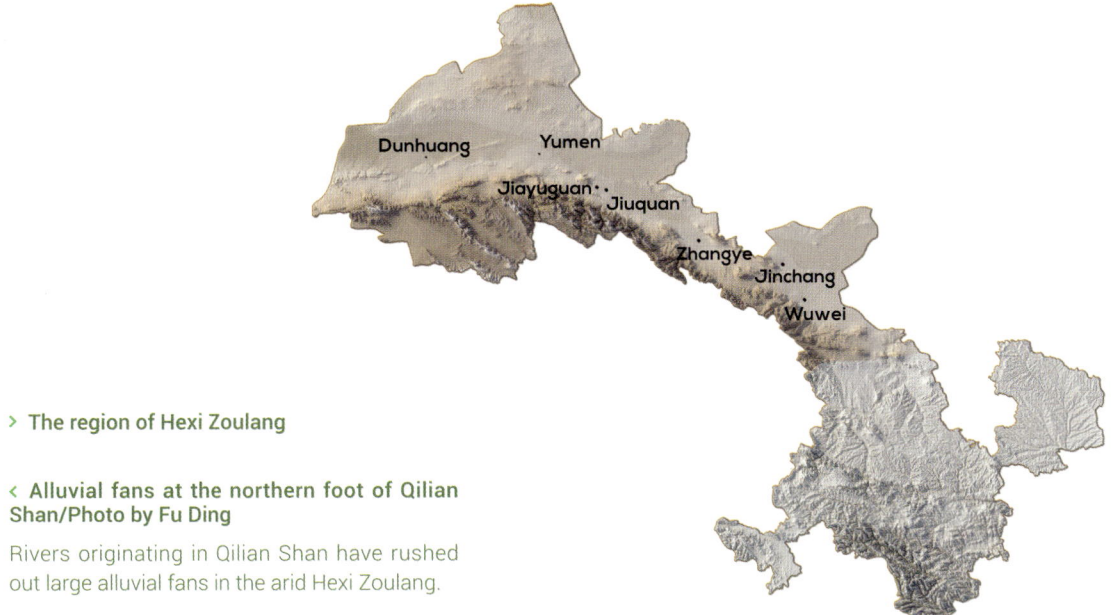

> The region of Hexi Zoulang

< Alluvial fans at the northern foot of Qilian Shan/Photo by Fu Ding

Rivers originating in Qilian Shan have rushed out large alluvial fans in the arid Hexi Zoulang.

Hexi Zoulang is located to the west of Huang He. Badain Jaran Shamo (Badain Jaran Desert) and Tengger Shamo (Tengger Desert), located on the north side of Hexi Zoulang, await an opportunity to expand south. However, Qingzang Gaoyuan, with its thin air, and the arid Qaidam Pendi in the south refuse to yield an inch of land. With the overwhelming Qilian Shan, Heli Shan (Heli Mountain), and Longshou Shan (Longshou Mountain), a narrow natural corridor with a width ranging from several kilometers to nearly 100 kilometers was formed. During the Han Dynasty, people from Zhongyuan had no choice but to travel through this narrow corridor to reach Xiyu.

Hexi Zoulang is arid and has little rainfall. When seen from the air, the land is full of cracks making it look as if it had been burned by flames.

Fortunately, the towering Qilian Shan stands on the south side of Hexi Zoulang. The snow-capped mountains form a strong contrast against the arid corridor.

The Qilian Shan range stretches some 800 kilometers and has an average elevation of more than 4,000 meters. The tall mountains intercept the clouds that are rich in water vapor. The eastern section of Qilian Shan has abundant rainfall and dense forests. At the northern foot of Qilian Shan, there are also grasslands that stretch over a total area of 24,000 square kilometers. Wild flowers dot the vast pastures.

The Shandan Army Horse Ranch, a world-famous warhorse farm, is located here. The area has been a large-scale army horse ranch since the Western Han Dynasty. Various tribes have fought numerous wars throughout history to occupy this precious land.

By the Han Dynasty, the defeated Xiongnu were forced to abandon Qilianshan Caoyuan (Qilian Mountain Grassland), and their songs expressed their sorrow:

> *Take away our Qilian Shan, our livestock cannot reproduce;*
> *Lost our Yanzhi Shan (Yanzhi Mountains), our brides fade without rouge.*

> Shandan Army Horse Ranch/Photo by Liu Zhongwen

The ranch is located in the Damaying Caoyuan (Damaying Grassland), which nestles in the middle of Hexi Zoulang and at the northern foot of Qilian Shan. The grassland, featuring a gentle terrain, plenty of water and lush grass, has been a famous military horse breeding ground since the Western Han Dynasty.

Qilian Shan has also given birth to many glaciers. At present, there are more than 3,000 glaciers, with a water storage capacity of about 132 billion cubic meters, about 100 times that of Miyun Shuiku (Miyun Reservoir) in Beijing. The largest is Touming Mengke Glacier, located in Subei County, Gansu. *Mengke* means *eternity* in Mongolian. There are rich ice scenes, towering and steep snow peaks, and large firn areas. The vast snowfields stretch to the horizon, forming a pure and transparent world.

Meltwater from glaciers and rainwater from mountains flow into rivers in the valleys, including Shiyang He, Hei He, Shule He, and Dang He (Danghe River). They form multiple river systems that flow toward Hexi Zoulang.

Qilian Shan/Photo by Li Chun
The photo was taken in Sunan Yugur Autonomous County, Zhangye, Gansu.

An aerial photo of the Touming Mengke Glacier/Photo by Chen Jianfeng

The largest river among them, Hei He, which was called Ruo Shui in ancient times, is the second-largest inland river in China after Tarim He. It starts from Qilian Shan and passes through oases, salt marshes, and deserts to Juyan Hai (Juyan Lake) in Ejin Qi, Nei Mongol Autonomous Region (Inner Mongolia). Due to this flow, the downstream of the river is also called Ejin He (Ejin River).

Dang He is the only river that irrigates Dunhuang Pingyuan (Dunhuang Plain). Without it, there would be no Dunhuang culture. Wowa Chi (Wowa Lake) in Dunhuang created a water town on the edge of Gobi Shamo (Gobi Desert).

These rivers flow to Hexi Zoulang, nourishing a string of oases on the arid land. Wuwei, Jinchang, Zhangye, and Jiuquan at the northern foot of Qilian Shan were built on different oases.

The existence of this chain of oases allowed Zhang Qian and others to enter Xiyu. Emperor Wu of the Han Dynasty also set up four prefectures, Wuwei, Jiuquan, Zhangye, and Dunhuang, in these oases. They were collectively known as the "four prefectures of Hexi." In addition, oases enabled farming civilizations to survive and develop in these prefectures and counties. This was also related to the fact that the prefectures and counties were able to be firmly controlled by the dynasties of Zhongyuan for a long time, even if they were under frequent attack from the nomadic tribes from the north and south.

After opening Hexi Zoulang, the dynasties based in the Zhongyuan no longer isolated themselves and began to communicate frequently with the vast outside world. This kind of exchange reached its peak during the Tang Dynasty and promoted the economic development of Hexi Zoulang. At that time, Liangzhou (now Wuwei) became the largest city in Hexi, and the grain stock of the entire region accounted for as much as 1/3 of the country's total, which made the prefecture the richest in the nation.

An open nation created a splendid civilization. At that time, Hexi Zoulang was not a border or barren land. Instead, it was a thoroughfare and a place where the empire displayed its ambitions.

⌃ **The pasture near the Mati Temple in Sunan Yugur Autonomous County/ Photo by Li Chun**

After a heavy snowfall, the golden grass and white snow complement each other with particularly vivid colors.

⌄ **Wowa Chi, Dunhuang/Photo by Jiang Hong**

Wowa Chi is to the south of Dunhuang. The snow-capped Altun Shan can be seen in the distance.

4 Gannan Gaoyuan (Gannan Plateau)

Hundreds of years later, before the establishment of the Yuan Dynasty (1206-1368), Godan, the second son of Ogedei, the third son of Genghis Khan, attacked the Kingdom of Tubo from three sides and invited Sakya Pandita, a Tibetan spiritual leader, to Liangzhou. After negotiations, the two sides agreed that Tubo should be subject to the Mongols. In exchange, Godan converted to Tibetan Buddhism. After that, Tibetan Buddhism was able to go beyond the Qingzang Gaoyuan and spread to the Mongolian Plateau and even the entire nation. This meeting of sovereigns was called the "Liangzhou Meeting," and it took place in 1247.

Here, Gannan Gaoyuan, Gansu's fourth geographic region, entered the scene.

Gannan Gaoyuan is located on the fringe of Qingzang Gaoyuan. During the Han and Tang dynasties, part of it was included in prefectures and counties under the jurisdiction of these dynasties, but it did not fall into the jurisdiction of the central government as a whole until the Yuan Dynasty.

Min Shan, Xiqing Shan (Xiqing Mountain), Jishi Shan (Jishi Mountain), and Qin Ling converge in southern Gansu, creating large, uniquely shaped mountainous regions. Among them, Zhouqu County and Tewo County on the eastern fringe of the plateau boast towering mountains, deep valleys, and dense forests, with a warm and humid climate. There are many little-known villages hidden at the foot of the mountains, such as Zhagana, where clouds and mist often drift along like in a paradise. Luqu County and Maqu County, which are in the hinterland of the plateau, are characterized a high altitude with a cold climate and vast grasslands. The winding rivers on the grassland cause people to pause and linger.

Gansu got its name during the Yuan Dynasty. The name Gansu is a combination of Ganzhou (now the main urban district and seat of Zhangye) and Suzhou (an old name and the seat of modern Jiuquan). Gannan was officially included as part of Gansu during the Qing Dynasty. At this point, the main body of Gansu, consisting of the four regions of Huangtu Gaoyuan, Longnan Shandi, Hexi Zoulang, and Gannan Gaoyuan, had taken shape.

▲ **Maqu Caoyuan (Maqu Grassland), Gannan Tibetan Autonomous Prefecture/Photo by Zuo Xuelan**

Maqu County in southwestern Gansu is part of Qingzang Gaoyuan. The land here is flat with winding rivers.

▽ **The region of Gannan Gaoyuan**

Zhagana, Têwo County, Gannan Tibetan Autonomous Prefecture/Photo by Zhu Jinhua

The name *Gansu* can be abbreviated as *Gan* or *Long*. Gansu, located in northwestern China, has an area of approximately 430,000 square kilometers. Situated at the edge of the First and Second Terrain Ladders, Gansu is at the intersection of Qingzang Gaoyuan, Huangtu Gaoyuan, and Nei Mongol Gaoyuan. The terrain in the area is complex due to the diverse landforms, including mountains, basins, plains, and deserts. Because of its special location, Gansu is the junction for many geographical regions in China.

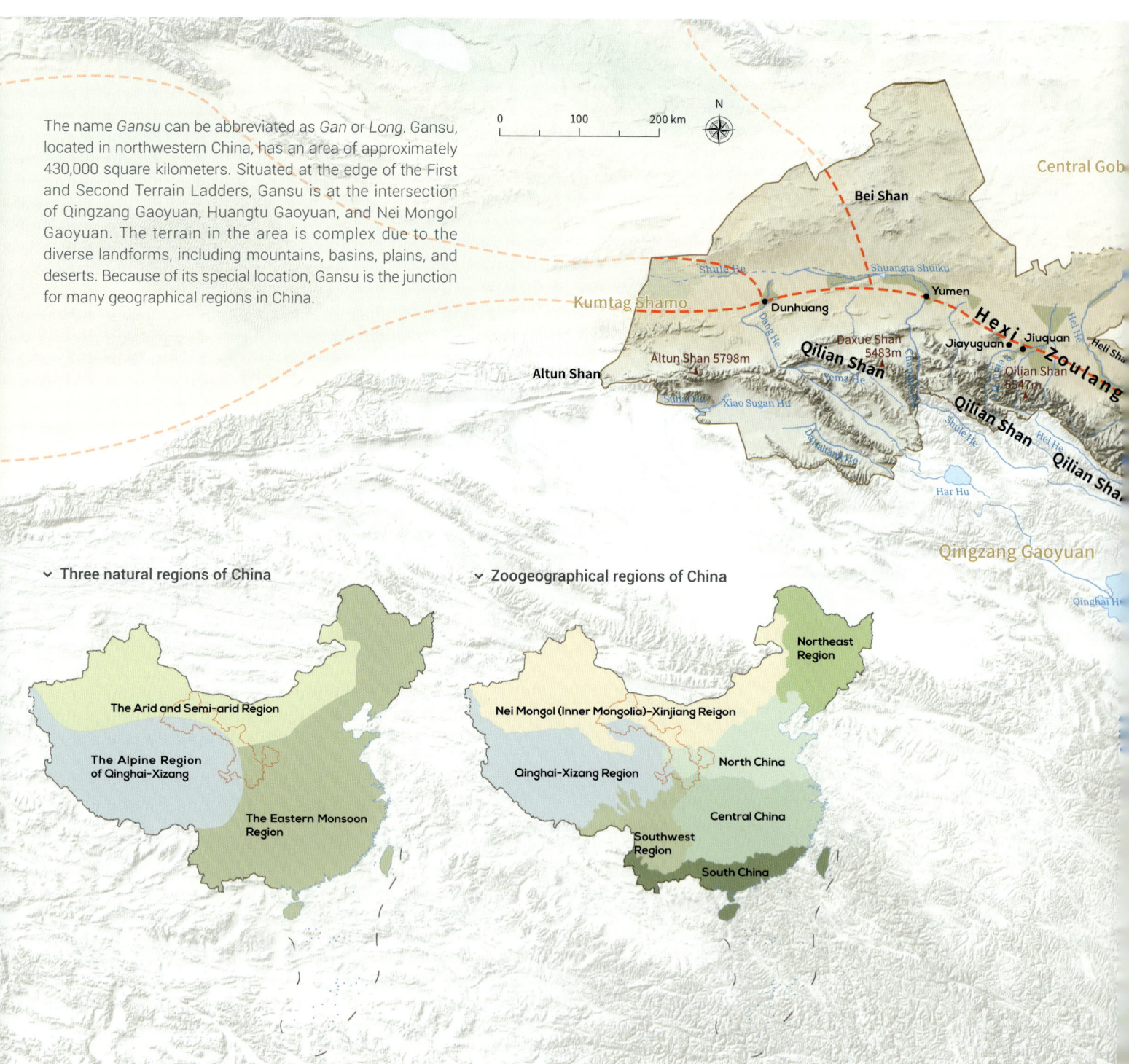

⌄ Three natural regions of China

⌄ Zoogeographical regions of China

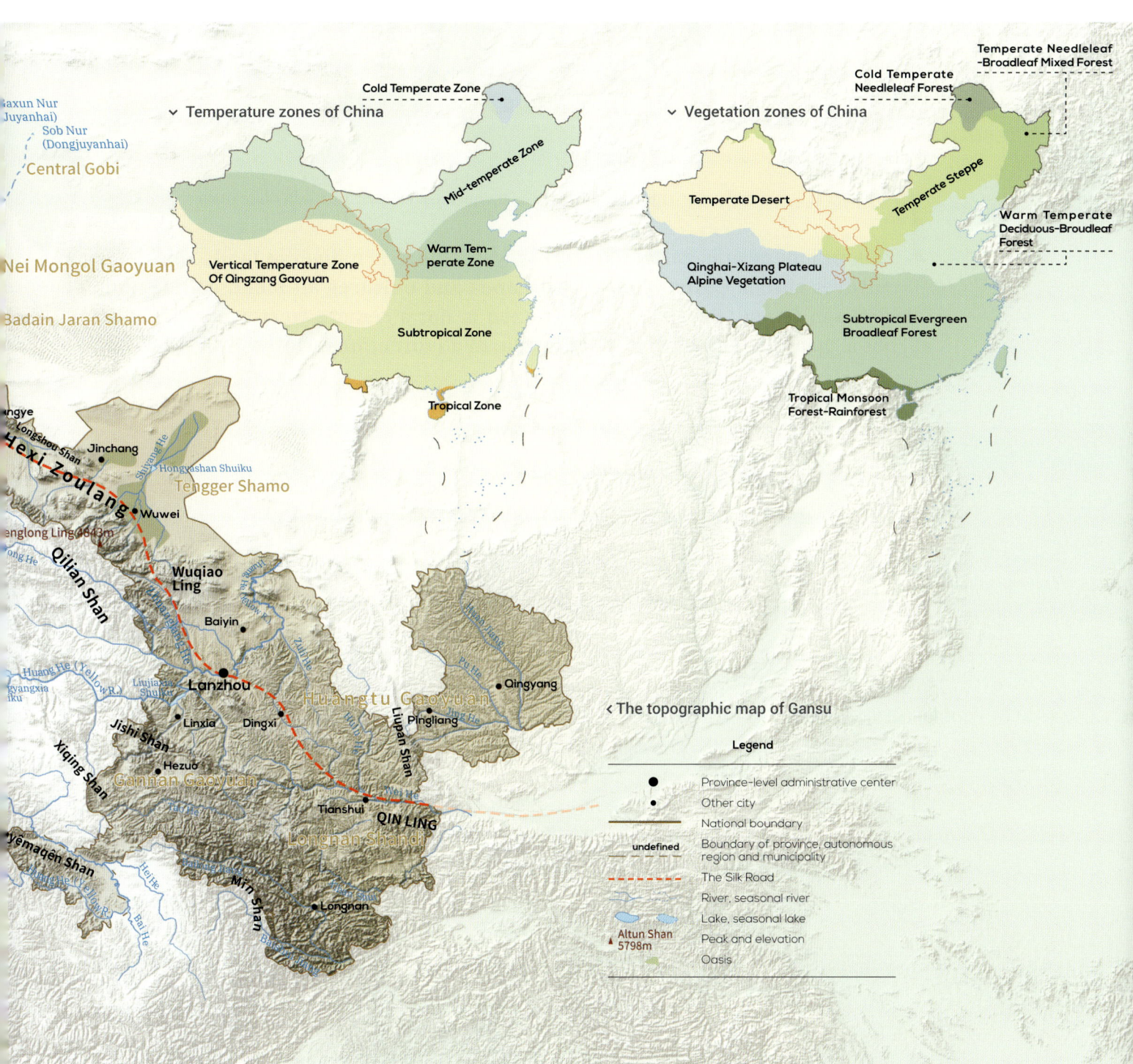

5 The More Diverse, The More Beautiful

If we look at Gansu from a broader perspective, its uniqueness within China can be seen clearly.

This uniqueness is reflected in this way: There are diverse landscapes and cultures across China. These landscapes and cultures all meet, collide, and integrate in Gansu. Because of this, Gansu is not a remote western province at all, but a "heart of China" that is accessible in all directions.

China's three natural regions, the Eastern Monsoon Region, the Northwestern Arid and Semi-arid Region, and the Alpine Region of Qinghai-Xizang, all meet in Gansu.

The four major temperature zones, the Mid-temperate Zone, the Warm Temperate Zone, the Subtropical Zone, and the Vertical Climatic Zone of Qingzang Gaoyuan, also converge and coexist in Gansu.

The same is true for the five vegetation division zones. There is a wide variety of species ranging from golden Euphrates poplar forests, to green faber fir (*Abies fabri*) and Chinese spruce (*Picea asperata*), to low Gobi grass.

The five major animal division zones also meet in Gansu. Even the giant panda, a national treasure, has found a suitable habitat in the arid and desolate region. They inhabit seven nature reserves in Gansu, including the Baishuijiang National Nature Reserve and the Jianshan Giant Panda Nature Reserve.

The intersection of various natural divisions makes extremely rich landforms coexist in Gansu—from the monotonous yardangs in Dunhuang to the splendid Danxia landform in Zhangye, from mountains to valleys, from grasslands to deserts.

> **Zhangye National Geopark, Gansu/Photo by Qiu Menghan**
> The Zhangye National Geological Park in Gansu is located at the northern foot of Qilian Shan. It is an area famous for its colorful hilly landscape. The area has high value for scientific research and tourism. However, there is still an ongoing debate on whether the landform here is part of the Danxia landform.

︿ Maijishan Grottoes/Photo by Hu Shu

Located in Maiji District, Tianshui, the Maijishan Grottoes boast clay figurines of matchless beauty in the world, hence its reputation as the "Oriental Sculpture Exhibition Hall."

﹥ Mogao Grottoes/Photo by Zhang Shihong

The Mogao Grottoes are located on the cliff at the eastern foot of Mingsha Shan (Mingsha Mountain), which is 25 kilometers southeast of Dunhuang city proper. The wooden architecture in this picture is Cave 96, the iconic nine-story building of the Mogao Grottoes. People often call it the "Great Buddha Hall." There is a giant painted stone-and-clay statue of Maitreya in a sitting posture.

The rich geographical environment connects the different directions and makes Gansu a melting pot of various ethnic groups, where different lifestyles and customs all merge and coexist.

Taoism, Buddhism, Tibetan Buddhism, Islam, and other religions all prosper in Gansu. As there is no dominant religion here, different sects have coexisted in a relatively tolerant environment. Taoism reveres Kongtong Shan (Kongtong Mountain) as one of its sacred mountains. The Labrang Monastery is one of the six great monasteries of the Gelug school of Tibetan Buddhism. Buddhist grottoes, such as the Mogao Grottoes and the Maijishan Grottoes, can be found throughout Gansu. Of the four major grottoes in China, two are in Gansu, which demonstrates the remarkable richness of grotto culture here.

These natural and cultural environments have enriched the diversity of Gansu.

However, starting from the Song Dynasty (960-1279), the dynasties of Zhongyuan lost control of Hexi Zoulang. In addition, navigation technology experienced rapid advances. The Maritime Silk Road gradually replaced the Silk Road on land. Gansu was no longer a thoroughfare. During the Ming Dynasty, the imperial court built a "luxury version" of the Great Wall in the vast northern regions, which included Gansu, and expended more manpower and financial resources than the Han and Tang dynasties. However, the stronger the Great Wall, the weaker the imperial sovereign. The once prosperous Zhongyuan dynasties gradually came to an end, and Gansu again became the desolate borderland it had been long ago.

As Gansu left the center stage, this once rich region became backwards and impoverished. In modern times, Europeans invaded China from the sea, forcing China to continue developing its coastal areas. The development of Gansu, an inland province, was of little concern. Its per capita GDP (gross domestic product) has been the lowest in China for many years.

What is the way out for Gansu? It is believed that its future depends on the great opportunities brought by the Belt and Road Initiative. History has proven that the more open and diverse a place is, the more beautiful it is.

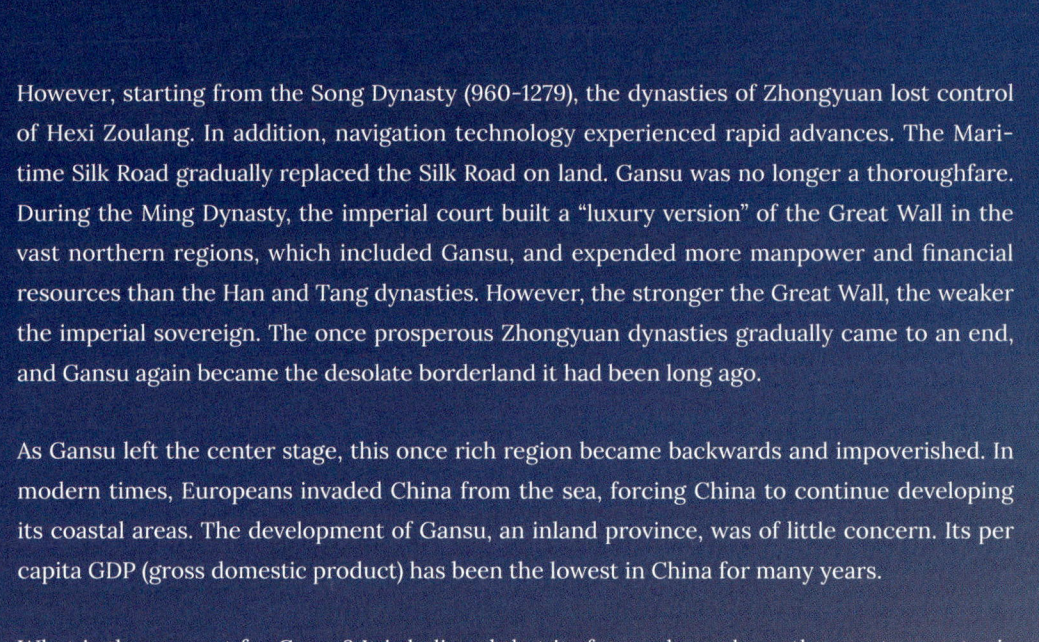

Jiayu Pass at sunset/Photo by Qiu Jianjun

The impression of Xi'an varies from person to person. It could be the Terracotta Warriors of the first Emperor of Qin, Chang'an City of the Han and Tang dynasties or the ancient city walls of the Ming and Qing dynasties that have made an impression on a person's heart. However, Xi'an is not only an ancient imperial capital but also a modern city of great vitality. After countless instances of destruction, it always has the power to be reborn.

2.4 Xi'an:
Rich and Affluent for a Thousand Years

Everyone has a different impression of Xi'an. It might be represented by the Terracotta Army of the First Emperor of Qin, the capital of Chang'an in the Han and Tang dynasties, or the ancient city walls of the Ming and Qing dynasties.

In this city located in the hinterland of China, there are countless historical sites left by past dynasties. Together, they make Xi'an a famous ancient city.

However, it seems that today Xi'an is more famous for its vitality than its history.

Today, Xi'an is joining the battle of "competing for talent." The number of new settlers in the first three months of 2018 was as high as 210,000, which is close to the total number throughout 2017. The city pays attention to details to improve residents' lives, such as requiring all motor vehicles to wait for the pedestrians in front of the zebra crossing. At the same time, numerous tourists swarm to Xi'an, experiencing the heroic way of drinking as locals and tasting local snacks such as the famous brush-shaped pastry. The innovation of traditional Xi'an cuisine is also impressive.

Is Xi'an a place of tradition or a city of vitality? What kind of city on earth is it?

According to the Institute for Planets, Xi'an is not just an ancient imperial capital but a vigorous city as well.

The city went through many times of destruction, but it still stands here to stay, and only looks even brighter.

‹ **The ancient city wall of Xi'an against the backdrop of modern buildings/ Photo by Li Wenbo**
In the lower part of the picture is the turret of Xi'an Ancient City Wall, echoing the modern skyscrapers in the distance. Further beyond is the tall Qin Ling.

⌄ **Xi'an and its surrounding areas**
Xi'an lies in the middle of Guanzhong Pingyuan (Guanzhong Plain). The city borders the northern foot of Qin Ling in the south, and the north mountain of Huangtu Gaoyuan in the north. The fertile plain here is easy to cultivate, and has long become the center of human activities. At the same time, the plain is surrounded by mountains. For the ancients, if the main traffic hub was guarded, a strong line of defense could be formed. As a result, Xi'an, located in the hinterland of Guanzhong Pingyuan, was always the first choice for the rulers of past dynasties to build their capitals.

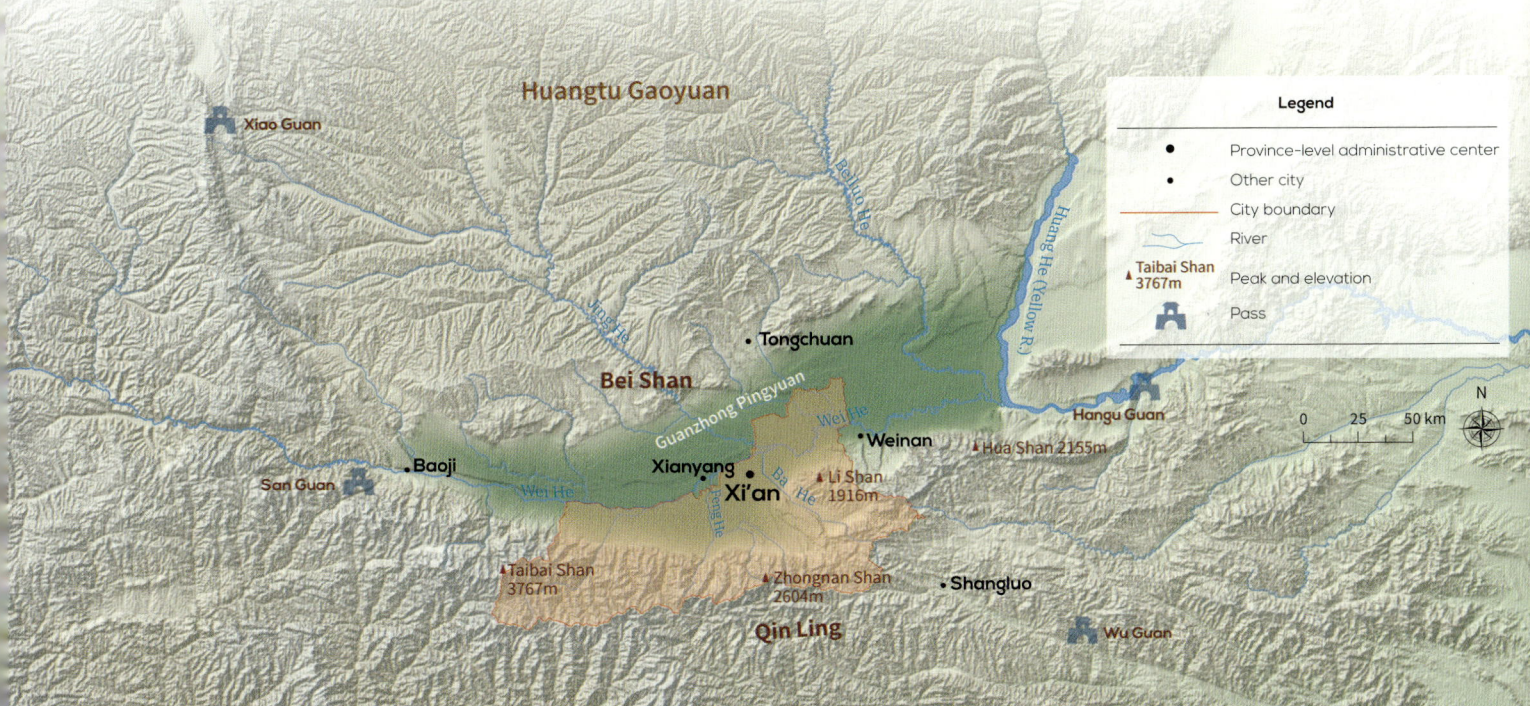

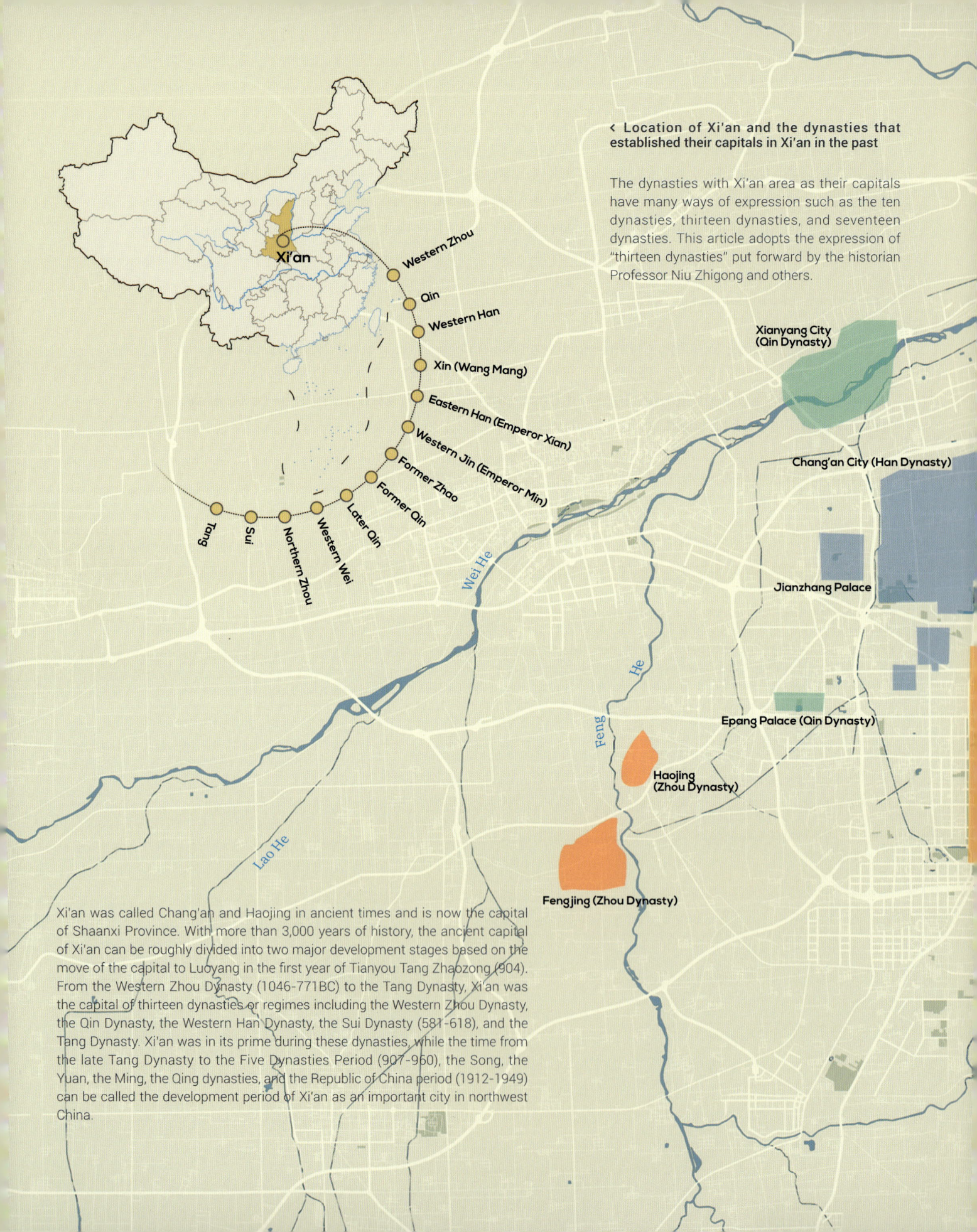

Location of Xi'an and the dynasties that established their capitals in Xi'an in the past

The dynasties with Xi'an area as their capitals have many ways of expression such as the ten dynasties, thirteen dynasties, and seventeen dynasties. This article adopts the expression of "thirteen dynasties" put forward by the historian Professor Niu Zhigong and others.

Xi'an was called Chang'an and Haojing in ancient times and is now the capital of Shaanxi Province. With more than 3,000 years of history, the ancient capital of Xi'an can be roughly divided into two major development stages based on the move of the capital to Luoyang in the first year of Tianyou Tang Zhaozong (904). From the Western Zhou Dynasty (1046-771BC) to the Tang Dynasty, Xi'an was the capital of thirteen dynasties or regimes including the Western Zhou Dynasty, the Qin Dynasty, the Western Han Dynasty, the Sui Dynasty (581-618), and the Tang Dynasty. Xi'an was in its prime during these dynasties, while the time from the late Tang Dynasty to the Five Dynasties Period (907-960), the Song, the Yuan, the Ming, the Qing dynasties, and the Republic of China period (1912-1949) can be called the development period of Xi'an as an important city in northwest China.

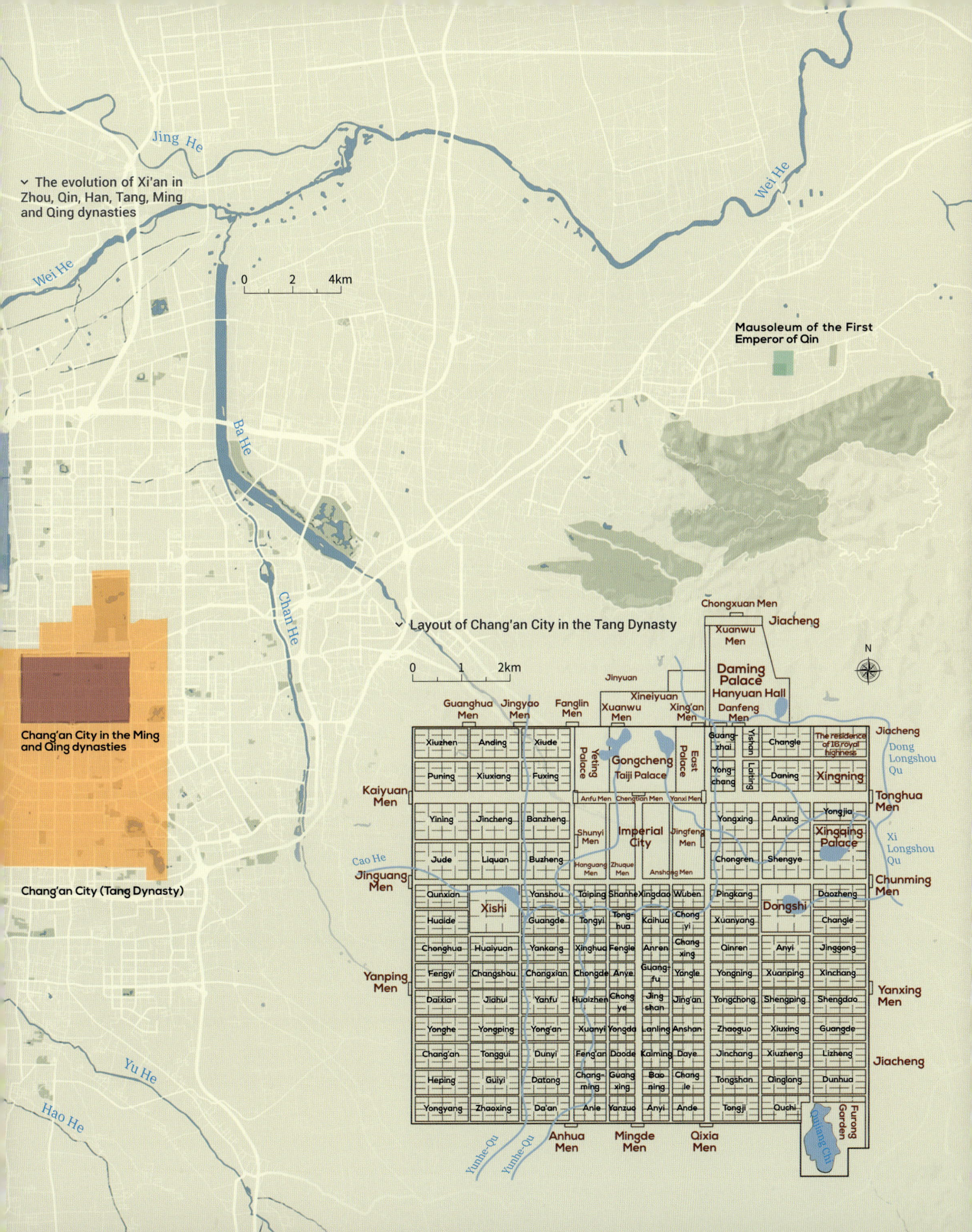

1 The Birth

First, we need to renew our understanding of the geography of Xi'an. It is not a pure plain, but half mountain and half plain. The mountain stands tall in front of the plain; the plain lays gently at the foot of the mountain.

Millions of years ago, the strata of today's Qing Ling region fractured due to tectonic movement, a huge fault zone started to develop. The north side of the fault zone continued to subside, forming a sedimentary basin, Guangzhong Pendi (Guanzhong Basin), while the southern part uplifted constantly and rose into Qin Ling. Taibai Shan (Taibai Mountain), Cuihua Shan (Cuihua Mountain), Zhongnan Shan (Zhongnan Mountains), Li Shan (Mount Lishan), and Hua Shan (Mount Huashan) spread from west to east. The mountains and the sea of clouds are magnificent.

Many river systems were bred in the mountains, which cut through the mountains to form valleys. On the side of Qin Ling facing Guanzhong Pendi, many valleys stand side by side, like a group of dragons spitting out water. These are the "72 Valleys of Qinling." Water rushes out of large and small valleys and flows towards Guanzhong Pendi. The basin has many lakes and marshes, with rivers crisscrossing. Feng He (Fenghe River), Lao He (Laohe River), Yu He (Yuhe River), Hao He (Haohe River), Chan He (Chanhe River), Ba He (Bahe River), plus Jing He (Jinghe River) in the north, all run into Wei He, which are referred to as the "Eight Rivers of Chang'an."

During geological time, rivers originated from surrounding mountains brought abundant sediments, which deposited in Guangzhong Pendi (Guanzhong Basin), formed a Cenozoic strata of thousands of meters. Thus, Guanzhong Pingyuan (Guanzhong Plain), known as "800 *li* of Qin land," was formed. The life of the Xi'an people unfolds on the stage of this fertile land.

˄ Qin Ling and Weihe Pingyuan (Weihe Plain)/Photo by She Hu

Rivers originating in Qin Ling give Xi'an fertile land, where both rural and urban areas thrive.

˅ An aerial photo of the distinct boundary between Jing He and Wei He/Photo by She Hu

On the left of the picture is Wei He, and on the right is Jing He. Due to the different sediment content of the two rivers, a clear boundary is formed between them.

2 Beautiful Clothes and Strong Horses

About 6,000 years ago, a group of early "Xi'an people" lived on the banks of rivers such as Chan He and Jing He. They had an appearance like that of modern southerners, and the average height of an adult would have been around 170cm. The utensils they used were simple and plain. They were fishermen, hunters, and wild fruit gatherers, and they practiced a mysterious worship of fish. Theirs was not a society of wealth, and they were threatened by diseases, beasts, and tribal enemies. The tragedy of infant deaths occurred frequently, and the life span of adults was only about 30-40 years. In their culture, they embodied their prayers for life as a symbol of a human-faced fish, which they painted into their pottery. The bowl with a human-faced fish that was unearthed at the Banpo site in Xi'an may be a testimony of this belief.

More than 3,000 years ago, the Zhou people, most of whom were good at farming, set out from Huangtu Gaoyuan in Gansu and Shaanxi and joined the ranks of the "Xi'an people." The Zhou people brought advanced production technologies and refined farmland management methods with them. They weeded, fertilized crops and used rainwater to wash away excessive salt and alkali in the soil. The fertile alluvial plains of Xi'an were quickly developed by the Zhou people into fertile fields planted with millet and other crops.

Developed agriculture allowed the Zhou people to become powerful. They built the twin cities of Fengjing and Haojing on the opposite banks of Feng He in southwestern Xi'an. This was the beginning of Xi'an as a capital.

Life in the capital was still simple. The Zhou people enthusiastically cast imposing pieces of bronze ware and then carved dozens or even hundreds of characters on them in an orderly manner. These characters recorded their appointment orders, official positions, wars, sacrificial ceremonies, and laws in detail.

> **Human-faced Fish Decorated Bowl/Photo by Liu Yanting**

The Human-faced Fish Decorated Bowl unearthed at the Banpo site in Xi'an is representative of the painted pottery work of the Yangshao culture. The human face on the bowl has a strange headdress, and there are two small fish in its mouth. The human face is ingeniously combined with the fish pattern. There is still controversy as to the purpose of the Human-faced Fish Decorated Bowl. One of the theories is that it is a burial vessel for deceased children, symbolizing the shaman asking the fish god to possess the child's body and a prayer for blessings.

⌄ **The Beacon Tower on Li Shan (Lishan Mountain)/Photo by Wei Wei**

This picture is an aerial photo of the Beacon Tower on Li Shan. Below it lies Weihe Pingyuan.

Then, real change came with the craftsmen and soldiers of the Qin Dynasty.

In 771 BC, the Quanrong people, a nomadic tribe active in the northwestern part of China, sacked Haojing (today's Xi'an) and overthrew the Western Zhou Dynasty. Xi'an fell as a capital for the first time. Immediately afterward, the Qin people moved from Gansu to Guanzhong Pingyuan, filling the vacancy left by the Zhou people. They implemented a military merit system. Anyone, regardless of social status, could be granted land and official rankings for their military accomplishments.

This effective incentive system allowed the Qin Dynasty to build one of the most powerful armies in the world at that time. Peasants put down their hoes and became soldiers. Fathers and sons, brothers and fellow villagers charged forward together on the battlefields. As sung in a pre-Qin poem:

> *Who can say we have no clothing? I will share the war skirts. When the King sends us to war, we will strengthen the armor, and march side by side.*
> —"Wuyi" in "Odes of Qin," a chapter of *Shijing (Classic of Poetry, or The Book of Songs)*

The Qin people united with one heart and finally conquered the other six states, unifying China. The Qin Dynasty then declared Xianyang as its capital.

The Qin government gathered the best craftsmen from Xi'an and the surrounding. Some of these craftsmen's names were fortunate enough to be preserved, they were Jiading, Xiao, An, Wen, Ran, and Xing while many more craftsmen's names were not. They perfectly "reproduced" the majestic army of the Qin Dynasty in terracotta to safeguard Qin Shi Huang, the First Emperor of Qin, in the afterworld.

‹ No. 1 Pit of Terracotta Warriors/Photo by Zhang Tianzhu

The terracotta warrior pits were the burial place of Emperor Qin Shi Huang, with three excavated so far. No. 1 pit is the largest, with a total area of about 14,260 square meters.

Green Terracotta Warrior/Photo by Zhang Tianzhu

Among the Terracotta Warriors of the First Emperor of Qin, it is the only one using green mineral pigment to color the face that has been discovered so far.

This is the Terracotta Army. The craftsmen sculpted the Terracotta Warriors and horses one by one, and each piece was given a unique appearance. These Terracotta Warriors are very lifelike, and even their hair and muscles were carefully sculpted. Each of the one-ton bronze chariots and horses is composed of more than 6,000 parts that were cast separately. The No. 1 bronze chariot and horse is equipped with offensive and defensive weapons such as crossbows, swords, and shields, and it is responsible for clearing the way for the No. 2 chariot. The No. 2 bronze chariot and horse are equipped with a luxurious carriage, in which its passenger can sit or lie freely.

Despite what we see from the statues today, the Qin people liked bright colors. The colors of the warriors, horses, and chariots were originally very eye-catching. For example, the terracotta warriors are typically 175 cm tall. Their long purple jackets and dark red armor were embellished with blue, pink, black, and white colors, making them the most dazzling warriors of the empire. More than 7,000 soldiers wearing gorgeous armor and riding magnificent steeds formed the square formation that guarded the Qin Empire.

^ **Each of the Terracotta Warriors looks unique/Photo by Zhang Tianzhu**

Above, from left to right are a kneeling and shooting warrior, an intermediate-ranking officer, and a warrior in gown; below, from left to right are a warrior in armor, a warrior in gown, and a warrior in armor.

Craftsmen and soldiers became key figures in the city. At that time, a very imaginative work was waiting for completion, that is, to build a capital like a heavenly palace.

The Qin people took Wei He as a representation of the "Milky Way" and built palaces on both banks of the river. The Xianyang Palace corresponded to the polar star and its surrounding stars. It was also known as the "Purple Palace," which inspired the name of the Forbidden City in Beijing. The Chinese name of the Forbidden City, Zi Jin Cheng, literally means "Purple Forbidden City." The Epang Palace corresponded to the "Yingshi Star" (Pegasus constellation), which was also the residence of the emperor. The two palaces were connected by a bridge across Wei He, corresponding to the "Gedao Star." This kind of layout is known as "making urban planning based on the pattern of celestial phenomena," and it could be called the most imaginative capital city planning in the world at that time.

As it was stated in historical records: "The other six states were conquered, and the country was unified. The trees in the mountains of Sichuan were cut down to provide timber for building the Epang Palace." However, the excessive use of resources and manpower triggered rebellions at the end of the Qin Dynasty. Eventually, the Xianyang Palace was burned down, while the Epang Palace was never completed.

Xi'an in the Qin Dynasty gradually became lackluster compared to its former shine. Could it come to life again? Was building a divine capital an impossible task?

‹ **The Ruins of the Front Hall of the Epang Palace/Photo by Gou Bingchen**
The Epang Palace was a huge palace complex of the Qin Dynasty. Its ruins are near Epang Village, 15 kilometers from western Xi'an, Shaanxi. According to findings by Chinese archaeologists, the Epang Palace was never completed.

3 The Divine City of Chang'an

In the early years of the Western Han Dynasty, Liu Bang—Emperor Gaozu of the Han Dynasty—was choosing the location of the capital for the new Dynasty. His meritorious generals and statesmen, who came from the same place as the emperor, all wanted to build a capital closer to their hometown. However, a soldier named Lou Jing boldly proposed to make the war-torn Guanzhong the capital again. According to *Shiji (Records of the Grand Historian)*, Lou Jing said:

> *Besides, the former Qin state's territory was surrounded by mountains and Huang He, and there are strong frontier defenses around them to resist the enemy. Even if a sudden attack occurs, we can gather millions of soldiers to prepare for a battle.*

The Guanzhong area was surrounded by mountains on three sides and Huang He on the fourth. Only a few passes needed to be guarded to form a strong line of defense. Liu Bang was persuaded. He named the new capital Chang'an, after Chang'an Township, and the city was built on the south bank of Wei He. Chang'an City began its first formal appearance on history's stage.

Several subsequent dynasties continued to develop Chang'an. In the Sui and Tang dynasties, the rulers built a larger new city—also named Chang'an—to the southeast side of the location of the Han capital. The new Chang'an was 2.4 times the size of the Han capital and 1.4 times the size of Beijing during the Ming and Qing dynasties. During the Tang Dynasty, the following five types of people in the city worked together to gradually build Chang'an into a divine city.

> **The miniature landscape of the Daming Palace/Photo by Li Wenbo**
> The Daming Palace National Heritage Park is located on the east side of the Daming Palace Site Museum, which restored the entire Daming Palace complex in the heyday of the Tang Dynasty at a ratio of 1:15. In this way, we can get a glimpse of the magnificence of the Daming Palace in its prime.

The reconstructed Danfeng Gate of the Daming Palace/Photo by Li Wenbo

After a snowfall, Danfeng Gate has a pure, pristine appearance. This architecture is reconstructed, while the interior is a museum that houses the original ruins of the Danfeng Gate.

Emperors

Emperors built several magnificent imperial palace complexes. The Daming Palace of the Tang Dynasty covered an area of 3.2 square kilometers, which was 4.5 times the size of the Forbidden City in Beijing. The central southern entrance of the Daming Palace was the Danfeng Gate. The gate consisted of five doorways. The gate faced a 176-meter-wide street. Emperors held large-scale ceremonies there, such as enthrone-

ment or the changing of reign titles. It was a symbol of the authority of the great empire.

Outside the city were the royal mausoleums, which consisted of tall burial mounds and wide cemeteries with their walls, doorways, gates, tombs of queens and imperial concubines, and satellite tombs. To the north of Wei He, from Qianxian County in the west to Pucheng County in the east, the 18 Tang Dynasty imperial mausoleums spread out one after the other, forming a huge fan shape with Chang'an City in the south.

City Planners and Administrators

City planners and administrators were responsible for maintaining order in Chang'an. Residents were strictly confined to the grid-shaped neighborhoods called "li" and "fang." The Tang Dynasty poet Bai Juyi once commented:

> *The distribution of hundreds of thousands of families in Chang'an City resembles a chessboard, and the twelve streets divide the city like neat vegetable fields.*
> —Bai Juyi, "Climbing the Guanyin Platform to Overlook the City"

No one in the "li" or "fang" was allowed to overstep their limits to build a house privately or to add door openings. Curfews were strictly implemented in the city. Offenders, even including those who held government positions, would be executed by flogging on the spot.

In addition to strict order, administrators also needed to provide citizens with an environment for leisure.

Trees were planted extensively in the city. Officials had once disputed over the choice of tree species. In the end, locust trees, elms, willows, poplars, phoenix trees, pine trees, and more were all allowed to grow and reproduce in the city, spreading all over the roads and shading the courtyards.

Manmade waterscapes were even more popular. The city administrators used the low-lying areas in the southeast corner of the city as a site to excavate the ground and form a lake. The water forming the lake zigzagged like a river. People call it Qujiang (literally, "Zigzagging River"). In the Tang Dynasty, a vast waterfront recreational area was formed with Qujiang Chi (Qujiang Lake) as the center. Unlike an enclosed royal garden, it was open to the public, who gathered there for feasts and amusement. Emperors often gave banquets for their officials here to show how they shared joy and prosperity with the people. This was rare in ancient Chinese history.

^ Tang Paradise/Photo by Song Hongfei

Furong Garden was a royal garden in the Sui and Tang dynasties. It was located on the south bank of Qujiang Chi. The current Tang Paradise was rebuilt to the north of the Furong Garden site, incorporating features of the traditional royal gardens of the Tang Dynasty. It is a large royal garden-styled cultural theme park, showcasing the style of the prosperous Tang Dynasty.

v The Ancient Ginkgo in the yard of the Ancient Guanyin Temple/Photo by Han Fei

Monks

The intensive construction period of Chang'an City coincided with one of the most creative periods of Buddhism. Kumarajiva traveled east from Xiyu (Western Regions) to Chang'an to spread Buddhism. The Chinese Buddhist monks Faxian and Xuanzang traveled west from Chang'an to seek to introduce Buddhist sutras from India. These monks not only established different sects in Chang'an but also built a staggering number of Buddhist temples. Among them, Daxingshan Temple is considered the cradle of Chinese Esoteric Buddhism. It occupied a vast area and was very majestic. It was the largest temple in Chang'an City. Daci'en Temple is the cradle of the Dharmalaksana Sect of Buddhism in China. The renowned Buddhist monk Xuanzang oversaw the building of the Giant Wild Goose Pagoda, a monumental Buddhist pagoda which adopted the Indian style of architecture. It has been standing inside the Daci'en temple complex for more than 1,300 years. A smaller pagoda was later built in Jianfu Temple, another famous Buddhist temple in Chang'an. It was named the Small Wild Goose Pagoda, as it is slightly smaller than the Giant Wild Goose Pagoda.

1 | 2

1 Giant Wild Goose Pagoda/Photo by Li Wenbo

It was built in 652 for keeping the collection of Buddhist sutras brought back from India by Master Xuanzang, about 60 meters high. The Giant Wild Goose Pagoda seen today was rebuilt in 1604.

2 Small Wild Goose Pagoda/Photo by She Hu

Built in 707, it was a pagoda with dense eaves. Initially, the pagoda had 15 stories. Due to factors like earthquakes, only 13 stories have been left, with a total height of 43 meters.

People from Ethnic Minorities

One of the most eye-catching aspects of the city was the novel lifestyle in Chang'an. The economic and military strength of the Han and Tang empires guaranteed that the Silk Road remained unobstructed. People from ethnic minorities opened jewelry stores, warehouses and wine shops in Chang'an. These shops were very popular among local residents. Li Bai's poem "Youth Journey" vividly portrays this scene:

> *The young master of a rich family in Chang'an was playing in the east of the gold jewelry market, riding a white horse with a silver saddle triumphantly. The hooves of his horse traversed the falling flowers in Chang'an without stopping. Where would he go after this? He smiled and entered the wine shop where there are female singers of ethnic minorities.*

The food of ethnic minorities also became popular in Chang'an. From ordinary people's dining tables to palace banquets, exotic food could be seen everywhere. Most of these foods were made from wheat flour. At that time, the staple crop in northern China was mainly millet. To meet the new flour demand of the Chang'an people, almost every available place on Guanzhong Pingyuan began growing wheat. The increased wheat production allowed the further popularization of wheat foods. With wheat as their main staple, the Chang'an people gradually created a great variety of delicacies made from wheat. In addition, influenced by ethnic minorities, the Han people of Chang'an, who typically used to sit on the ground, began to use tables and chairs.

The easiest way to evaluate whether an era is progressive is to look at how women lived at the time. This is obvious if you examine the life of the women during the Tang Dynasty. They could be dressed very modestly, but could also at any time enter the scene with a flamboyant outfit, or they could put on a suit at any time and take on the world. In 1966, a tri-colored work of pottery was unearthed from a Tang tomb at the construction site of the Xi'an Pharmaceutical Factory. The pottery depicts a girl dressed up as a man on a galloping horse, and it is the best portrayal of the multifaceted lifestyle from this period in Chang'an.

∧ Terracotta women playing musical instruments on horses/Photo by Li Wenbo

The picture shows Tang Dynasty women in men's clothes playing pipa on horses.

∨ Sancai ware depicting a woman/Photo by Li Wenbo

A piece of Tang Sancai, now displayed in the Shaanxi History Museum.

Poets

The palaces in Chang'an were very magnificent. The order in Chang'an was admirable. The scenery in Chang'an was extremely pleasant. The religions in Chang'an were fully developed. The life in Chang'an was quite fashionable. The poets gathered in Chang'an began to extol the city.

They praised Chang'an in great joy:

> *Successful, faster runs my horse in vernal breeze; I've seen within one day all flowers on Chang'an trees.*
> —Meng Jiao, "Success at the Civil Service Exam"

Leaving Chang'an, they felt lost and lamented:

> *Clouds always cover the sun, and leaving Chang'an makes me sorrowful.*
> —Li Bai, "Climbing Jinling Phoenix Terrace"

Chang'an at that time had surpassed itself in the previous dynasties, becoming an ideal place and a divine city for people. As contemporary Chinese novelist and essayist Wang Xiaobo said:

> **Zhenling, the tomb of Emperor Xuanzong of the Tang Dynasty/Photo by Chang Zhiqiang**

Zhenling is one of the 18 tombs of the Tang Dynasty. It is the tomb of Li Chen, Emperor Xuanzong of the Tang Dynasty. It is located on Zhong Shan (Zhongshan Mountain), northwest of Jingyang County, Xianyang, Shaanxi. The existing stone carvings of the tomb, consisting of stone horses, stone figurines, ornamental columns, winged horses, and the Vermilion Birds, are all broken.

It is not enough for people to merely have their mundane life. They should also have a poetic world. For me, the world is in the city of Chang'an.

—Wang Xiaobo, *Hongfu Elopes at Night*

As an ancient poem reads: "The blooming chrysanthemums are dazzling, and the fragrance permeates Chang'an. The whole city is carpeted by chrysanthemum blossom as if dressing a golden armor." However, rebellions were already incubating during the late Tang Dynasty and eventually put an end to the once-powerful empire. In 881, the rebels led by Huang Chao captured and ruined the Tang capital Chang'an. Thus, the divine city of Chang'an effectively disappeared.

4 Inheritance and Innovation

From the Qin Dynasty to the Tang Dynasty, Xi'an was a rich and affluent place for more than a thousand years. After the Tang Dynasty, the political center of China was relocated, and Xi'an was reduced from a capital city to a prefectural city. The size of the city greatly shrank, but its military importance became even more prominent. The Song, Yuan, Ming, and Qing dynasties all considered Xi'an a city of strategic significance in northwest China.

The city walls built during the Ming and Qing dynasties were the best proof of its military importance. With a perimeter of 13.74 kilometers, it is the best-preserved city defense system of ancient China. The bottom layer of the wall was made of a mixture of lime, tamped earth, and glutinous rice. The top layer was rammed-earth construction using loess, and the top and exterior faces of the earthen walls were reinforced with black bricks. The defense system of the city gates was more complete, and barbicans were built out-

Xi'an City Wall/Photo by Wang Xudong

This picture shows the Yongning Gate of the Xi'an City Wall. Xi'an City Wall mainly refers to the Ming City Wall of Xi'an. There are four main gates: Changle Gate (East Gate), Yongning Gate (South Gate), Anding Gate (West Gate), and Anyuan Gate (North Gate). The Xi'an City Wall is the largest and most preserved of the many city walls left from ancient China. It is in the first group of Major Historical and Cultural Sites Protected at the National Level.

side these gates to defend the entrances. From the outside to the inside, a gate includes a sluice tower, an archery tower, and the main tower. The three towers were situated next to each other.

The Bell Tower of Xi'an was built in the early Ming Dynasty. It is the largest and best-preserved tower of its kind from ancient China. It is located in the center of Xi'an at the intersection of the four streets that radiate out to the four directions of the compass. In ancient times, guards could watch over the entire city from atop the Bell Tower.

Today, the city walls and the Bell Tower of Xi'an have lost their former military significance, and the city has ushered in a period of rapid development. It has become one of the key cities of the country and the hub of the northwest region. The city's status has once again been elevated. A quarter of the city is the historical area, which preserves the traditional Qin opera. Different religions exist here in harmony, and the city has many famous universities. It is also an important manufacturing center and a large-scale transport hub in China. It is teeming with innovation and vitality.

This is Xi'an, a city that will remain rich and affluent for many years to come.

What kind of a city is Chengdu? Why is it so charming?

This may be due to its accommodation of three religions, nine schools of thought, and people of all classes. Over the past three thousand years countless people, from princes and generals to commoners, have stepped onto the stage of Chengdu one by one. Together, they have built a grand Chinese city full of the hustle and bustle of daily life.

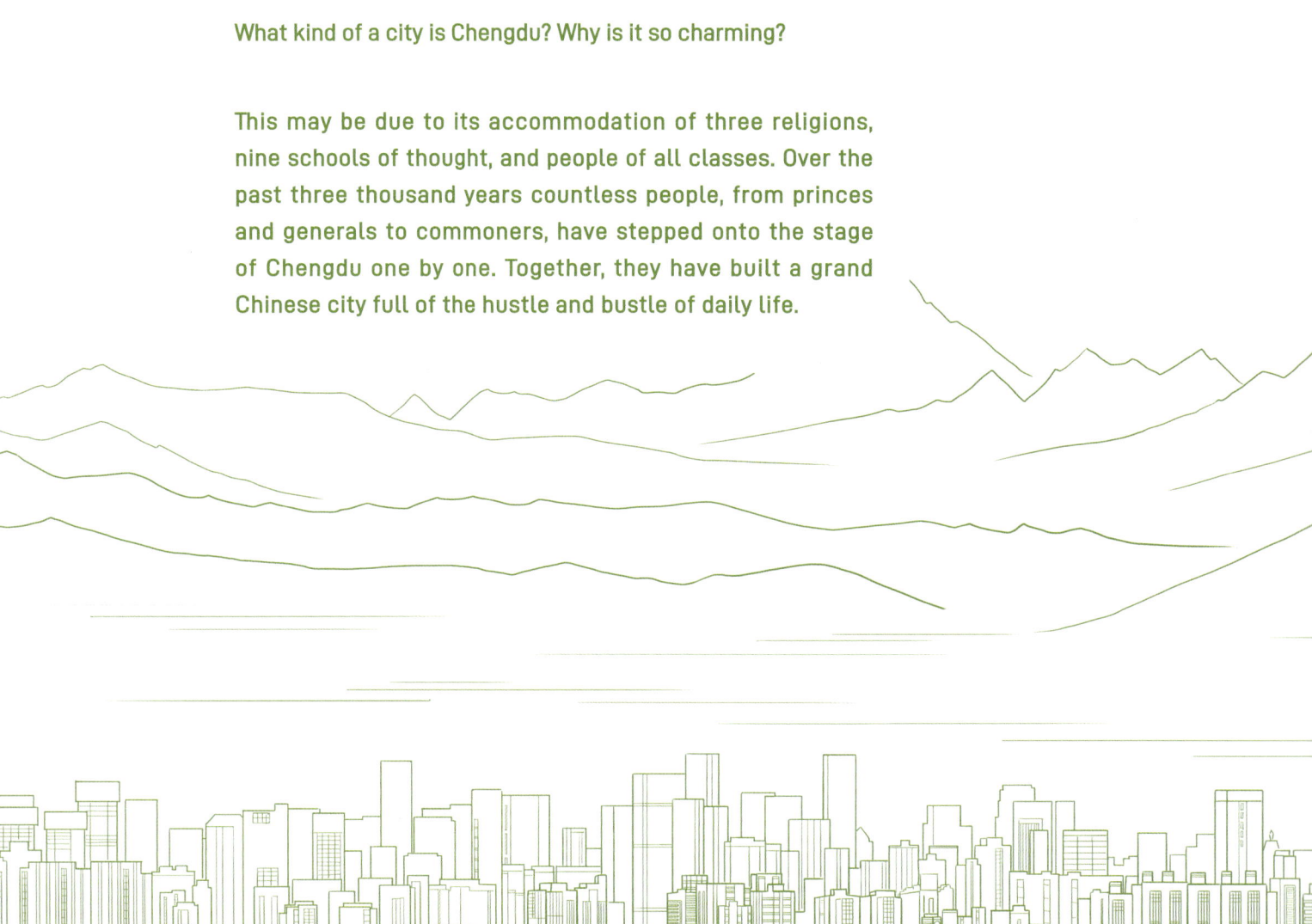

2.5 Chengdu:
Three Thousand Years of Vibrant Traditional Lifestyles

Not many people have had the opportunity to enjoy a full view of Chengdu. This city spreads over a large area and is often shrouded in fog. Jia Nan, a Jiangxi-born photographer working in Chengdu, is determined to capture every opportunity he can. Every morning, for three consecutive years, he climbed Longquan Shan (Longquan Mountain) on the east side of Chengdu at six o'clock, waiting for the sky to clear.

On the early morning of June 5, 2017, the weather was better than ever. Jia seized the opportunity and took 32 photos in a row, finally creating a real panorama of Chengdu.

It is called "real" because it not only includes the urban parts of Chengdu but also fully demonstrates the basic geographical pattern of the city, which features a plain sandwiched between two mountains. Around Longquan Shan, ten thousand lush trees stand side by side. The over 7,000-meter-high Konggar Shan, the over 6,000-meter-high Yaomei Feng, and many other peaks of Longmen Shan (Longmen Mountains) are visible in the distance. The densely arranged buildings between the two rows of mountains stand on the vast plain. This wide area with so many houses is also teeming with life. This is Chengdu, a super city with a permanent population of 21 million.

However, even after gazing on the full picture, Chengdu still has many mysteries to unravel. It is located deep inland in southwestern China. It is without the convenience of coastal cities to connect it with the world; it is far away from Chang Jiang with its developed shipping, and it does not have the advantages of water transportation in cities along Chang Jiang such as Chongqing. But business elites are optimistic about its future development. Apart from first-tier cities including Beijing, Shanghai, Guangzhou, and Shenzhen, Chengdu is the best choice for them to pursue their dreams of wealth.

Common people speak highly of its way of life. The beauty, food, mahjong, and teahouses here seem to embody everything about the daily life of the people in Chengdu. Its high standard of comfortable living attracts people from all over the country. Among the major provincial capitals, Chengdu has outdone the others for a long time, ranking first on internet search lists, far surpassing other popular and attractive cities—Hangzhou and Nanjing.

What kind of a city is Chengdu? Why is it so charming?

This may be due to its accommodation of three religions, nine schools of thought, and people of all classes. Over the past three thousand years countless people, from princes and generals to commoners, have stepped onto the stage of Chengdu one by one. Together, they have built a grand Chinese city full of the hustle and bustle of daily life.

Chengdu is now the capital of Sichuan province and a megacity in western China. Today's Chengdu is the continuation and development of Chengdu in history. Its most special feature is that since the city was founded in the 4th century BC, the city site has not been moved and the city name has not been changed for more than 2,300 years. Throughout the ages, Chengdu's urban area has spread out with roughly the same center, which is the region between the two main tributaries of Jin Jiang (Jinjiang River) today. The main stories of Chengdu in the past were also staged here. Apart from the four first-tier cities of Beijing, Shanghai, Guangzhou, and Shenzhen, Chengdu has become more and more popular in recent years, which is well reflected in the online search index and various rankings of cities.

Major landscape of Chengdu

Landmarks:
- Jinsha Relic Site
- Wenshu Monastery
- Du Fu's Thatched Cottage
- Kuanzhai Xiang
- Sanhua Lou
- Huanhua Xi
- Tianfu Square
- Chunxi Road
- Jinli
- Temples of the Marquis Wu
- Hejiang Ting
- Wangjianglou Park

Rivers: Fu He, Jin Jiang

The topographic map of Chengdu

Chengdu is located at the western edge of the Sichuan Pendi and the eastern edge of the Qingzang Gaoyuan, with plateau mountains, plains, and hilly landforms. The most central area is Chengdu Pingyuan (Chengdu Plain) between Longmen Shan and Longquan Shan. The deposition of sediments carried by Min Jiang and Tuo Jiang (Tuojiang River) as well as their tributaries formed Chengdu Pingyuan, providing fertile lands. The rich resources of water was well controlled by ancient Sichuan people, thanks to Dujiangyan, an irrigation system designed by Li Bing, the governor of Shu, in the 3rd century Before Christ, aiding local development of agriculture. Chengdu Pingyuan soon replaced Guanzhong as "the Land of Heaven."

Features on topographic map: Xiaoxuelongbao, Jiuding Shan, Gangguang Shan, Longmen Shan, Siguniang Shan, Zipingpu Shuiku, Dujiangyan, Shiting Jiang, Jian Jiang, Qingcheng Shan, Qingbai Jiang, Pi He, Qionglai Shan, Daxuetang, Min Jiang, Fu He, Jiang'an He, Chengdu Pingyuan, Chengdu, Xi He, Dongfeng Qu, Tuo Jiang, Longquan Lake, Longquan Shan, Danan He, Pu Jiang, Sancha Shuiku

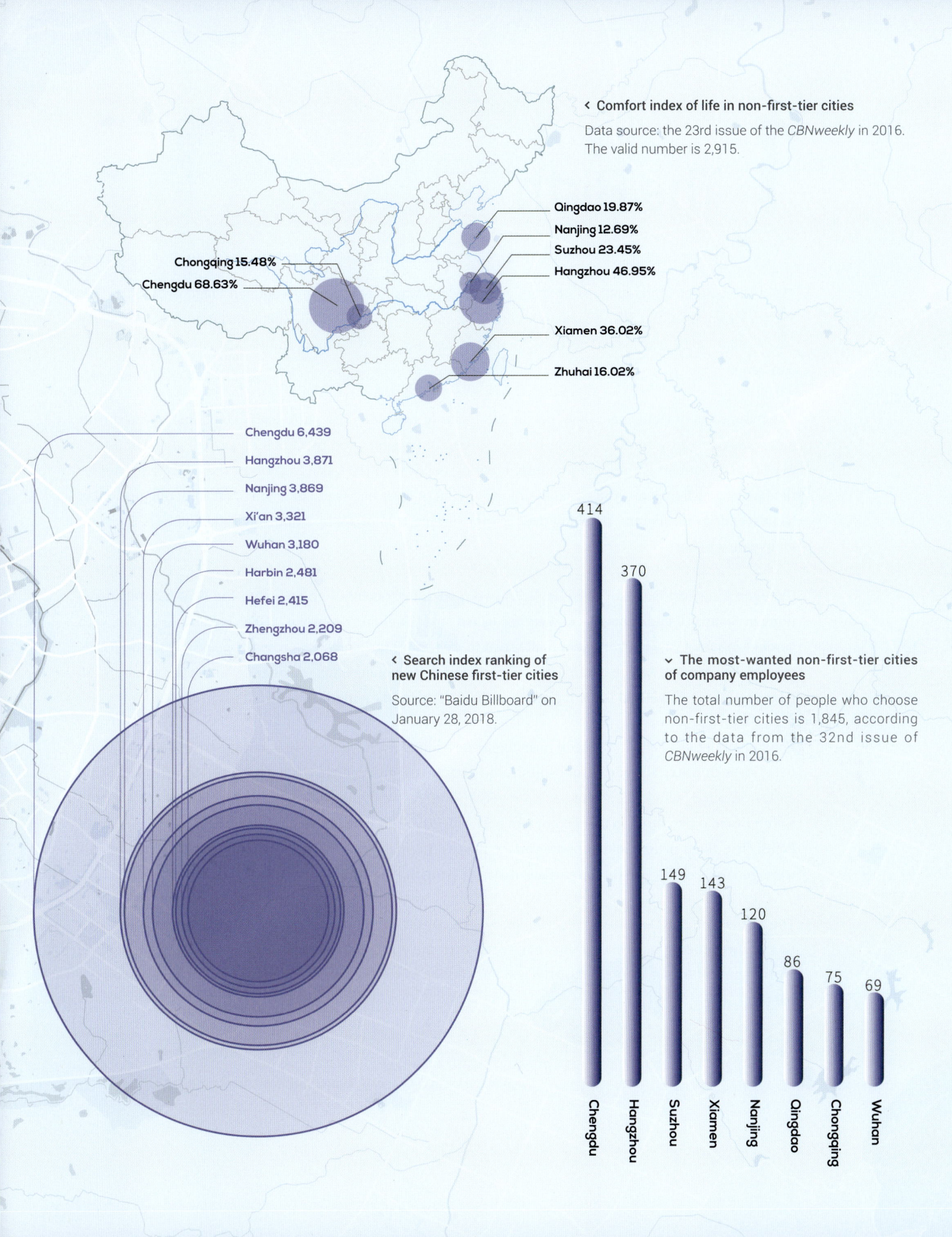

1 The Birth

In the land of China millions of years ago, orogeny was in full swing. Hengduan Shan, Daba Shan (Tapa Mountains), Wu Shan (Wushan Mountains), and Dalou Shan (Dalou Mountains) gradually took shape through uplift. They stand at the west, north, east, and south, forming a huge basin in the center, Sichuan Pendi.

The mountains of Hengduan Shan, on the west side of the basin, are particularly steep and covered with huge glaciers. Water from the rivers formed by melting glaciers and precipitation carries gravel and sand out of the mountain gorges, continuously creating deposits in the basin in front of the mountains. Across the last two million years, the thickness of the sediment layer between Longmen Shan and Longquan Shan has exceeded 500 meters, reaching over a total surface area of about 9,000 square kilometers. Chengdu Pingyuan was born.

Chengdu Pingyuan is sandwiched between two mountains, occupies an area with the best natural conditions in Sichuan Pendi, and it is sometimes called "the jewel on the crown." It has beautiful scenery, with verdant mountains, which are commonly seen in eastern China, and snow-covered peaks, which are common in the west and can be appreciated all year round. Daxuetang Shan (Daxuetang Mountain) stands 5,353 meters above sea level and is the highest peak in the region of Chengdu.

The tall mountains helped Chengdu form highly developed river systems. Murmuring streams flow through here, stacked waterfalls gurgle and splash, and crisscrossing rivers run through the plains. After Min Jiang enters onto the plain, the current becomes gentle, and the river splits into several branches. There is a large watercourse every three to five kilometers here. Together, they form the densest river network in Sichuan Pendi. The flood plain could support variant flora to flourish here, thick soils full of nutrient-rich humus were generally developed on the surface, making Chengdu Pingyuan increasingly fertile.

The fertile land and the natural vertical belt—which consists of a huge height difference from the plain area to the surrounding high mountains—have bred extremely rich animal and plant resources. This includes more than 2,600 species of seed plants and 237 species of vertebrates, including rare giant pandas and red pandas.

> A waterfall in Qingcheng Shan (Qingchen Mountain)/Photo by He Lei

Chengdu is close to Hengduan Shan, which is geologically active and has frequent earthquakes. However, because the seismic energy decays rapidly in the direction vertical to the seismogenic fault, and the thick coarse sediments underground in Chengdu Pingyuan may also have a certain ability to absorb seismic energy, the earthquake damage in Chengdu Pingyuan is relatively small.

With beautiful scenery, well-developed river systems, fertile land, rich flora and fauna, and very few earthquakes, Chengdu's natural conditions can be described thus:

> *Chengdu was built by the nine heavens. Thousands of households are as beautiful as pictures.*
> —Li Bai, "Ten Songs of the Emperor's West Tour of Nanjing"

Now the stage was set, waiting for the arrival of humans.

˅ Giant panda/Photo by Zhou Mengqi
˂ A red panda/Photo by Yan Su

320

2 Powerful and Noble People

The ancient Shu people in the upper reaches of Min Jiang were the first to discover the value of Chengdu. They descended along the rivers, climbed over the mountains, entered Chengdu Pingyuan, and established the Kingdom of Shu in Chengdu, where the natural conditions were optimal for development.

About 3,000 years ago, a large-scale capital city appeared in the northwestern part of today's Chengdu City, the Jinsha Site. The kings of Shu governed the kingdom from here. Exquisite goldware and huge works of ivory decorated the ceremonies presided over by the kings of Shu.

More than 200 pieces of goldware have been unearthed at the Jinsha Site. This is the largest amount of this type of goldware from a pre-Qin site ever discovered in China. Tons of ivory ware were also unearthed, and the sheer quantity is jaw-dropping. The superb craftsmanship and advanced aesthetics of these artifacts reflect the spiritual belief of the kings of Shu. For example, on one famous piece, four flying divine birds were carved on a gold leaf only 0.2mm thick, symbolizing eternal rotations around the sun in the middle.

1	2
3	

1 Gold masks of the Jinsha Site/Photo by Li Bin

Various objects such as gold masks, gold ribbons, round gold ornaments, and flared gold ornaments were unearthed at the Jinsha site. This gold mask is the same in style as the bronze mask of Sanxingdui in Guanghan. Other types of gold ornaments are unique to the Jinsha site.

2 Gold Sun Bird of the Jinsha Site/Photo by Zhang Yan

The Gold Sun Bird of the Jinsha Site is a cultural relic, and it is forbidden to be exhibited abroad. In 2005, the State Administration of Cultural Heritage stated that the artifact symbolized Chinese history.

3 Jinsha Museum/Photo by Li Bin

The Jinsha Site is in Jinsha Street, Qingyang District, Chengdu. The site was accidentally discovered in February 2001 when the China Real Estate Development Group was constructing the Shufeng Huayuancheng. In 2007, the Jinsha Museum was constructed to display the artifacts and features found here.

About 2,300 years ago, the Kingdom of Shu was conquered by the Qin State. Li Bing, the newly appointed governor of Shu, accepted a very ambitious mission—Chengdu should not only serve as the administrative center of Shu, but also take on the important task of unifying China's far-flung areas. The construction of Dujiangyan, an unprecedented water conservancy project of immense size, began.

Li Bing organized the Shu people to move mountains and dig canals to divide the frequently flooded watercourse of Min Jiang into two parts. The inner river was used for irrigation and the outer river was used for flood diversion. The successful construction of Dujiangyan has greatly promoted agriculture, and the vast Chengdu Pingyuan has remained fertile without a single period of famine since then. Soon, Chengdu Pingyuan replaced Guanzhong Pingyuan as the "land of abundance."

In the subsequent 30-year war of the Qin State to conquer other states, army provisions, including food and weapons from Chengdu, were continuously sent to the front line, helping the king of Qin complete the great cause of unifying China.

Not only the king of Qin but also Liu Bang, the first emperor of the Han Dynasty who competed with Xiang Yu for power, both regarded Chengdu as one of the important rear bases. Liu Bang arranged for Xiao He to "collect taxes from Bashu (in present-day Sichuan) and provide food to the army." Xiao He was hailed by Liu Bang as the most meritorious statesman who helped found the Han Dynasty because of his effective tax collection.

The Chengdu people were grateful for Li Bing's work and regarded him as the river god that protected Sichuan. Li Bing's second son, Li Erlang, was also venerated as the famous "Erlang God," which manifested a belief of the people which divinized the rulers at that time. That was popular in Sichuan at the time. There were more than 500 temples dedicated to these "Lords" in the heyday of this belief.

About 1,700 years ago, the Three Kingdoms—the Wei, Shu, and Wu states—coexisted in China. The resourceful Zhuge Liang, chancellor and later regent of the state of Shu, helped govern Shu with Chengdu as the center. However, the key to winning the competition among the three kingdoms was not simply intelli-

> Part of the Dujiangyan Irrigation System/Photo by Yu Ming
This aerial picture shows part of the Dujiangyan Project. The narrowest and longest river channel on the left of the picture is Shahei Zonghe (Shahei River); the middle is the outer stream, and the right is the inner stream.

The Dujiangyan Irrigation System/Photo by Tang Chao

gent ideas. Instead, the key was winning the competition for economic strength in the three core areas of Zhongyuan, Wuyue, and Bashu. Although the people of Shu enjoyed the agricultural benefits of Chengdu Pingyuan, its territory was relatively small, and its national economic strength was weak by comparison. Regent Zhuge needed to find a new source of wealth for the state. He focused on a kind of premium luxury product, namely Jin (brocade).

During the Qin, Han, and the Three Kingdoms periods, Chengdu was noted for producing Shu brocade. The quality of this brocade topped its counterparts in China. It was not only popular with local high-ranking officials and nobles. It was also popular as an export to the Wei, the Wu, and even foreign countries.

To control the production of Shu brocade, the Shu government built an official workshop in the west of Chengdu and named it the City of the Brocade Official. Thereafter, Chengdu was known by its beautiful nickname Brocade City or City of the Brocade Official. Many place names with the character jin also began to emerge in Chengdu. The location of the brocade workshop is called Jinli, and the river where workers washed the brocade was called Jin Jiang.

However, Regent Zhuge passed away before he "won the war," and Shu brocade was later surpassed by silk from Jiangsu and Zhejiang. Nevertheless, Zhuge Liang's merits in helping govern Shu have been permanently remembered by the Chengdu people. They have built a large ancestral temple, Wuhou Temple, which has been planted with pine, cypress and bamboo and is quiet and solemn. Just as Du Fu wrote in *"Regent of Shu"*:

> *Where to find the ancestral hall of Regent Zhuge? It is among the dense cypress trees outside the Brocade City.*

The kings and emperors of the ancient Shu, Qin and Han, as well as Li Bing and Zhuge Liang all together represent generations of powerful and noble people who once attained remarkable achievements in Chengdu; now, batches of newcomers were waiting for their debut.

▲ **Wuhou Temple/Photo by Zhang Yan**
Wuhou Temple is the only temple site in China where an emperor and his generals and civilian officials are worshipped together. It is composed of Wuhou Temple, Han Zhaolie Temple, and Hui Mausoleum, and they are usually referred to as Wuhou Temple as a whole. This picture shows the walls in Wuhou Temple and the bamboo that grows here.

▼ **Jinli/Photo by Liu Chengyao**
This picture shows Jinli today. Jinli has become a famous commercial area in Chengdu.

Du Fu Thatched Cottage/Photo by Fan Zhe

This picture shows the simple yet unique thatched cottage in the plum garden of the Du Fu Thatched Cottage Museum.

3 The Literati

In the pre-Qin period and during the Qin and Han dynasties, although Chengdu's economy had developed to a certain level, it still lagged far behind Zhongyuan in terms of cultural development. The Shu people described this in this way:

Originally, there were no scholars in the Shu.
—"Biography of Qin Mi" in *Sanguozhi (Records of the Three Kingdoms)*, referring to the situation in the early Western Han Dynasty

In the Tang and Song dynasties, Chengdu's economy reached its peak. A saying at the time went: "Yangzhou ranks first, and Yizhou (Chengdu) second." When the political situation was stable, scholars such as Wang Bo, Lu Zhaolin, Li Bai, and Lu You all considered it fashionable to travel in Chengdu.

When the Zhongyuan region was turbulent, scholars retreated to Chengdu as their refuge, especially during the An-Shi Rebellion and the wars in the late Tang Dynasty and the Five Dynasties Period.

In 759, 47-year-old Du Fu, a famous poet, fled to Chengdu. After staying in a temple for a few days, he began to build a new home for himself. He borrowed money from relatives and some bamboo seedlings from local county officials. Even his porcelain bowls were all given to him by friends. A few months later, the famous Du Fu Thatched Cottage was completed. Both sides of the path in front of the cottage were planted with flowers and trees. When friends visited, Du Fu wrote happily in his poem:

My floral path has never been swept for guests. Today, for the first time, a gentleman reaches the rough gate.
—Du Fu, "Guest Is Coming"

After settling down, Du Fu was in the mood to finally appreciate the beauty of Chengdu. Xiling Xueshan also became famous due to his poem:

My window frames the western mountains cloaked in autumnal snow,
My boat, resting at the doorway, will take me thousands of miles to Eastern Wu.
—Du Fu, "A Quatrain"

More than 30 years after Du Fu arrived in Chengdu, the poetess Xue Tao went to Shu with her father. Unfortunately, her father soon died of illness in Chengdu, and she was forced to become a government courtesan, playing music, serving wine, and composing poetry to entertain high-ranking officials at banquets.

‹ Wangjiang Pavilion/Photo by Wang Xingang
Wangjiang Pavilion is in Wangjianglou Park on the south bank of Jin Jiang (Jin River), near Jiuyan Bridge outside the east gate of Chengdu. It was built in the Ming and Qing dynasties to commemorate the female poet Xue Tao of the Tang Dynasty.

At that time, the paper on which people wrote poems was large sheet, and male poets wrote poems on it freely with their brushes. Xue Tao, who was thoughtful, believed that there should be a kind of exquisite paper that was more in line with her preference. She then drew water from a well and made small-format paper by herself. She even dyed her paper a romantic pink. As soon as this kind of small-size writing paper—known as "Xue Tao Style Paper"—came out, it became popular among the literati.

Xue Tao lived by Huanhua Xi (Flower Rinsing Creek) in her later years. A group of magnificent buildings were built along Jin Jiang to commemorate her after her death. The Wangjiang Tower is one of them.

With the gathering of more scholars, Chengdu gradually became a city rich in artistic atmosphere. People all over the city were talking about poetry, painting, and music. Du Fu wrote in the poem "To General Hua":

> *In Silk City music instruments everyday sing aloud,*
> *Half floating into river wind, half drifting into cloud.*
> *Such music can be heard only in the heavens.*
> *How many times has it been played for humans?*

The Chengdu people were optimistic by nature. Their life was full of humor and joy. For a time, the city was overflowing with leisure and enjoyment. People were enjoying food, wine, singing, dancing, having banquets, and playing musical instruments. Li Shangyin wrote in his poem:

> *One can spend one's later years here with Chengdu's wine, not to mention that there are beauties like Zhuo Wenjun selling wine.*
>
> —Li Shangyin, "Leaving Chengdu"

The outdoor entertainment events were particularly grand, attracting both government officials and ordinary people. The Song Dynasty's *Suihuajilipu (Festival Life)* recorded:

> *Chengdu is the most prosperous place to travel, which can rank first in western Sichuan. With a vast territory, it is a land of abundance, and people here like entertainment. If the prefectural governor holds banquets or festivals... gentlemen and ladies dressed in gorgeous clothes, alongside their old parents and young children, roam down the bustling streets.*

The Chengdu people also made great efforts to renovate many scenic spots such as Huanhua Xi. They planted a variety of flowers and trees, including begonia, gardenia, rhododendron, plum, ginkgo and more. The most famous variety is hibiscus, which is why Chengdu is also known as the "City of Hibiscus." To better enjoy the beautiful scenery, they built or repaired many pavilions, including the famous "skyscraper for viewing," the Sanhua Tower.

^ **Hejiang Pavilion/Photo by Wang Xingang**

Hejiang Pavilion is located at the intersection of Fu He (Fuhe River) and Nan He (Nanhe River) in Chengdu, Sichuan. It was first built during the Zhenyuan reign of the Tang Dynasty. After being rebuilt in the Northern Song Dynasty (960-1127), it reached its peak of fame and became a popular place among citizens.

Religious activities also flourished at this time. During the Sui and Tang dynasties, there were as many as 43 Buddhist temples in Chengdu, and Xuanzang was initiated into monkhood in one of them. The beautiful Qingcheng Shan (Mount Qingcheng) had many Taoist temples and became a famous center of Taoism.

Li Bai, Du Fu, Xue Tao—many poets and scholars gathered in Chengdu, enriching the cultural atmosphere of the city. Subsequently, outbursts of cultural creativity made Chengdu even more eye-catching.

The Jianfu Palace on Qingcheng Shan (Mount Qingcheng)/Photo by Tang Chao

Qingcheng Shan (Mount Qingcheng), sitting in the southwest of Dujiangyan City, is a famous Taoist mountain. The building in the picture is the Jianfu Palace on Qingcheng Shan, which was built in the Tang Dynasty.

4 Ordinary People

At the time when the Yuan, Ming, and Qing dynasties changed, Chengdu was no longer a stable rear base. Frequent massacres depopulated Chengdu. The two massacres led by Zhang Xianzhong in the late Ming Dynasty were the most terrifying. Chengdu was almost destroyed and became an empty city.

During the periods that took place from the end of the Yuan Dynasty to the beginning of the Ming Dynasty, from the end of the Ming Dynasty to the beginning of the Qing Dynasty, and the War of Resistance against Japanese Aggression in the 20th century, new immigrants from other provinces, and Chinese People's War of Resistance Against Japanese Aggression on a massive scale. The population structure of Chengdu underwent unprecedented changes.

New villages and towns, both big and small, mushroomed on Chengdu Pingyuan. Influential landlords built super manors, the Hakka people introduced *tulou* (earthen buildings) to Chengdu, and the Manchus built the Kuanzhaixiangzi alleys in accordance with the northern architectural style. The immigrants lived and intermarried with each other while maintaining their respective living habits and dialects, but eventually, they turned into brand-new Chengdu residents in this city that had become like a melting pot.

The previous Chengdu culture that was led by kings, generals, civil officials, and the literati had given way to folk culture.

> **Pingle Ancient Town, Qionglai/Photo by Yin Guicheng**

Pingle is southwest of Qionglai under the jurisdiction of Chengdu, Sichuan. Pingle Ancient town has preserved the ancient houses from the Ming and Qing dynasties very well. The houses on both sides of the ancient street are mostly wooden structures with two floors. Generally, the lower floor is used for running a store and the upper floor is used as a living room, which exhibits a typical western Sichuan style.

Here, people have merged the culinary styles of southern and northern China to create the popular Sichuan cuisine: Hot Pot, Chuan Chuan Xiang, Dandan Noodles, Lai Sweet Dumplings, Intestine Noodles, Zhong Dumplings, Sliced Beef and Ox Tongue in Chili Sauce, Sad Bean Jelly, Mapo Tofu, Rabbit Head, Crusty Pancake, Chili Oil Wontons, and more. People of all statures, be it high-ranking officials, noble lords, small tradesmen, and porters, they can all enjoy Sichuan cuisine.

They have merged Jiangsu's Kunqu Opera, Hubei's Han Opera, Shaanxi's Qin Opera, Sichuan's Gaoqiang Opera and Lantern Opera, and many other local traditional operas to form the Sichuan Opera. Face-changing and fire-breathing remain hallmarks of Sichuan Opera today.

Teahouses are ubiquitous in Chengdu. People from all walks of life gather here, enjoying tea while chatting with each other.

Mahjong has been an essential part of most local people's lives. Almost every local, regardless of age, social status and time of year, enjoys the game. Mahjong tables constitute the largest "social network" in Chengdu.

The popularity of mass culture made Chengdu's small commodity economy more prosperous during the Ming and Qing dynasties. During the late Qing Dynasty and the Republic of China period (1912-1949), Yang Sen, a general of the Sichuan clique, built a Western-style road in Chengdu, which was called "Senwei Road" at that time. Merchants from Jiangsu, Zhejiang, Beijing, and Sichuan set up shops along the road. The commercial capital concentrated on this road alone accounted for 70% of commercial capital in all of Chengdu, making the road the city's central business district at that time. Later, Senwei Road was renamed Chunxi Road, the name by which it is now more widely known.

^ A Chengdu teahouse/Photo by Zhu Jianguo

Teahouses are one of the most representative public places in Chengdu. This picture shows an open-air teahouse in Chengdu.

< Fire breathing in a Sichuan Opera/Photo by Zhu Jianguo

The prosperity of commerce and the increase in population drove Chengdu to start planning road construction around the city in 1936. The 1st Ring Road is close to the city wall and is about 15 kilometers long; the 2nd Ring Road surrounds the urban area and has a total length of nearly 55 kilometers. Therefore, Chengdu has become a city that incorporates typical ring-road traffic.

Western-style higher education was also introduced into Chengdu during this period. In 1910, Christian churches of several Western countries jointly established the West China Union University. The location of the university was called Huaxiba. The architectural style of the campus is a combination of Chinese and Western styles and is a fusion of Chinese classical gardens and Western palace gardens.

Most of the tens of thousands of residents in the city may not have left a lasting mark, but they have jointly promoted the prosperity of Chengdu. Sichuan cuisine, Sichuan Opera, teahouses, mahjong, commercial streets, Ring Roads, and new-style education all make Chengdu a vibrant, inclusive city.

1 West China Dental Health Education Museum/Photo by Wang Xingang

In front of the museum stands the life-size sculpture of Dr. Ashley Woodward Lindsay, the founder of Chinese stomatology.

2 Chunxi Road/Photo by Zhang Sheng

Chunxi Road is named after Laozi's *Dao De Jing* (*Tao Te Ching*). "Everyone is happy and joyous, just like enjoying the spring scenery." During the Republic of China period, Chunxi Road was the commercial center of Chengdu.

3 The Clock Tower of the West China Medical Center of Sichuan University/ Photo by Zhu Jianguo

The Clock Tower is an architecture combining Chinese and Western styles. It is made of grey bricks and tiles, painted and carved beams, as well as a Western-style clock.

5 Chengdu Today

Today's Chengdu has gone through 3,000 years of vicissitudes. All kinds of modern buildings now rise from this historical ground. Commerce is prosperous, transportation is highly developed, and the city is closely connected with the world. People's lifestyles are avant-garde, diverse, and there is an artistic atmosphere.

Tianfu Square/Photo by Zhu Jiannan

Tianfu Square is in the first section of Renmin South Road, Jinjiang District, and is at the center of Chengdu. A statue of Mao Zedong stands in the north of the square.

This is Chengdu, which has gone through 3,000 years of change in the mundane world.

What makes Fanjing Shan (Mount Fanjing) stand out is not its scenery or religion but the life it nurtures. Through the ages, Fanjing Shan has been like a solitary island in the world of mortals. It has repeatedly supported the survival of endangered species at critical moments. As ecologist Jim Thorsell said during his visit to Fanjing Shan, it is like an ecological island with a diversity of species in the ocean of human activities.

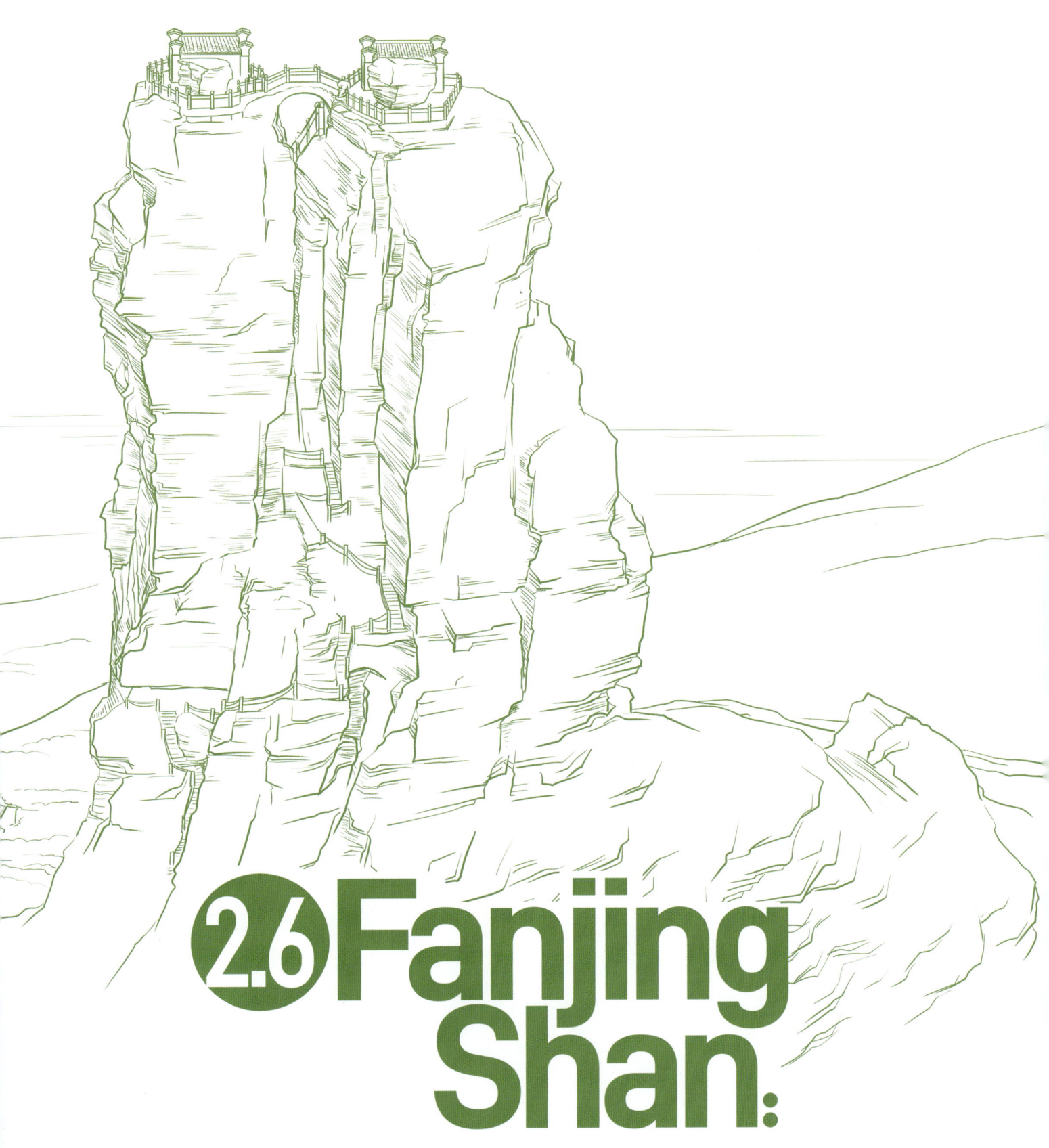

2.6 Fanjing Shan:
A Paradise in the Secular World

An earth-shaking change is taking place in Guizhou, China. The development of the tourism industry is particularly impressive, with a growth rate of more than 40%. The province has continued to reach new milestones. On July 2, 2018, Fanjing Shan in Guizhou became China's 53rd UNESCO World Heritage site.

Many people may already be familiar with the famous Huangguoshu Waterfall, Chishui's Danxia landform in Chishui, and Libo's karst landform in Guizhou. However, most may know little about Fanjing Shan.

Why is Fanjing Shan a World Heritage site? Many Chinese mountains that are more famous, such as Changbai Shan (Changbai Mountains), Heng Shan (Mount Hengshan, Hunan), and Heng Shan (Mount Hengshan, Shanxi) fail to be listed among World Heritage sites, not to mention Hua Shan, which has been struggling for applying for the status of World Heritage for more than 20 years. Why is Fanjing Shan so lucky? Because of its reputation as one of the five sacred mountains of Buddhism in China or its outstanding landscapes?

Neither is right.

First, although the landform of Fanjing Shan is special, but that of Huang Shan (Mount Huangshan), Lu Shan (Mount Lushan), and Hua Shan are more unique, not

to mention the numerous towering snow-capped mountains in the west.

Second, the so-called "five sacred mountains of Buddhism in China" have not been widely accepted. In fact, there are only four universally recognized "sacred mountains of Buddhism"–Jiuhua Shan (Mount Jiuhua), Putuo Shan (Mount Putuo), Wutai Shan (Wutai Mountain), and Emei Shan (Emei Mountain). Fanjing Shan can be regarded as a regional religious mountain at best.

It seems that to truly understand the value of Fanjing Shan, we can no longer use the way we usually view famous mountains and rivers. Because what is outstanding is not its appearance, nor religion, but the life it nurtures.

Since ancient times, Fanjing Shan has been like an isolated island in the world. It helps the creatures to multiply and survive three times at critical moments. As the ecology expert Jim Sancerre said during his field trip to Fanjing Shan:

Fanjing Shan is like an ecological island, with many species living and developing on it, which is surrounded by an ocean of human activities.

Fanjing Shan's Xin Jin Ding (New Golden Summit)/Photo by Shi Yaochen

1 The Birth

Fanjing Shan is in the northeast of Guizhou. The core area and buffer zone of the World Heritage site cover a total of 775 square kilometers, which is less than one ten-thousandth of China's land area of 9.6 million square kilometers.

During hundreds of millions of years, most of Southern China, where Fanjing Shan was located, changed between land and sea for several times. Biological debris and other particles in the ocean were continuously accumulated to form carbonate rocks.

About 230 million years ago, the once-submerged Southern China finally rose to land. Many carbonate rocks were also exposed on the surface. The exposed area was 500,000 square kilometers, with a total thickness of 10 kilometers, like an ocean of carbonate rocks. These carbonate rocks were easily eroded by

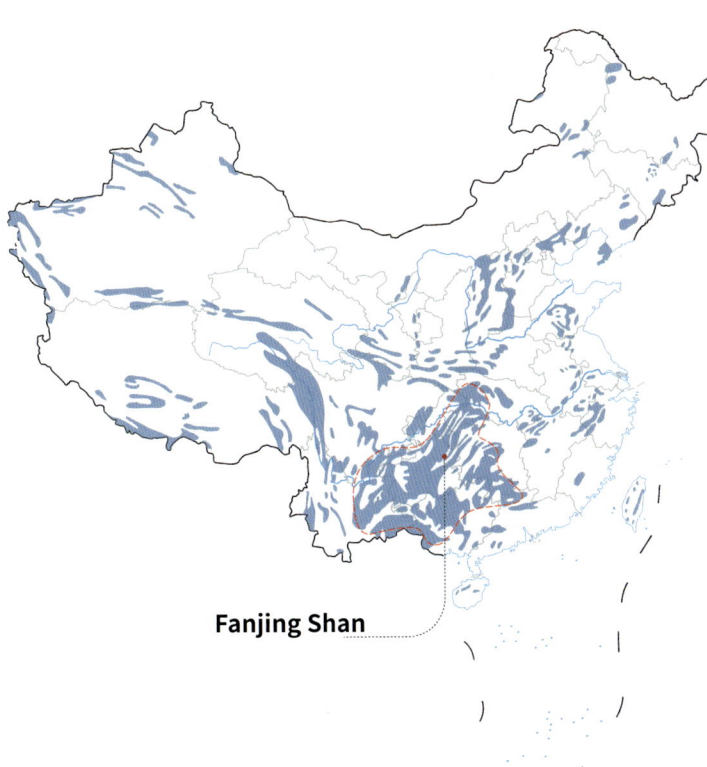

> China's carbonate rock distribution

The area shown by the red line in the picture is the concentrated distribution area of carbonate rocks in southern China.

< Libo Karst, Guizhou/Photo by Wei Jian

Libo County, located in the southernmost part of Guizhou, is home to a typical landscape of karst peaks and forests. As part of "South China Karst," it was included in the World Natural Heritage List in 2007.

water, forming the famous karst landform. After long-lasting geological movements, the land of Guizhou was eroded and torn apart. The uplift of Fanjing Shan broke this pattern.

For 65 million years, the Indian Plate had been colliding with the Eurasian Plate, and the northeastern part of Guizhou rose sharply. The carbonate rocks on the periphery of Fanjing Shan were gradually eroded by currents during the uplift, and the original appearance of the mountain was exposed. The main body of Fanjing Shan is metamorphic rock, which is completely different from carbonate rocks and is not easily corroded by water.

Fanjing Shan appears as a peach kernel, bulging in the middle and narrowing at both ends. The mountain appears like an island of metamorphic rock in the ocean of carbonate rocks.

Its highest peak, Fenghuang Shan (Phoenix Mountain), towers 2572 meters above sea level.

Lao Jin Ding (Old Golden Summit) is the second highest peak, with an elevation of 2,493 meters. The rugged peak is formed by layers of stacking plate-like metamorphic rocks.

Xin Jin Ding of Fanjing Shan/Photo by Yang Xiufang
What is the most striking in this picture is Xin Jin Ding of Fanjing Shan, and Fenghuang Shan, the highest peak of Fanjing Shan, is in the distance.

Between Fenghuang Shan and Lao Jin Ding stands the unusually prominent Xin Jin Ding (New Golden Summit). At sunrise or sunset, the peak is basked in the glows and surrounded by red clouds, creating a vista called "Golden Summit in Red Clouds." Xin Jin Ding stands on a narrow ridge with a height difference of several hundred meters. After centuries of weathering and erosion, the hard rock mass broke and formed a crack, tearing the peak into two parts. The peak is eye-catching no matter which angle it is viewed from.

Viewed from the distance, Fenghuang Shan, Xin Jin Ding, Lao Jin Ding, and the ridge connecting them form an illusion like a man lying on his back, known as the "10,000-meter sleeping Buddha."

Numerous metamorphic rocks of the mountain have been sculpted into strange and unique shapes across hundreds of millions of years. For instance, the Eagle Rock, Ten Thousand Volumes of Sutras and Prince Stone... There are many lifelike and grotesque-shaped stones.

In this way, Fanjing Shan composed of metamorphic rocks has been born. The process is different for the surrounding carbonate rocks, and the three impacts on life were about to be launched soon.

> "Ten Thousand Books from Heaven" in Fanjing Shan/Photo by He Xiongzhou

Among the many metamorphic rocks at the top of Fanjing Shan that have formed unique shapes after erosion over hundreds of millions of years, one is like a stack of scriptures, figuratively dubbed "Ten Thousand Scrolls of Scriptures."

Fanjing Shan's Xin Jin Ding/Photo by Qin Guanghui

This picture shows Xin Jin Ding of Fanjing Shan after snow. From this angle, you can see that there is a crack in the upper part of Xin Jin Ding. The peak is split into two, and a temple is built on each peak.

Xin Jing Ding of Fanjing Shan/Photo by Xu Jun

Guanyin Waterfall/Photo by Yang Xiufang

Guanyin Waterfall is in the Heiwan He (Heiwan River) Scenic Area of Fanjing Shan. It is named after its shape resembling Guanyin.

2 The First Impact

Fanjing Shan is the highest peak rising from the surrounding areas. The East Asian Monsoon from the Pacific Ocean and the South Asian Monsoon from the Indian Ocean converge here after crossing the mountains. The warm and humid airflow brought by the monsoons is blocked by the mountains and begins to climb upwards along the mountainsides. When it gets cold, the water vapor condenses, so there are always clouds and mists in the mountains. The towering Xin Jin Ding is also hidden in such an ethereal environment. The small water droplets in the cloud diffract sunlight, forming a fascinating view like the Buddha's halo under certain conditions. The Mushroom Rock, Jiuhuang Cave, and Xin Jin Ding in Fanjing Shan are where such a natural phenomenon occurs frequently.

The rising moisture transformed into abundant precipitation, and the annual precipitation of Fanjing Shan is as high as 1,100 to 2,600mm. The abundant precipitation is centered on the top of the mountain, giving birth to a radial river system around it that rushes all around. There are 23 waterfalls with a drop of more than 20 meters. Guanyin Waterfall, Heiwan He (Heiwan River) Waterfall, and Baishuidong Waterfall, are all spectacular.

If so much water had flowed in the carbonate rock area around Fanjing Shan, it would have eroded the rocks quickly and barely left any soil on the ground. If the precious thin soil layer is washed away due to deforestation, it will be hard to recover, and a large area of rock surface will be exposed, which is called a "rock desert." At this time, no matter how much precipitation there is, water will quickly flow away through underground fissures and caves, making surface water extremely scarce.

However, things are different in Fanjing Shan. The metamorphic rocks which cover most area of Fanjing Shan are difficult to dissolve, so they can produce soil in large depth in a short time. As a result, there will be no problem of rocky desertification. Meanwhile, the precipitation will not flow away through the underground, and can converge into surface water such as streams and rivers, providing a superior environment for the survival of animals and plants.

With sufficient water sources, fertile soil, and the subtropical environment where Fanjing Shan is located, the hydrothermal conditions are superior, providing an excellent environment for the survival and habitat of flora and fauna. According to incomplete statistics, there are 4,394 species of wild plants in Fanjing Shan, with a forest coverage rate of more than 80%. Both the quality and quantity of the wild plants here are better than those in the surrounding carbonate rock areas.

This was the first time Fanjing Shan helped life to get rid of rocky desertification. And, the second impact started from the ice age.

3 The Second Impact

Fanjing Shan is in the subtropical zone. As the altitude increases, the temperature gradually decreases. On the top of the mountain, the annual average temperature is only 5-6 degrees Celsius. The lower part of the mountain is often lush but the upper part is usually covered with snow.

Within a vertical distance of several kilometers, Fanjing Shan spans four temperature zones, namely the Middle Subtropical Zone, the Northern Subtropical Zone, the Warm Temperate Zone, and the Middle Temperate Zone, which is equivalent to a change of several thousand kilometers horizontally.

Temperature zones at different altitudes can meet the needs of growth of various types of vegetation, including Evergreen Broad-leaved Forest Belts below 1,300 to 1,400 meters, Evergreen and Deciduous Broad-leaved Mixed Forests between 1,400 and 2,200 meters, and Subalpine Coniferous and Broad-leaved Mixed Forests and Shrub Meadow Belts with a range of 2,200 to 2,572 meters. These are the vertical natural belts of the mountain.

Davidia involucrata/Photo by He Xiongzhou

Davidia involucrata, the relict of the Tertiary ancient tropical plant, is endemic to China and is a national firstclass protected plant. It likes to live in a humid and shady environment, and the moist surroundings in the deep ravine of Fanjing Shan meet its growth needs.

Liriodendron tulipifera x chinense/Photo by He Xiongzhou

Liriodendron tulipifera x chinense photographed in Fanjing Shan, Guizhou, is a hybrid of Liriodendron Chinese as the female parent and Liriodendron tulipifera as the male parent. The flower is generally yellow.

During 2.58 million years, every time an ice age comes, the global temperature would drop sharply. Some animals and plants disappeared because they could not adapt to the cold. In Fanjing Shan, the vertical natural belts came into play, and the plants that originally lived at higher altitude areas gradually migrated to lower warmer places. When the ice age was over and the temperature went up, they moved back to cooler heights. During this process, certain ancient species, the so-called relict species[1], survived the vicissitudes of climate changes. Here, you can see rare tulip trees with beautiful leaves and flowers, as tall as 40 meters.

The rarer *Davidia involucrata* is distributed in patches in Fanjing Shan, and the tree can reach more than 20 meters. At the end of spring and early summer each year, the plant blooms with large white bracts fluttering in the wind, like white doves. Therefore, it is also called the "Chinese Dove Tree."

The rarest is *Abies fanjingshanensis*, which is unique to the Fanjing Shan area. It grows slowly in the juvenile period, but begins to grow fast after 40 years of sprouting. Its life span can exceed 300 years.

In this way, Fanjing Shan became Noah's Ark of life during the ice age. *Primula*, *Gentiana*, *Enkianthus*, *Pedicularis*... many species with a history of tens of millions of years have survived in the mountain area.

Fanjing Shan's role as a kind of Noah's Ark of life continued, and how did it save lives next?

---

1 Relict plants refer to species that once flourished and were widely distributed in ancient geological epochs but are restricted to limited geographic regions currently.

4 The Third Impact

The ancestors of modern human left Africa and migrated to all over the world, and their footprints were also spread around Fanjing Shan.

People cultivated farmland around Fanjing Shan and mined cinnabar. During the Ming and Qing dynasties, local chieftains attacked each other constantly and there were many bandits:

> *Residents around the mountain were robbed and killed by bandits, and no fewer than 700 houses were leveled, with more than 4,000 killed.*
> —Record of the Zhenguo Temple Tablet

The imperial court continued to engage in large-scale battles with the Wuling local tribe and invested huge sums of funds to build the 190-kilometer-long southern Great Wall.

Intensive human activities had significantly disturbed the ecological environment around Fanjing Shan. It was said:

> *The evil Mei Wanyuan and others cut down the trees on the mountain and opened a kiln to produce charcoal for prof0it.*
> —From the inscriptions on *The Leshichui Stele* which was erected in 1832

1 | 2

1 Guizhou snub-nosed monkey/Photo by Ding Kuanliang

Guizhou snub-nosed monkey, endemic to China, a national first-class protected animal, is only distributed in the Fanjing Shan area. The population of Guizhou snub-nosed monkeys has grown from the estimated 200 at the time of discovery to 700 to 800, but it is still the most endangered species in China, even rarer than giant pandas. This picture shows two mothers and their kids.

2 Guizhou snub-nosed monkey/Photo by Cui Duoying

In this picture, you can see the tail of a Guizhou snub-nosed monkey, which is like an oxtail.

The mountainous biological corridor that originally connected Qingzang Gaoyuan, Yungui Gaoyuan (Yunnan-Guizhou Plateau) and Jiangnan Qiuling (Jiangnan Hills) to the mountains of Taiwan was severely damaged.

Humans pushed forward while animals and plants retreated. Fanjing Shan once again had a life-saving function, and many primates took refuge here. The most famous is Guizhou snub-nosed monkey. Because of the destruction of other habitats, Fanjing Shan became their last paradise.

The Guizhou snub-nosed monkey has a body length of 60 to 70cm, and its tail is slender and long, like an oxtail, which is striking. Like the Sichuan snub-nosed monkey and the Yunnan snub-nosed monkey, the Guizhou snub-nosed monkey belongs to the *Rhinoceros* genus. Originally living in tropical rainforests, they gradually differentiated during migration. The Guizhou snub-nosed monkey is one of the rarest species, with its total estimated population fewer than 800. They live at an altitude of 1,300 to 2,000 meters and feed on plant shoots, tender leaves, flower buds, and fruits.

Guizhou snub-nosed monkeys live in groups. To look for food, each group moves around Fanjing Shan in a certain order. They jump among the tree canopies over four or five meters. Their daily life is to repeat the cycle of "moving-feeding-resting-moving," and occasionally comb and play with each other. They change living locations at least three to four times every day. They never stay in the same location for a long time, and quickly flee away when sensing danger.

^ Moving routes of Guizhou snub-nosed monkey in Fanjing Shan

The two routes indicate the moving of two large groups of Guizhou snub-nosed monkeys in Fanjing Shan area. The data is based on Yang Yeqin and others' *Fangjingshan Research: Ecology of the Wild Guizhuou Snub-nosed Monkey*.

Guizhou Snub-nosed monkey/Photo by He Xiongzhou
One of the rarest and most endangered species in China, even rarer than the giant panda, it is called "the Only Child of Mother Nature."

Golden pheasant/Photo by Zhang Qiang

The golden pheasant was originally a bird species endemic to China, mainly distributed in the mountainous areas of central and southwestern China. They often inhabit broadleaf forests Mixed coniferous forest, and forest marginal shrubs at an altitude of 500 to 2,500 meters. Later it was introduced to European countries because of its beautiful appearance. The picture shows a male bird.

5 Protecting Fanjing Shan

At each of the three critical moments, Fanjing Shan played a significant role in rescuing living creatures from extinction. Today, as the domestic ecological environment is in a general state of emergency, the natural vegetation in a small "island" like Fanjing Shan still maintains a relatively primitive state. Fanjing Shan has become home to more than 6,000 species of animals and plants.

At present, Fanjing Shan has the largest continuous distribution of beech forests in the subtropical region of the world, ancient tea trees more than 600 years old, and the world's largest crape myrtle tree. There are also Tibetan macaques that habitually live on the ground and cliffs, Chinese giant salamanders that live in creeks, underground rivers, and deep pools, and Chinese Green Tree Viper *(Trimeresurus stejnegeri)* that likes to hang around treetops. Besides, there are more than 200 bird species, such as Temminck's tragopan, golden pheasant, white-browed laughingthrush, crested serpent eagle, and more. They together made Fanjing Shan one of the places with the greatest biodiversity in the world.

Today, the development of Guizhou is rapid and the province is changing with each passing day. At the same time, it is hoped that this "island" of life can be protected well so that it can continue to stand gloriously in the world.

3

The Third Terrain Ladder

3.1 Henan:
Mountains, Water, and Contributions to China
371

3.2 Zhengjiang:
A Province of Invincible Productivity
401

3.3 Fujian:
The Legend of Pioneers
437

3.4 Qingdao:
A History of Urban Aesthetics
465

3.5 Jiangnan:
A Great Feast of River, Lake, and Sea
493

Henan has not only a vast plain area but also undulating mountains. With mountains and hills accounting for more than 44% of the province, it could be described that half of the province is mountains and half is plains. This topography is also the key to answering what Henan is. Because the "hands of God" shaped the plains, rivers and mountains with repeated geological movements, wonderful geographical landscapes and historical miracles were created one after another. Henan was gradually pushed to the peak of glory and directly established the foundation of Chinese civilization.

3.1 Henan:
Mountains, Water, and Contributions to China

Henan is located in the middle and lower reaches of Huang He. Henan covers an area of approximately 167,000 square kilometers. It is located in the transitional zone between the second and third terrain ladders. The terrain is high in the west and low in the east. The north, west, and south sides are surrounded by Taihang Shan, Qin Ling, Tongbai Shan (Tongbai Mountains), and Dabie Shan (Dabie Mountains). The central and eastern parts are the vast Huabei Pingyuan (North China Plain). from the pre-Qin to the Song Dynasty, Henan has always been the political, economic, cultural, and transportation center of China. More than 20 dynasties have established their capitals in Henan. It is the province with the largest number of dynasties (more than 20) which established their capitals there.

The topographic map of Henan

The location of Henan in China

It is difficult to answer what Henan is.

People would say that the Shandong people are bold and forthright while Sichuan is the "land of abundance." However, it is difficult to accurately describe Henan in one word because it is not a province with distinctive characteristics. It is just like its location in the middle of China, being quite "moderate."

However, from a historical point of view, Henan has a prominent feature. Counting from the establishment of the capital of the Xia Dynasty in the 21st century BC, Henan, as one of China's political, economic, and cultural centers, had led the Chinese culture for more than 3,000 years. Starting from the fall of the Northern Song Dynasty in 1127, Henan's decline lasted 800 years. This decline was almost too dramatic, that is, it fell directly from the peak of the Northern Song Dynasty to the bottom of the valley, and has since become one of the most turbulent and conservative regions in China's mainland. Its drastic decline was pitiful. Just as the saying goes:

If you ask about the rise and fall of all dynasties, please only look at Luoyang City.
—Sima Guang, "Passing the Former Luoyang City"

There is no province in China like Henan that has fallen so suddenly, so heavily, and for so long that people's negative impressions of it are deeply rooted. Even though Henan's economy has been gradually revitalized in recent years, many people still cannot erase their stereotype about Henan as a poor, backward province. With a long period of decline and a huge population base, Henan has become the most vulnerable target of ridicule for people who discredit others because of their native place. People tend to generalize and echo the views of others, but the real Henan has become obscure.

The most remarkable point is that many people mistake Henan as an endless plain; they do not realize that the province also has rolling mountains. The mountains and hills together account for more than 44% of the province's area, which can be described as half mountains and half plains. This geographical feature is the key to understanding what Henan is.

Because the "hands of God" built mountains and waters in Zhongyuan repeatedly, not only an excellent landscape of mountains and rivers but also a series of historical miracles were created. As a result, Henan was gradually pushed to the apex of glory, and even directly laid the foundation of Chinese civilization.

Taihang Shan/Photo by Liu Chen
These craggy peaks, sitting in Huixian County, Henan, are part of Nan Taihang Shan (Southern Taihang Mountains).

1 The Era of Taihang Shan

Taihang Shan were the first to help Henan stand out.

Taihang Shan, which stretch for more than 400 kilometers from north to south, were formed by faults of the ancient North China Plate. They are constantly uplifting on one side. Up to now, the ridge of Taihang Shan is 1,500-2,000 meters above sea level, and the mountains also constitute the natural boundaries of Shanxi, Hebei, and Henan. In Henan, they hang like an arc-shaped machete in the north, with a mountain area of 15,000 square kilometers, which is equivalent to the area of Beijing.

This kind of orogenic process caused a series of extremely steep cliffs and valleys to appear on the side of Taihang Shan that faces Henan. Among them, the Taihang Shan Grand Canyon in Linzhou is particularly magnificent. It extends 50 kilometers from north to south, with a relative height difference of nearly 1,000 meters. The mountains are majestic and the rocks are towering. Local people have to cut through the mountains to build roads, which either hang directly on cliffs or circle valleys.

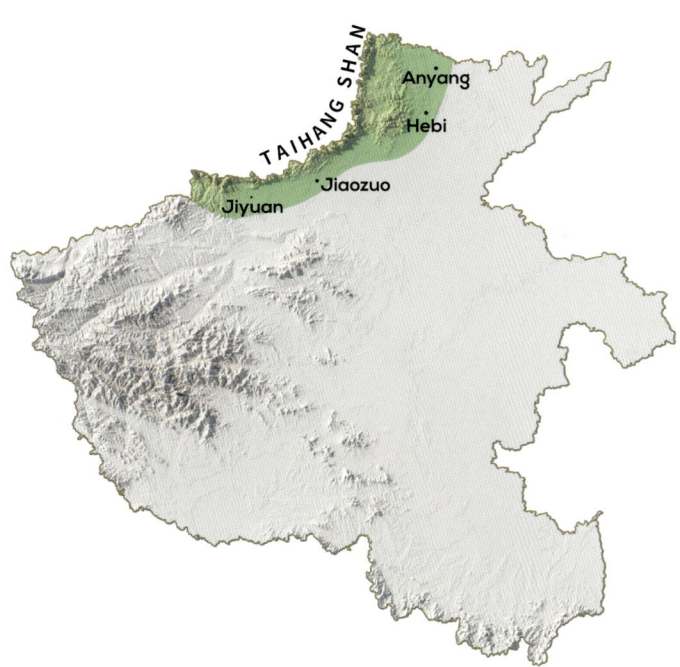

> The Taihang Shan region in Henan

< Guoliang Hanging Tunnel Road/Photo by Dong Jianjun

There are many hanging roads in the Taihang Shan Grand Canyon, among which the hanging road from Guoliang Cave is the most famous. The Guoliang Hanging Tunnel Road is also known as the Guoliang Tunnel, which was manually excavated by villagers of Guoliang Village in the 1970s.

The tall mountains intercepted the vapor-filled East Asian Monsoon, and a rainy belt was formed along the windward slope of the mountains. The highest annual precipitation is close to 1,000 millimeters, which is equivalent to many places in the middle and lower reaches of Chang Jiang. With numerous canyons and cliffs, Taihang Shan in Henan boasts the most outstanding waterside scenery in northern China. Waterfalls with a height difference of several hundred meters drop down the rocky cliffs like silver silk. Water then forms lakes as blue as sapphire and zigzagging streams like azure dragons.

When the water rushed out of the valley, the slope became gentle and the river channel widened. The river flowed freely with mud and sand, forming a vast area like a folding fan, called an alluvial fan. The soil here is fertile and water is abundant.

The edge of the alluvial fan not only benefits from water sources but also avoids floods. The ancients lived by the water and established many ancient villages on the edge of the alluvial fan.

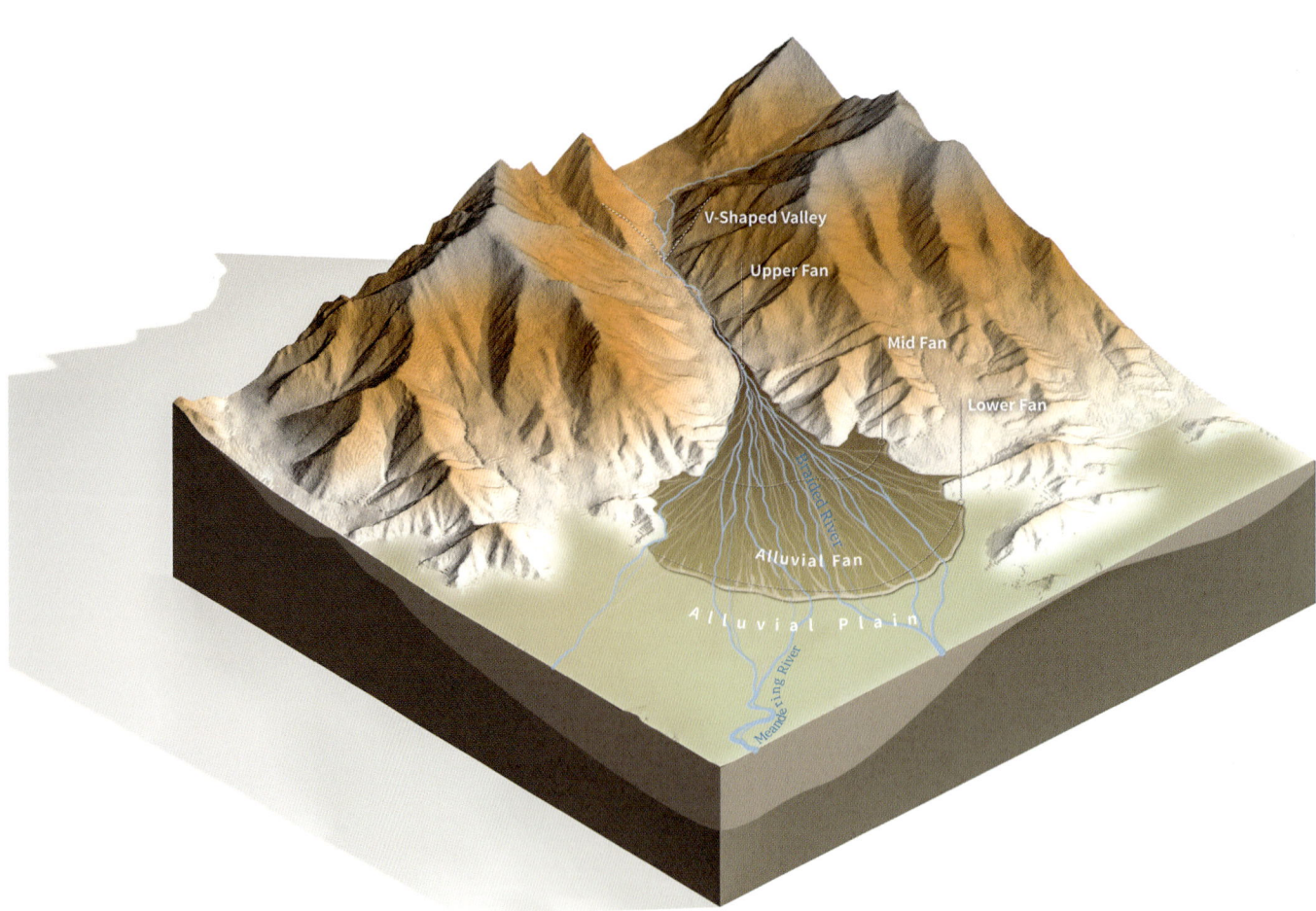

^ **Alluvial fan under the Taihang Shan/Photo by Deng Guohui**

The photo was taken in Niezhuang, Zhicheng Town, Jiyuan, which is a transitional zone from mountain to plain.

< **The formation of alluvial fans and alluvial plains**

After the river flowed out of the mountain, the sediment carried by the river accumulated in front of the mountain to form an alluvial fan. Alluvial plains take shape when alluvial fans, which were formed after large rivers or many rivers flow out of the mountain, are vast and connected. Huabei Pingyuan mentioned later was formed by the accumulation of sediment carried by Huang He, Hai He (Haihe River), and Huai He (Huaihe River) in North China. It is also one of the three major plains in China. Among them, Huainan Pingyuan (Henan Plain) is a part of Huabei Pingyuan, mainly formed by alluvial and fluvial deposits of Huang He and Huai He. Nanyang Pendi (Nanyang Basin), located in southwestern Henan, was formed by alluvial and fluvial deposits of Tang He (Tanghe River) and Bai He (Baihe River).

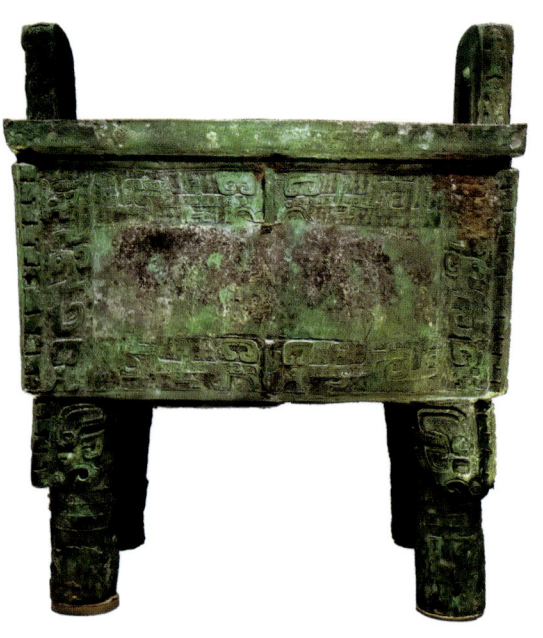

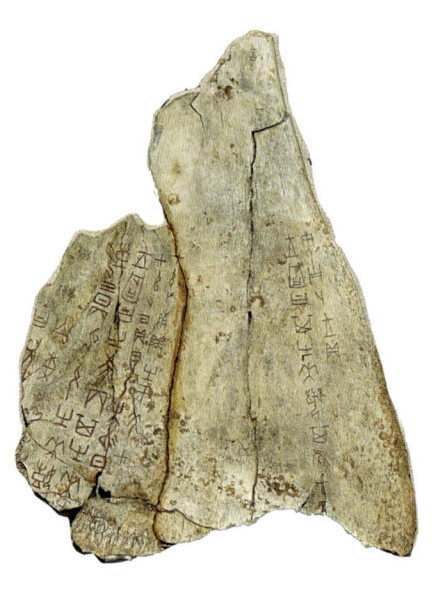

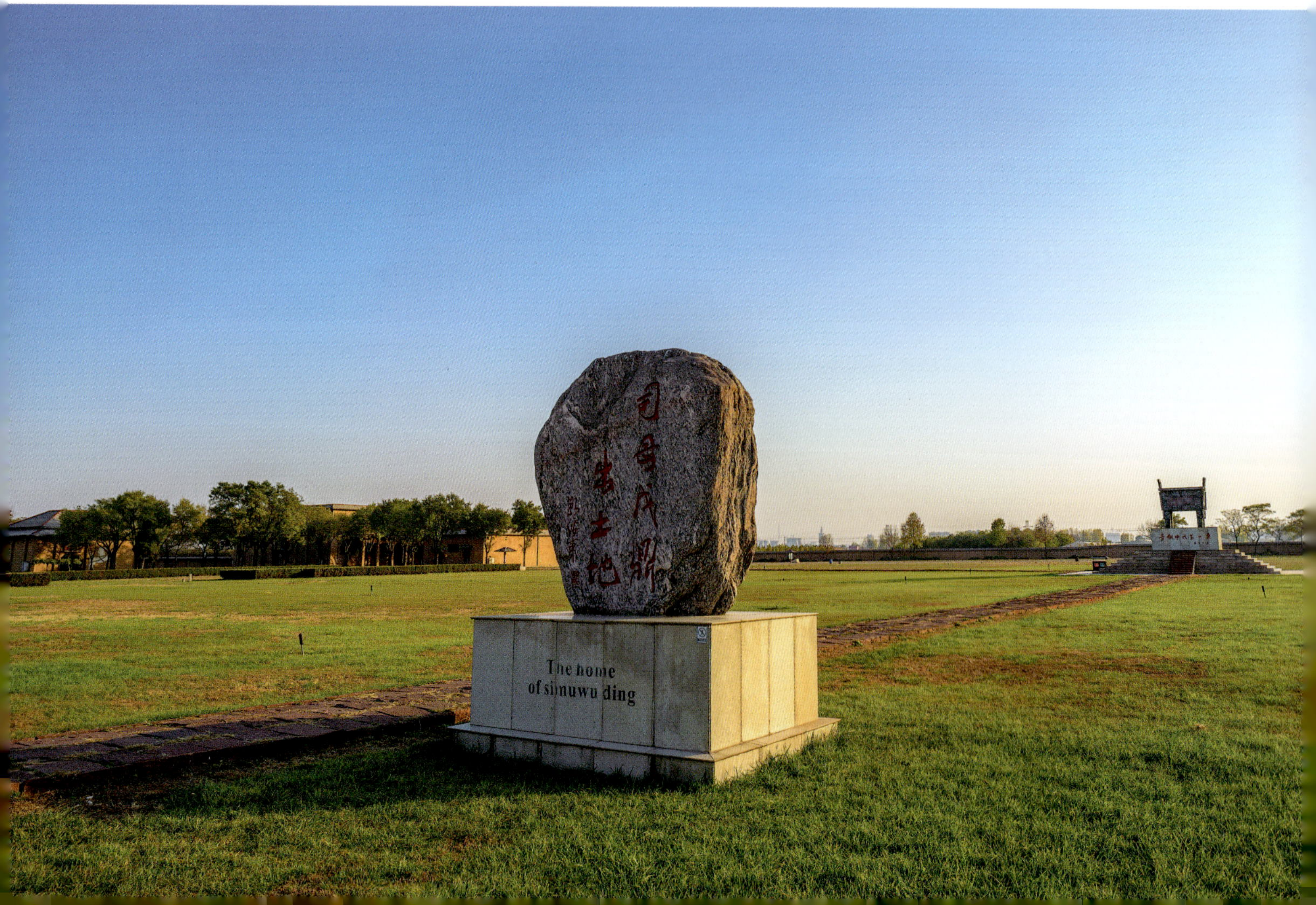
司母戊鼎
出土地
The home
of simuwu ding

Around 1300 BC, Pan'geng, a king of the Shang Dynasty, moved the capital of his kingdom to the edge of the alluvial fan of Zhang He (Zhang River) and Huan He (Huan River), at the foot of Taihang Shan. This move was known in history as "*Pan'geng Qianyin* (Pan'geng moving the capital to Yin)." Thus, Anyang emerged as the first permanent in Chinese history.

Taihang Shan provided the Yin people with abundant resources in terms of wild animals and plants. People could hunt, forage, make clothing, and build houses and temples. The strong uplifting movement of surrounding horst-block mountains also made the resources buried deep underground easier to mine. Some resources were even directly exposed on the surface, the most important of which was copper. As a result, the Yin people (the subjects of the Shang Dynasty) were able to forge bronze ware on a large scale, including ritual vessels, musical instruments, weapons, and drinking vessels. The wide application of bronze and the exquisite craftsmanship that resulted are breathtaking.

The Yin people lived in Anyang for more than 200 years. During this period, the Yin people built a magnificent palace, a pit for extremely cruel sacrifices, and the unparalleled Tomb of Fu Hao. They inscribed all the information they knew about astronomy, geography, hunting, farming, animal husbandry, and sacrificial ceremonies on oracle bones and bronze ware. The earliest known form of Chinese writing was thus recorded.

After the Shang Dynasty, the Anyang area, which was centered on Yecheng, successively became the capital of six kingdoms during the Wei, Jin, Northern and Southern Dynasties Period (420-589), and was the ancient capital of seven dynasties.

This was the Taihang Shan era of Henan.

1	2
3	

1 Houmuwu Ding (a king of cooking vessel)/Photo by Su Lihuan

The Houmuwu Ding, unearthed in Anyang in 1939, is now in the National Museum of China and is a first-class national cultural relic. The amount of raw metal needed to cast this Ding exceeded 1,000 kilograms, and the techniques used were quite complicated. It is the heaviest piece of bronze ware to survive from anywhere in the ancient world.

2 Oracle bone script/Photo by Wang Yang

Oracle bone script, also known as Voynichese, oracle bone inscriptions, or "tortoise-shell and animal-bone script," is the earliest known form of Chinese and East Asian writing. It was first unearthed at the archaeological site of Yin Xu (Ruins of Yin) in Anyang, Henan.

3 Yin Xu/Photo by Shi Yaochen

The picture shows the place where the Houmuwu Ding was unearthed at the archaeological site of Yin Xu in Anyang.

2 The Era of Qin Ling

After the era of Taihang Shan, Henan ushered in the more glorious era of Qin Ling.

On the foundation of an ancient orogenic belt formed by the continental collision of North China Plate and Yangzte Plate more than 300 million years ago, the north part of it subsided due to normal fault activities somehow about 60 million years before. The south part, however, was relatively uplifted as a young mountain range that trended from east to west, forming today's Qin Ling, and it has a total length of more than 1,000 kilometers. It inserted itself into Qingzang Gaoyuan at its western end, and it connects with Kunlun Shan at the border of Qinghai and Gansu. Its eastern end directly extends into the western part of Henan, giving birth to a series of mountains such as Song Shan (Mount Songshan), Xiao Shan (Mount Xiaoshan), Xiong'er Shan (Xiong'er Mountain), and Funiu Shan (Funiu Mountains). This region is Henan's largest area with the most mountains.

These mountains have different characteristics, but all of them are

> Taishi Shan (Taishi Mountain)/Photo by Liu Kebai

Taishi Shan is part of Song Shan, located north of Dengfeng City, Henan. It is characterized as the eastern peak of Song Shan. This is the lingering area of Qin Ling's mountain range as it extends eastward.

Laojun Shan (Laojun Mountain)/Photo by Sun Jie

Laojun Shan is located in the southeast of Luanchuan County, Luoyang, Henan. At an elevation of 2,297 meters, it is the main peak of Funiu Shan, an eastern extension of Qin Ling.

sights to behold. The highest peak of Song Shan is only 1,512 meters above sea level, but as it rises abruptly far above the surrounding flat ground, the mountain appears tall and lofty.

Funiu Shan is the largest mountain range in western Henan. The huge mountain range features many towering and majestic peaks that rise above 1,500 meters. As one of the fold mountains, Funiu Shan does not have a huge fault-block body and steep cliffs like Taihang Shan, but its peaks are also precipitous. Its main peak, Laojun Shan (Laojun Mountain), stands about 2,200 meters above sea level and has a jagged ridge. The sharp rocks protruding from it are unique.

The Qin Ling region in Henan

The rolling slopes of Funiu Shan abound in water vapor. The mountains are densely covered with vegetation, and are surrounded by clouds and mists. The rivers that originate from these mountains form a dense river system. According to *Shuijingzhu* (*Notes on Book of Waterways*), there were as many as 170 rivers of various sizes in western Henan in ancient times. The alluvial area formed by the gathering of so many rivers is larger and thicker than a typical alluvial fan. It is called an alluvial plain.

An alluvial plain extends over a vast area and is more hospitable for human survival. Luoyang Pendi (Luoyang Basin), where the hundreds of water systems converge, is such a plain. In addition, it is surrounded by mountains, which helps to deter enemies coming from the outside. The river system here stretches both vertically and horizontally on the map reaching all directions. The ancients concluded: "Surrounded by mountains, Luoyang has six rivers flowing through it and eight gates, connecting to ten provinces."

⌄ Sea of clouds on Funiu Shan/Photo by Han Zihao
Water vapor brought by the monsoon causes a sea of clouds in Funiu Shan.

Since the beginning of the Xia Dynasty, 13 dynasties have established their capitals in Luoyang. It was the ancient capital seat of thirteen dynasties.

At the end of the 7th century AD, Wu Zetian focused on building Luoyang as Shendu, or Divine Capital, and Luoyang's development began to enter its prime. At that time, the people of the Tang Dynasty built extensive palaces, which were majestic and grand; when the giant statue of Buddha was carved out, thousands of people bowed in salute.

Luoyang had a profound psychological impact on people. People of the time were emotionally attached to Luoyang. Therefore, many places that were named after "Luoyang" appeared. Today, you can still see "Luoyang Village" and "Luoyang Town" in Jiangxi, Fujian, Chongqing, Guangdong, Hubei, Hunan, and Taiwan. Even the alternate name of Kyoto in Japan is "Luoyang."

This was the era of the Qin Ling of Henan.

Longmen Grottoes in Luoyang/Photo by Deng Guohui

The Longmen Grottoes are located on the cliffs of Longmen Shan and Xiang Shan (Xiangshan Mountains) on the banks of Yi He (Yihe River) in the southern suburbs of Luoyang. They were mainly carved out during the period from the Northern Wei Dynasty (386-534) to the Northern Song Dynasty. The Longmen Grottot, the Yungang Grottoes, and the Maijishan Grottoes, along with Mogao Caves, are called China's top 4 Buddhist Grottoes, and the former three were inscribed on the UNESCO World Heritage List in 2000, while the Mogao Caves made it in 1987.

3 The Dabie Shan Sub-Era

During the Qin Ling era, the third mountain combination in Henan—Tongbai & Dabie Shan also became very important.

Their influence was not as great as those of the first two mountain ranges, but they helped create the conditions necessary for the later emergence of an even more magnificent scene. It may be called the Dabie Shan sub-era.

Tongbai & Dabie Shan are the eastern extension of Qin Ling and are located slightly more southerly than Qin Ling. Their formation process is almost identical with that of Qin Ling. Their formation processes were quite familiar with Qin Ling, which was uplifted due to relatively young faults activities on the planation surface of ancient Qin Ling orogeny. The mountain range extends from northwest to southeast and serves as the border between the two provinces of Henan and Hubei.

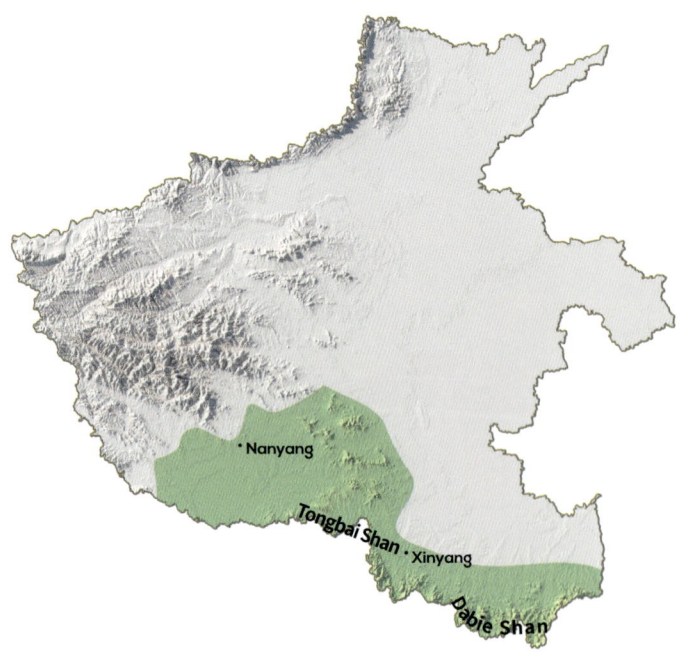

< Tongbai Shan-Dabie Shan and Nanyang Pendi

> A tea plantation in Xinyang/Photo by Jiao Xiaoxiang

The climate of Dabie Shan is very suitable for growing tea. Tongbai Shan & Dabie Shan region as well as the Nanyang Pendi region in Henan is known for its tea plantations, and Xinyang produces the famous Xinyang Maojian. The picture shows a tea plantation near Nanwan Hu (Nanwan Lake) in Xinyang.

Dabie Shan is in the transitional zone between the subtropical and warm temperate zones. The heating and cooling of air masses alternates frequently here, and Huai He (Huaihe River), one of the seven major river systems in China, has its origin in this area. The mountains are shrouded by clouds and mist all year round. The area also features frequent rainfall and dense, lush vegetation. Lakes are as placid as mirrors, composing views of the mountains that are like splash-ink paintings.

Dabie Shan and Funiu Shan of Qing Ling enclose the famous Nanyang Pendi (Nanyang Basin). On the north side of the basin, there is a sudden break between Funiu Shan and Tongbai Shan, forming a gap in the northeastern corner of the basin, which has become a major transportation hub between northern and southern China. Nanyang, one of the early cradles of Chu culture, emerged here, and it was also the early capital seat of Chu. In the Western Han Dynasty, Nanyang became one of the six largest cities in the country.

Huangbai Shan (Huangbai Mountain)/Photo by Han Zihao

Huangbai Shan in Shangcheng County, Xinyang, is located in the hinterland of China.

4 The Era of the Great Plains of Henan

Once the three mountain building eras transformed the region, the stage had been set for a climax to the story, that is, the era of the great plains of Henan.

Now, our focus needs to shift from tall mountains to a big river. It is the great Huang He, which originated from Qingzang Gaoyuan and flowing through Huangtu Gaoyuan.

When Huang He broke through the blockade formed by Taihang Shan and Qin Ling and entered Henan, a vast stage awaited it. The central and eastern parts of Henan—which are surrounded by Taihang Shan in the northwest, Qin Ling in the west, and Tongbai & Dabie Shan in the south—are lowlands formed by tectonic subsidence. Here, Huang He can run freely, capturing Hai He (Hai River) in the north and invading Huai He in the south. It carries from hundreds of millions of tons to more than one billion tons of sediment each year, contributing to the formation of the contemporary Huabei Pingyuan.

< The Huabei Pingyuan region in Henan

> Huabei Pingyuan/Photo by Chen Junjie
The picture shows farmland in Henan. The river in the distance is Huang He.

Huabei Pingyuan covers a total of 300,000 square kilometers, spanning seven provinces and municipalities including Beijing, Tianjin, Hebei, Shandong, Henan, Anhui, and Jiangsu. It is no exaggeration to say that Huabei Pingyuan is a fertile land stretching thousands of square kilometers, of which the Henan part is the most fertile.

The plain is rich with many river systems. In addition to natural rivers, many canals were also dug by the ancients. One major canal, Bian He (Bianhe River) originated from the gulf and was dug during the Warring States Period (475-221BC), connecting Huang He and Huai He. Its well-developed water transportation system was highly regarded in the Tang Dynasty:

> *The people of the entire land of the 43 states in the southeast were exploited through this river.*
> —Li Jingfang, *The Boats Directly enter the Bian He*

Qingming Riverside Landscape Garden in Kaifeng/Photo by Yue Kefeng

Kaifeng, known as the world's most prosperous city back to the Song Dynasty, always arouses infinite imagination in the minds of later generations.

In the Northern Song Dynasty, its capital Bianliang (today's Kaifeng) became the world's most prosperous city by virtue of its plains and river systems, and it was also the last super metropolis in the southern part of Huabei Pingyuan throughout China's imperial period.

The greatest achievement of the great plains era was not the development of one city or one place. Instead, Henan, with Kaifeng as the center, led the Song Dynasty to an unprecedented height in material affluence and cultural life. The historian Ray Huang once said:

> *With the rise of the Song Dynasty in 960 AD, China seemed to have entered the modern era, and an advanced material culture was developed during this period. The circulation of money was more popular than before. The invention of gunpowder, as well as the use of flame devices, navigational compasses, astronomical clocks, blast furnaces, hydraulic spinning machines, and watertight bulkheads for ships, all appeared in the Song Dynasty.*
>
> —Ray Huang, *China: A Macro History*

It was closer to a commercial civilization than to an agricultural civilization.

Starting from the time of Emperor Zhenzong of the Song Dynasty, government revenues from industrial and commercial taxes and levies exceeded the amount collected from agricultural taxes. During the Xining reign (1068-1077) of the Northern Song Dynasty, the proportion of revenue collected from agricultural taxes dropped to 30%, a surprisingly small amount. In contrast, government revenues from agricultural land taxes in the Ming and Qing dynasties accounted for as much as 70% of the total.

People left the countryside for cities.

According to the *Collections of the History of Chinese Urban Development* by the economic historian Zhao Gang, the urban population in the Northern Song Dynasty accounted for as much as 20% of the total population, while the urbanization rate in the mid-Qing Dynasty was only 7% of inhabitants.

People were getting richer.

According to estimates by Professor Liu Guanglin from the Hong Kong University of Science and Technology, the per capita annual income in the Song Dynasty was 7.5 taels of silver. In comparison, the per capita annual income during the heyday of Emperors Kangxi and Qianlong 600 years later was only 6.45 taels of silver.

This was the era of the great plains of Henan.

5 Contributions to China

After the mountains, river systems, and the great plains were formed, and after the Taihang Shan era, Qin Ling era, and Dabie Shan sub-era that followed, as well as the most glorious great plains era, a complete and clear image of Henan may take shape.

However, its evolution did not end there. During its period of prosperity, Henan continued to spread its civilization. In the later period of its decline, Henan also profoundly affected all of China. In every war and disaster, when people fled Zhongyuan, it also resulted in a spread of civilization across the land.

We can take Lin'an (today's Hangzhou) in the early Southern Song Dynasty (1127-1279) as an example. It was home to 260,000 households, which included generals and ministers as well as people from the lowest social status. Most immigrants to Lin'an came from Henan. Numerous shops, pharmacies, and temples were opened or built by people from Kaifeng. Until the Ming Dynasty, some people sighed in frustration over the Kaifeng accent of some Hangzhou people. Jiangsu, Fujian, Jiangxi, and many other provinces also had similar phenomena:

> *The dialect spoken in the city (Hangzhou) is easier to understand than in other places because many residents are the descendants of immigrants from Bianliang (today's Kaifeng). They migrated south in the early Southern Song Dynasty and have lived here ever since. Therefore, the accent of Hangzhou dialect is still quite similar to that of Bianliang.*
> —Lang Ying, *Seven Categories of Research, Volume 26*

Among the 4,820 Han surnames today—of those gathered by scholars in an as-of-yet incomplete count—1,834 are of Henan origin; of the 300 dominant surnames, 171 are of Henan origin. It is precisely due to the continuous spread of civilization from Henan, whether it underwent a rise or decline, that the population and cultural pattern of today's China has been established.

Henan has made great contributions to the formation of both China's landscapes and culture.

> Zhengzhou East EMU Train Yard/Photo by Jiao Xiaoxiang
> Today's Zhengzhou is the main national transport hub in central China. The bullet trains in the picture are like arrows darting out to their targets.

Among the 34 provincial-level administrative regions in China, you would be hard pressed to find another place that parallels Zhejiang for its positive image. It is prosperous, with a galaxy of talented people, canal towns bordered by waters, picturesque scenery and more. Yuan Hongdao, a Hubei native during the Ming Dynasty, made the following analogy when he arrived at Zhejiang: that there were more scholars there than fish in the sea. In addition, there is Xi Hu in Hangzhou, which has attracted people from all over the country to make a visit to its shores for more than a thousand years.

3.2 Zhejiang:

A Province of Invincible Productivity

When considering Zhejiang, people often think of many wonderful things: prosperity, a surplus of talent, Jiangnan canal towns, beautiful scenery and more.

Among the 34 provinces, municipalities, and autonomous regions in China, you can hardly find another place that enjoys the same great reputation as Zhejiang. When Yuan Hongdao, a native of Hubei in the Ming Dynasty, first arrived in Zhejiang, he made the analogy that "the scholars are more numerous than crucian carps here." One place which enjoys great reputation is the famous Xi Hu in Hangzhou. This popular destination has been admired by people from all over the country for more than a thousand years.

However, Zhejiang's near-perfect image is not simply innate to its given nature. It had four major disadvantages stemming from its history and geography, and any one of them could have been enough to subvert its development into what it is today. In the face of these major disadvantages, what could Zhejiang rely on to avert disaster?

In the eyes of the Institute for Planets, the answer to this question is attributed to the province's unparalleled productivity.

From the manufacturing of needles and thread to the production of exquisite and precious embroideries, from the construction of artificial rivers and lakes to famous cities and ancient towns, from the development of science and technology to commercial innovation, all of these factors have enabled Zhejiang to get out of predicaments time and time again. Zhejiang is simply a "super machine" that has been in operation for more than 7,000 years.

> Majishan Ore Transit Base in Shengsi County, Zhejiang/Photo by Zhao Gaoxiang

Different kinds of colorful ores are heaped together.

∧ The map of Zhejiang

Zhejiang is abbreviated as "Zhe." The largest river snaking through its territory, Qiantang Jiang (Qiantang River), is also known as "Zhe River" and "Zhi River," inspiring the name Zhejiang (literally "Zhe River"). Zhejiang's coast is on the East China Sea, and it is located to the south of Tai Hu (Taihu Lake). Zhejiang has an area of approximately 104,000 square kilometers, accounting for just 1.1% of the country's total land area. It is one of the smallest provinces in China. Zhejiang has many mountains and a complex topography. The four main mountain ranges extend from southwest to northeast, and the terrain gradually lowers from southwest to northeast. Overall, the hills and mountains in its territory account for 70.4% of its total land area, the plains account for 23.2%, and the rest is comprised of rivers and lakes. There is a saying that describes this distribution: "70% mountains, 10% water, and 20% farmland." In addition, with a vast costal area that includes 3,061 islands, Zhejiang is the province with the most islands in the country. Among them, Zhoushan Dao (Zhoushan Island) has an area of 502.65 square kilometers and is the fourth largest island in China. With numerous islands and tortuous coasts, Zhejiang's total coastline is as long as 6,700 kilometers.

^ The location of Zhejiang in China

< National GDP ranking (1978-2017)

Since China's reform and opening up, Zhejiang's ranking in its contribution to the national GDP has risen greatly.
Data source: *National Bureau of Statistics and provincial statistical yearbooks*, excluding Hong Kong, Macao, and Taiwan.

1 The Ancestors

A group of ancestors to modern humans arrived in northern Zhejiang 7,000 years ago. Their appearance included certain characteristics of modern Chinese people, but they were closer to the Austronesian peoples. They are called the Hemudu people.

In the Zhejiang region at that time, four columns of mountains stretched from southwest to northeast, including Tianmu Shan (Tianmu Mountain), Baiji-Qianligang-Yuling-Longmen Shan, Xianxialing-Dapan-Kuaiji-Siming-Tiantai Shan (Xianxialing-Dapan-Kuaiji-Siming-Tiantai Mountains), and Donggong-Yandang-Kuocang Shan (Donggong-Yandang-Kuocang Mountains).

Among this group of mountains, Huangmaojian Feng (Huangmaojian Peak), located in Donggong Shan (Donggong Mountains), has an elevation of 1,929 meters and is the highest peak in Zhejiang. At sunset, there is often a sea of clouds hovering around the mountaintops, creating a fairyland-like vista.

Located in the Kuocang Shan, Shenxianju is steep, with towering cliffs and strange rocks. Yandang Shan (Yandang Mountains) are represented mainly by rhyolites erupted during Cretaceous, and their landforms are more varied.

> Shenxianju/Photo by Liu Jie

Shenxianju in Kuocang Shan has many volcanic rhyolites, and the rocks have their own characteristics under external forces. The protruding mountain in the distance is called "Guanying Feng (Guanyin Peak)" because it resembles the Guanyin of the South China Sea with folded hands.

Jinji Shan (Jinji Mountain), Wenzhou/Photo by Su Lisuo

Jinji Shan is located in the northwest of Rui'an City, Wenzhou, and it belongs to the southern branch of Donggong Shan (Donggong Mountains). There are many peaks on the mountain which are often surrounded by clouds and mist.

Abundant river systems are bred in the mountains. Waterfalls cascade down and converge into streams, lakes, and many rivers. The largest among them, Qiantang Jiang, is 668 kilometers long, and the different sections are named Xin'an Jiang (Xin'an River), Fuchun Jiang (Fuchun River), and Qiantang Jiang. The river zigzags through the province. This is is the origin of the name "Zhejiang."

Rivers flood out onto the plains and are mainly concentrated in northern Zhejiang. As a result, Zhebei Pingyuan (North Zhejiang Plain) is covered by swampland and not relatively dry like Huabei Pingyuan. In the era when the Hemudu people lived, the climate was warmer than it is now, and the rainfall was even more abundant. On Zhebei Pingyuan, swamps, wetlands, and even some forests could only grow in water. Even now, the river system density in northern Zhejiang is still much greater than that in other parts of the province. Northern Zhejiang is an area with some of the densest river systems in China.

Zhejiang's first disadvantage is now clear, that is, it has too much water.

‹ Wulongxia Waterfall/Photo by Ye Qi

The Wulongxia Waterfall is in Pan'an County, Jinhua. The waterfall flows down from the cliff like a piece of flying white silk.

Dusk at the "Sanjiangkou" of Qiantang Jiang/Photo by Ding Junhao

Fuchun Jiang, after converging with Puyang Jiang (Puyang River) somewhere near Wenyan Town, Xiaoshan, is called Qiantang Jiang. The picture shows the confluence of Qiantang Jiang, Fuchun Jiang, and Puyang Jiang.

There is so much water in Zhejiang that just a dry place to sleep is precious. If the local settlers of antiquity had the opportunity to compare the advantages and disadvantages of northern China and northern Zhejiang, they would have chosen the former without hesitation. This assumption is consistent with reality. The early culture of Huabei Pingyuan discovered by archaeologists was much richer and more developed than that of Jiangnan. The Hemudu people, however, changed this perception. The prosperity they created around lower reaches of Chang Jiang was comparable to that of Huang He Pendi because they learned to use a kind of "weed."

This "weed" grew in the swamp. If it is well cared for, its seeds can be harvested regularly. We call this "weed" rice. The nutrients brought by the rivers made the soil of the alluvial plains very fertile, greatly enhancing the possibility of the growth of rice, allowing the local settlers to produce bumper harvests.

In addition to raising bumper harvests, the local settlers of antiquity here were also able to solve the housing problem. They cut end pieces of wood into a protruding bump, and they chiseled a hollow out of the ends of other pieces. Thus, two pieces of wood could be connected by inserting a protruding bump into a hollowed-out hole. With this technique, a solid wooden house could easily be built. The base of these wooden houses was built above the ground like current stilt houses, for the purpose of preventing water and moisture damage. This kind of wooden structure connected by bumps and holes was the earliest usage of the mortise and tenon joint in China. Its craftsmanship is amazing.

The Hemudu people laid the foundation for the affluent life in Zhejiang, which brought about a great deal of productivity.

> Harvesting rice/Photo by Pan Jincao

The photo was taken in Fuyang District, Hangzhou.

< Ancient bone *si* (ancient farm tool like a plough)/Photo by Liu Yanting

The picture shows an ancient si, unearthed at the Hemudu site in Zhejiang in 1974. A si was a shovel-like farm tool from ancient times. It was mainly used for leveling soil, digging ditches, and diverting and draining water. The appearance of the ancient si shows that the rice cultivation of the Hemudu culture had progressed beyond the initial slash-and-burn stage.

About 5,300 years ago, the residents of Zhebei Pingyuan were called the Liangzhu people. In addition to food and housing, the Liangzhu people developed a brand-new pursuit.

Thousands of jade articles of 61 different distinct types of decorations were used to adorn the lives of the Liangzhu people. The most luxurious piece, dubbed the "King of *Cong*" (a kind of cylindrical piece of jade ware with an inner hole), weighs 6.5 kilograms.

A certain kind of worm that grew on mulberry trees in the region, the silkworm, was carefully collected. The Liangzhu people extracted fine silk from silkworm cocoons. More than 20 pieces of cocoon silk were wound into every thread of raw silk, which was then woven into clothing with a density of 122 to 134 pieces of raw silk per inch. Amazingly, this complicated silk production technology was mastered 5,000 years ago.

Wood also found a brand-new usage by the locals. After cutting and polishing, the world's earliest wooden clogs were born.

Ever since, the Liangzhu people have worn jade ornaments, silk, and clogs. Rice is still their staple food. This was the most fashionable, luxurious way of life in the Neolithic Age. Other ethnic groups in Huang He Pendi during the same period could not reach comparable living standards.

About 3,000 years ago, another ethnic group began to thrive in Zhebei Pingyuan, and they were called the Yue people.

⌃ Liangzhu *Cong*/Photo by Su Lihuan

This piece of *cong* (a long hollow piece of jade with rectangular sides), weighing 6.5 kilograms and decorated with intricate patterns, is known as the "King of *Cong*."

< Liangzhu jade *cong*/Photo by Liu Yanting

A *cong* was a cylindrical jade item that was round inside and square outside. It was an important ritual vessel during the Neolithic Age, and the jade *cong* unearthed in the Liangzhu site is the most exquisite example known. Some scholars believe that the larger upper part and inner round structure of it symbolized heaven, and the smaller lower part and the squarer shape at the bottom symbolized earth. It is a kind of artifact intended to connect heaven and earth. The animal face patterns on the four sides of the jade *cong* in the picture were highly symbolized, which showed the degree of development of craftsmanship in the Liangzhu culture.

> The Sword of Goujian, King of Yue, and the bird-worm seal script on one side of the blade/Photo by Su Lihuan

The sword of Goujian, King of Yue, a bronze sword of the Yue Kingdom in the late Spring and Autumn Period (770-476BC), was unearthed in ancient Chu Tombs in Jiangling County, Hubei in 1965. The sword is engraved with "bird-worm seal script." The characters in the right picture on the right page are the bird-worm seal script on one side of the blade.

The Yue people considered birds to be their totems, and both men and women went naked and were covered with tattoos. They spoke a language that was difficult to understand by people from Zhongyuan. Their characters were the bird-worm seal script, which was decorated with bird patterns. The pursuits of their ruler, the King of Yue, surpassed simple wealth and fashion, and he was eager to defeat his strong neighbors and achieve hegemony.

The bronze sword was the best weapon at that time. After years of war, the casting skills of the Yue sword became increasingly exquisite. This has been verified by modern scientific tests. Among the thousands of existing Eastern Zhou (770-256BC) bronze swords, the Yue swords from the late Spring and Autumn Period to the mid-Warring States Period are of the best quality.

In 473 BC, with the support of the Yue sword, Gou Jian, the king of Yue, lay on firewood and tasted gall, annexed the State of Wu and became a hegemony in the Spring and Autumn Period. And it's time for a group of new ethnic groups to land.

∧ Jinhua ham/Photo by Yang Meiqing

The picture shows Jinhua ham being hung up to dry in the sun. In the Song Dynasty, Jinhua ham rose to fame and was used as tribute to the imperial court.

∨ Chrysanthemum produced in Tongxiang, Zhejiang/Photo by Yuan Peide

Tongxiang chrysanthemum is a type of high-quality chrysanthemum flower tea.

2 The Immigrants Were Coming

Following the Qin and Han dynasties, due to events from the Rebellion of Yongjia Reign in the Western Jin Dynasty (265-317), to the An Lushan Rebellion in the Tang Dynasty and the Jingkang Incident in the Northern Song Dynasty, many Han people fled the wars, migrating from the north to the south and merging with the Yue people. They spoke Wu dialect, saying "nong" when they spoke about themselves, and "yi" or "qu" when they meant "he" (in some dialects today "nong" means "you"), and adding the "a" sound in front of a number of titles of relatives, such as agong (grandpa), apo (grandma), a'ge (elder brother), amei (younger sister), agu (aunt) and ashu (uncle). They were the new Zhejiangese.

Zhejiang is one of the smallest provinces in China, only larger than Ningxia, Taiwan, and Hainan. Of its total land area of about 100,000 square kilometers, 70% are mountains and hills, with only a small amount consisting of plains distributed in its northern and eastern parts. The terrain of neighboring Jiangsu is just the opposite, with nearly 70% of its land area being vast plains. For the development of human civilization, plains hold a huge advantage. This alone makes Zhejiang's innate conditions less hospitable than the surrounding regions.

This is the second disadvantage of Zhejiang: a terrain of many mountains and few plains.

How could Zhejiang respond to the challenges of its own terrain?

The first response was agriculture. Quick-maturing rice—Champa rice—was introduced from Vietnam to Zhejiang, where its use quickly spread. The imperial court sent specially assigned persons to guide farmers in planting, and the emperor also gave symbolic demonstrations of agricultural labor. Farmers planted rice in summer, harvested it in autumn, planted winter rice after the fall harvest, and harvested again the following summer. In this way, crops were harvested twice a year. It was a substantial increase in land utilization. Jiangnan began to replace Zhongyuan as the country's main grain-producing region. As the saying goes, "the grain harvested in Suzhou and Huzhou are enough to feed the entire population of China."

In addition to grain, value-added cash crops, including mulberry, tea, fruit, flowers, and vegetables, were also planted extensively in Zhejiang. In this way, farmers could obtain a greater income on limited land. The scale of raising livestock and poultry was also widely expanded. Jinhua people salted the hind legs of pigs, and then dry-cured and fermented them to make Jinhua ham, which has a red-toned meat and is very well-known around China.

In addition to agriculture, handicrafts also flourished. The silk fabric made by the people of Huzhou was as light as a cicada's wings and as thin as the morning mist. In the kilns set up by the people of Longquan, the celadon pottery that was produced was very firm, having a glaze that was as smooth as jade, displaying a craftsmanship that was superb. People from Zhoushan living by the sea opened many salt pans, and Zhoushan was one of the nine major salt-producing areas in the country during the Tang Dynasty.

Tea, ham, silk, celadon, boiled salt, brewing, papermaking, and woodblock printing—all these industries realized remarkable achievements during this period. It was commonplace to see vendors carrying a variety of merchandise as they hawked them along the streets and alleys, just like a mobile "Taobao Mall (an online shopping application)."

Diverse goods and materials from Zhejiang were distributed across the country by means of Jinghang Yunhe (Beijing-Hangzhou Grand Canal), opened during the Sui Dynasty. The transportation of grain and other goods from the south to the north lasted for more than 1,000 years in this period of Chinese history.

In addition to domestic transportation, Zhejiang's location close to the sea facilitated the export of local products. Zhejiang earned huge profits from international trade. During the Five Dynasties Period, Wuyue, a small coastal kingdom in Zhejiang, paid millions in coins from its income gained from maritime trade as tribute to the Zhongyuan regime every year. This demonstrated the huge scale of trade that took place here. In the Song Dynasty, Zhoushan had 597 large ships with a width of over one *zhang*[1] and 3,324 boats with a width of less than one zhang. Ningbo also developed into a famous overseas trading port at this time.

Great commodity production capacity and prosperous domestic and foreign trade boosted Zhejiang's construction of urban infrastructure. From the plains to the mountainous areas, a wave of urban construction set in. Places such as Shaoxing and Huzhou experienced vigorous development.

The most praise-worthy gains occurred in Hangzhou. This once-insignificant small town developed rapidly and prospered greatly in just one to two hundred years due to the increase in population and the trade of commodities, becoming a famous metropolis ever since the Sui and Tang dynasties.

The governors of Hangzhou, Bai Juyi and Su Shi realized the value of a gradually dammed lake on the edge of the city. They heightened the lake embankment to increase its water storage capacity, providing irriga-

---

1 a Chinese unit of length equal to about 3.33 meters

tion for farmland and water for the city. The beauty of the lake also became important as a "business card" for the city. This small lake was Xi Hu.

People of later generations continued to add scenic spots and build temples and towers around Xi Hu. The lake has gradually developed into a sacred place in the minds of literati and scholars all over the country, known for "the scent of flowers across the water intoxicating countless guests." Hangzhou, and even the whole of Zhejiang, became more charming because of this. A lake benefited a city and an entire province, and it can be called the greatest creation of the Zhejiang people.

The increase in productivity overcame the disadvantages of Zhejiang having many mountains and few plains and created the prosperity of the Tang and Song dynasties. However, in the Ming and Qing dynasties, the third disadvantage, caused by certain policies, became apparent.

⌄ The Broken Bridge and withered lotus of Xi Hu in snow/Photo by Hu Han
The lotus flower of Xi Hu is always strongly associative of beauty, and even the withered lotus remnants are of appeal to the literati.

3 The Forbidden Sea

The coastline of Zhejiang is long and tortuous. There are as many as 3,061 islands, accounting for two fifths of the total number of islands in China. Among them, Zhoushan Qundao (Zhoushan Archipelago) is composed of 1,390 islands. It is the largest archipelago in the country and a world-famous fishing ground. It has many protruding headlands, beautifully curved bays, clear seawater, soft sand, a wide sky, and bright stars. One of the most beautiful places is the funnel-shaped Hangzhou Wan (Hangzhou Bay) at the mouth of Qiantang Jiang. Whenever the tide comes, the seawater rolls in, making for magnificent, unparalleled scenery.

However, the advantages created by Zhejiang's proximity to the ocean did not continue forever. During the Ming and Qing dynasties, the open trade policy was replaced by a strict ban on maritime trade.

A lighthouse on Xia Dachen Dao (Lower Dachen Island)/Photo by Zhao Gaoxiang

Dachen Dao (Dachen Islands), off the east coast of Taizhou, Zhejiang, consist of Shang Dachen Dao (Upper Dachen Island) and Xia Dachen Dao, both belonging to the Taizhou archipelago.

According to Daming Lü (*Statutes of the Ming Dynasty*):

Those who bring prohibited goods into the sea, go to other countries to buy and sell, collude and conspire with pirates, and act as their guides to rob good people shall be beheaded in public according to the law, and their whole family shall be exiled to the frontiers for military service. Those who build sea-going ships and sell them to the barbarians for profit, like those who bring prohibited weapons to the sea, shall be deemed as having committed a crime due to the disclosure of military information. The principal offender shall be beheaded, and any accomplices shall be exiled to the frontiers for military service.

The ban on maritime trade caused the ports to be deserted and the people living there to lead miserable lives. Because of this, some maritime merchants and coastal residents who couldn't make a living chose to join with Wokou (pirate), who plagued almost all the coastal areas of Zhejiang.

The population of Zhejiang, which had lost its advantage in maritime trade, was still increasing rapidly. The population of Zhejiang today is about 65 million, but in the Qing Dynasty, its population had already reached 30.4 million. The population density had soared from 114 people per square kilometer during the Ming Dynasty to 300 people per square kilometer in the Qing Dynasty, and the per capita of arable land had dropped from 4.15 *mu* to 1.77 *mu*. Zhejiang was the province with the highest population density and the lowest per capita of arable land in the Ming and Qing dynasties.

> Gouqi Dao (Wolfberry Island) in Zhoushan/Photo by Zhu Jinhua

Zhoushan is China's largest archipelago, comprised of 2,085 islands in total. The island on the right is Gouqi Dao.

Linhai Ancient City Wall, dubbed the "Great Wall of Jiangnan," Taizhou/Photo by Ke Jianbo

The Great Wall of Jiangnan is located in the coastal area of Zhejiang and was once reinforced and built by the famous anti-Wokou general Qi Jiguang.

How could Zhejiang respond to its policies?

Improving the utilization rate of agricultural land was once again on the agenda. High-yield crops such as sweet potatoes and potatoes, which had been introduced after the contact with European traders, were promoted. Farmland began to appear in the mountainous areas in addition to on the plains. However, the agricultural development of mountainous areas caused soil erosion, and it was often difficult to increase the output of agricultural products. Therefore, planting more and better cash crops became even more important, considering the limited amount of arable land. Zhejiang substantially increased the production of mulberry, cotton, and tea. After all, the income from an acre of a tea plantation was far more than that of an acre of rice fields. Longjing tea became famous all over the world in this context.

At the same time, the handicraft industry and various workshops became more prosperous. Shaoxing wine, Huzhou brush pen, Jili silk—all kinds of local products were gaining popularity in the market.

The popularity of locally produced products further boosted the development of commerce. Many farmers put down their hoes and started to do business. The Longyou and Ningbo business guilds came into being. Qing He Fang in Hangzhou became the most bustling commercial district. There were many shops and stalls in the streets and alleys, attracting numerous customers.

In 1675, Nikolai Spataru Milescu, an envoy of the Russian Empire to China, described Hangzhou in a tone which hardly concealed his admiration :

> *"The population of this city is so large that 10,000 bags of rice are consumed, and 1,000 pigs are slaughtered every day."*
>
> —Quoted from *General History of Zhejiang*

The infrastructure construction was once again a major concern. Instead of big cities, countless small towns were built at that time. In the middle and late Ming Dynasty, there were more than 100 industrial and commercial towns in Zhejiang. In the Qing Dynasty, the number soared to more than 1,000. This was an unprecedented urbanization process in Chinese history. Xitang, Nanxun, and Wuzhen all rose to prominence during this period.

< A Longjing tea plantation/Photo by Jin Liang

This picture shows a tea plantation in Longjing Village, Hangzhou. Rows of tea trees cover the mountains. They not only are an excellent cash crop, but also prevent soil erosion.

4 We Can Produce Everything

⌄ **Fishing boats off Gouqi Dao/Photo by Lu Jiamin**
Gouqi Dao, located in the east of Shengsi Liedao (Shengsi Islands), is relatively close to Zhoushan and Shanghai.

After the Opium War, Ningbo and Wenzhou were again opened for trade, and Zhejiang was once again able to use its sea ports. However, much time had passed, and the rise of Shanghai produced a huge siphon effect. Much of the capital from Jiangsu and Zhejiang gathered in Shanghai. Ningbo Port and Wenzhou Port remained undeveloped.

After 1949, Zhejiang was once again regarded as the front line of coastal defense, and almost ruled out as a part of the country's economic and industrial layout. From 1953 to 1978, Zhejiang's per capita investment in state-owned fixed assets was the lowest in the country.

In agriculture, Zhejiang's per capita arable land area in 1978 measured 0.68 *mu*, less than half of the national average. When reform and liberalization began in the late 1970s, the province was neither a state-owned industrial base like regions in northeastern China nor did it enjoy preferential policies of special economic zones like Shenzhen. All that Zhejiang could rely on were its people—people from all walks of life living in every corner of the province.

Xu Wenrong in Hengdian Town, Dongyang set up the Hengdian Reeling Silk Factory. Later, he established the most famous film studio in China: Hengdian World Studios.

In 1982, Li Shufu, a Taizhou native who just graduated from high school, made money by taking pictures for tourists. After amassing a certain amount of funds, he opened a photo studio. With the money earned from the photo studio, he then opened a refrigerator accessories factory. After the accessories factory made money, he opened a refrigerator factory. Later, he founded Geely, an automotive company.

In the same year, Xie Gaohua—the party chief of a small county known to few people—made a bold decision to establish a local small commodities market and allow farmers to do business. Now, people all over the country know the name of this place: Yiwu.

There are many people with similar stories. In 1987, Zong Qinghou, the founder of Hangzhou Wahaha Group, started by contracting a school-run business. To make money, he once rode a tricycle to hawk popsicles in the streets.

In 1993, several young people in Tonglu County started four separate express delivery and logistics companies, known as "Kuaidi" in Chinese, including STO Express, Best Express, YTO Express, and ZTO Express. They are called the Tonglu guild of China's logistics industry.

In 1995, English teacher Jack Ma began to make web pages for others.

Almost everyone started their own businesses, and almost every village had factory chimneys. Zhejiang's productivity began to develop fully in many directions. The sea ports became busy again, and containers and resources were piled up on the docks.

⌃ **Hengdian World Studios/Photo by Zhao Gaoxiang**
Hengdian World Studios is in Hengdian Town, Dongyang, Jinhua, Zhejiang. It was built in 1996 for Director Xie Jin's filming of the historical blockbuster *The Opium War*. Now it has become the largest film studio in China.

⌄ **A night market in Yiwu/Photo by Ding Junhao**
At the night market on Santing Road, Yiwu, the street is densely packed with stalls.

三姨路夜市

New "super business cards" appeared, and cities are changing with each passing day. Magnificent bridges span rivers and extend to the ocean. Zhejiang's economy grew suddenly. In terms of disposable income per capita, Zhejiang has ranked first among all provinces and autonomous regions in China for 17 consecutive years.

If you ask me, "What is Zhejiang?"

I will answer, "Zhejiang is unparalleled productivity."

Wenzhou/Photo by Ni Qianhui

The photo was taken on the Shizishan Viewing Deck, Sanjiang Street, Yongjia County, Wenzhou. In the picture, the Ouyue Bridge is at the forefront and the skyscraper in the distance is the Wenzhou World Trade Center.

Fujian is a mountainous province, with mountains and hills accounting for more than 80% of the total area. Fujian is also a place with high precipitation, with an average annual rainfall of over 2,000mm. Water converges to form rivers, waterfalls and lakes. The currents erode mountains day after day. Over the course of thousands of years, mountains are split and valleys take shape. Water flows around mountains and mountains block the water's path. The two gradually become interdependent. These are the mountains and rivers in Fujian. Nevertheless, the dream of Fujian lies in the ocean. It faces the sea and blossoms in the warmth of spring.

3.3 Fujian:

The Legend of Pioneers

Its history was extremely turbulent 1,700 years ago. The Rebellions of the Eight Princes of the Western Jin Dynasty and the Rebellion of Yongjia Reign completely reduced the originally prosperous Zhongyuan to nothing more than a battlefield. The Han people in Zhongyuan were forced to migrate on a massive scale to Jiangnan (the areas south to the Chang Jiang), historically referred to as "Yiguan Nandu" (South Migration of Zhongyuan Civilization).

However, before the memory of displacement dissipated, Jiangnan also became a region of many troubles. The rebellions of Wang Dun, Su Jun, Sun En, and Hou Jing broke out in Jiangnan one after another. As is shown in the verse titled *Ai Jiangnan Fu* ("*Mourning the Fall of the Liang Dynasty*"):

> *Hou Jing usurped the Liang throne and the capital Jinling fell. It was difficult to find people in villages and towns during the war, and people couldn't find shelter and were displaced.*
> —Yu Xin, *"Mourning the Fall of the Liang Dynasty"*

The suffering people could only flee to Fujian. The question was: Would Fujian be a newfound paradise?

‹ The map of Fujian

Fujian, referred to as "Min," is located on the southeast coast of China, with an area of approximately 124,000 square kilometers. The terrain of Fujian is high in the northwest and low in the southeast. The northern and central parts are all high mountains.
Mountains and hills account for more than 80% of the province's land area. Only a few plains are distributed on the southeast coast. Affected by this high terrain, most of Fujian's rivers form their own closed systems. At the same time, this geographical environment also makes it inconvenient for Fujianese to communicate with other inland provinces, and so more of its focus is placed on the ocean. Fujian boasts a unique history and has become a province with distinctive regional characteristics.

1 Thousands of Mountains and Rivers

To answer whether Fujian is a paradise, we need to start with a geographical overview of Fujian.

Fujian is a mountainous province with slopes and hills accounting for more than 80% of its total area.

Two large mountain systems run diagonally through the central and western parts of the province. The border between Fujian and Jiangxi in the west is the famous Wuyi Shan (Wuyi Mountains), and the middle part is the Minzhong Shan (Minzhong Mountain) system, composed of Jiufeng Shan (Jiufeng Mountain), Daiyun Shan (Daiyun Mountain), and Boping Shan (Boping Mountain).

Many peaks of Wuyi Shan are more than 1,500 meters above sea level. The highest peak, Huanggang Shan (Mount Huanggang), stands 2,161 meters above sea level, which is the highest mountain in the six surrounding provinces and one municipality in southeastern China. As far as the topography of the mountain is concerned, the side of Wuyi Shan facing Jiangxi is steep and mainly comprised of cliffs; The side facing Fujian is relatively gentle, with a stepped downward trend to its slope. Fujian is like a person sitting on a chair with a tall backrest, facing the sea and looking out over the blooming spring flowers.

There are two major types of landscapes in Wuyi Shan, the granite landform and Danxia landform. The most remarkable type is Danxia landform, which is composed of red sandstone. The vegetation in the mountains is dense. The green vegetation and the red mountains create contrasting echoes with each other, which is extraordinarily splendid to behold.

In addition to Wuyi Shan in the west, there are many other granite mountains in Fujian. Taimu Shan (Taimu Mountain) in northeastern Fujian is famous for its spectacular granite formations. The strange rocks seem to protrude above the clouds and fog as they overlook the sea.

› Dawang Feng (Dawang Peak) of Wuyi Shan/Photo by Wang Shimin

Dawang Feng is in the north of Jiuqu Xi (Nine-bend Stream). It is also called Gauze Cap Rock because of its shape that resembles a eunuch's gauze cap.

› Taimu Shan (Tianmu Mountain)/Photo by Lin Min

Taimu Shan is in the northeastern part of Fujian. It is a mountainous area composed of granite peaks and forests. In this picture, there are stone eggs formed by centuries of weathering on the top of the forest-covered peaks.

These tall mountains intercept water vapor, causing the average annual precipitation in the mountains of Fujian to exceed 2,000mm. The humid climate makes the forests grow densely, resulting in Fujian having the largest mid-subtropical forest ecosystem among areas at the same latitude around the world. Today, the amount of land covered by forest is as high as 65%, ranking among the top provinces in China.

The mountains have not only lush forests but also many waterfalls. They either drop straight down with all their might from mountaintops, or they fall layer by layer like a veil of water. Various waterfalls and springs gradually converge, forming large rivers and small streams that densely cover the entire province of Fujian, including Min Jiang, Jiulong Jiang (Jiulong River), Jin Jiang (Jinjiang River), Ting Jiang (Tingjiang River), Dai He (Daihe River), Huotong Xi (Huotong Stream), Jiao Xi (Jiaoxi Stream), Mulan Xi (Mulan Stream), Shangqing Xi (Shangqing Stream), and more. On average, there are about 100 meters of watercourse in every square kilometer, a density that is simply amazing.

Among these rivers, the upper reaches of Huotong Xi have the most abundant vegetation, which maintains the soil and water quality extremely well. It is the river with the smallest sediment content in Fujian. Xiashan Xi (Xiashan Stream) in Fuding winds and flows, and it looks like a big "S" if looked at from above. The famous Min Jiang is 562 kilometers long and is the longest and largest river in Fujian. Its runoff volume even exceeds that of Huang He, although the latter is about 10 times longer.

The river current cuts through the mountains day after day, carving deep grooves in the rocks. Thousands of years later, this splitting of the mountain has created river valleys both large and small. The water wraps around the mountain, and the mountain blocks the water. The two mutually reinforce, neutralize and complement each other.

1 | 2

1 Xiashan Xi/Photo by Lin Min

The picture shows Xiashan Xi in Chixi Village, Fuding, where the river takes a huge "S" turn.

2 Jiuqu Xi/Photo by Wu Yuchen

Jiuqu Xi originates from Wuyi Shan and meanders in a deep gorge among these hills.

Green mountains, clear waters, green trees, the Danxia landforms and the granite landscapes have already formed a beautiful picture. Now it's time to consider the waters that converge into still lakes in the mountains. At the foot of Sancai Feng (Sancai Peak) in Wuyi Shan, a lake glimmers with golden light under peaks shrouded in mist. Even more amazing is Wushan Tianchi (Heavenly Lake) in Changshan, Zhangzhou. The mountain and the water create a refreshing echo of each other. Wushan Tianchi is surrounded by striking peaks and rocks, combining elegance and magnificence.

These are the mountains and rivers of Fujian.

Confronted by the beautiful scenery of mountains and rivers, Jiang Yan, a poet and writer who moved from Henan to Fujian during the Southern Dynasties (420-589), once praised Fujian in his poem:

> *Some of the numerous rocks are red and some are green, and some of the overlapping mountains are dear and some are vague.*
>
> –Jiang Yan, Imitate the Analects

Zhu Xi, a master of Neo-Confucianism of the Song Dynasty, whose family originated from Jiangxi Province, was born in Fujian. He is well-known for his poems depicting Fujian:

The half-acre square pond is like a mirror. The light of the sky and the shadow of the cloud are shining and floating on the water.

—Zhu Xi, *After Reading a Book*

⌃ Wushan Tianchi/Photo by Zhang Yuanfeng

Wushan Tianchi is located in Zhangzhou, Fujian. Many granite peaks tower around the lake. The bare rocks and green vegetation find reflections in the calm water, creating something ethereal.

2 New Arrival

Thousands of mountains and numerous waters embellish Fujian.

Historically, especially for migrating refugees, Fujian seemed inaccessible. To enter Fujian, they had to climb over mountains and cross endless rivers. Torrential waters run through the mountains with formidable force and momentum, leaving a grid-like network. After finally crossing a mountain, the migrants had to cross a river; after crossing a river, they had to climb another mountain. The process repeated again and again. You can imagine the difficulty of the journey. This also made Fujian famous all over the country for its inconvenient and difficult terrain for travel. *Transport Monthly*, a magazine in the early years of the Republic of China period, once wrote:

> *In the hinterland of Fujian, there are numerous mountains and bumpy roads. These dangerous and narrow mountain roads are meandering. It often takes 10 days to walk for a distance of a hundred li (each li is equal to 0.5 kilometers) here.*

The most efficient "express delivery" system in ancient China, the so-named "800-li express" and "600-li express" post system, had to slow down by 50% in the mountains of Fujian and became "slow delivery." The Gazetteer of Fujian Province once described the delivery of official documents of Junji Chu, or the Grand Council, in Fujian during the Qing Dynasty as follows:

> *Once the important official documents sent by the Grand Council enter the border of Fujian, no matter the required delivery speed is three hundred li or six hundred li, they can only travel at a speed of no more than three hundred li each day and night.*

The high mountains and fragmented terrain allow different kinds of flora and fauna to thrive here. Take the Wuyi Shan area as an example: It has 2,527 species of plants and nearly 5,000 species of wild animals. In the eyes of the migrating refugees, however, the area was difficult to walk through due to the dense forests, pervading swampy miasma, and entangled vines. What was more, tigers and leopards might kill the refugees traveling amidst the mountains at any time.

Even if the refugees successfully struggled to find ways in the mountains, crossed the rivers, and narrowly escaped from any dangers along the way, they would be in dire need of a suitable piece of flat land to settle down. However, there were very few such places in the mountains, and most of the limited pieces of flat land had already been occupied. The rest of the land was covered by deep forests, lush grasses, or dense swamps. With backward tools and limited manpower, the refugees could not take advantage of the undeveloped land.

During this time, settlers were very likely to be looted, taken as slaves or killed by the locals. During the reign of Emperor Wu of the Han Dynasty, the court sent troops to forcibly relocate the Min people to the areas between Chang Jiang and Huai He, and Fujian almost became an uninhabited land. During the Three Kingdoms Period (220-280), the Eastern Wu (222-280) often ransacked the Min people, enlisting them forcibly into the army to go north to fight. Understandably, the local settlers were not friendly to outsiders.

Due to the abundant mountains and near-impossible transport conditions, it was very difficult to make a living in Fujian back then, which significantly limited the number of immigrants that settled in the province. The total population of Fujian in the Western Jin Dynasty was only 8,600 households. During the Sui Dynasty, there were only 12,000 households. On average, there was only one household per 10 square kilometers. It was the least populated area in southern China at that time. Such a small population could not produce the group effect that results in a "civilizational leap" and could only maintain a very basic standard of living.

However, changes were about to take place. A group of new immigrants would bring more advanced technology into Fujian. They would overcome their inner fears and the barriers to development, and they would fight not just to ensure their survival but also to realize their dreams.

Dawang Feng and Jiuqu Xi in Wuyi Shan/Photo by Lin Wenqiang

From the picture, we can see the luxuriant vegetation and dense water systems in Fujian.

Terraces in Fujian/Photo by Lin Wenqiang
Photographed in Zherong County, Ningde

3 The New Fujianese

About 1,300 years ago, the outlying prefectures of the Tang Dynasty often burst into conflict as the military governors attempted to seize power and wealth, and the Han people in the Zhongyuan region once again migrated to the south on a large scale. The turning point for the development of Fujian had arrived. The immigrants brought new tools to "conquer" mountains, rivers, forests, and swamps one by one. They cut down trees, opened roads in the mountains and built bridges over the rivers; they dug ditches, drained swamps, and turned wasteland into farmland; they intercepted streams, built water conservancy projects, and turned all four plains of Fujian into grain producing areas.

In the Sui Dynasty, Putian Pingyuan (Putian Plain) formed by alluvial deposits in the lower reaches of Mulan Xi was still a swamp filled with cattails, but after the water conservancy reform, it became a developed area. The same was true for Fuzhou Pingyuan (Fuzhou Plain), Quanzhou Pingyuan (Quanzhou Plain), and Zhangzhou Pingyuan (Zhangzhou Plain) formed by the alluvial accumulation of Min Jiang, Jin Jiang, and Jiulong Jiang.

For mountainous areas where farming was inconvenient, they used superb dam-building techniques and invested no less manpower than what had been required to build the Great Wall in the north, cultivating tens of thousands of acres of terraced fields. In Youxi County and Zherong County, the terraced fields extend layer by layer to the top of the mountains, looking like dense contour lines on a map if viewed from above.

The increase in arable land continuously attracted immigrants. In the heyday of the Tang Dynasty, there were 100,000 households in Fujian, and this number rose to 460,000 households in the early Song Dynasty. In the late Northern Song Dynasty and the early Southern Song Dynasty, the Jin army invaded, the Zhongyuan region fell into war once again, and northern residents moved south once again. They often migrated collectively, ranging from hundreds to thousands of people of the same clan. Not only were they large in number, but their social positions were also more diverse, including aristocrats, scholars, the poor from lower classes, street peddlers, and stragglers. By that time, the number of households in Fujian had reached 1.3 million, and Fujian had changed from the most sparsely populated area in the country to a densely populated area.

A *tulou*, or earthen building/Photo by Liu Yanhui
This picture shows the Chengqi Tower in the Gaobei Tulou Cluster in Gaotou Township, Yongding District, Longyan, Fujian. The picture presents the scene of a dragon parade during the Lantern Festival.

‹ Wenshan Kiln, Minhou County, Fuzhou/Photo by Qiu Jun

The ancient Wenshan kiln in Minhou County, Fuzhou is several stories high. People stand on a "ladder" made from bricks and then remove the bricks from top to bottom. In recent years, most of the bricks and tiles used in the renovation of Sanfang Qixiang, literally Three Lanes and Seven Alleys, were produced here.

› An ancient street in Taining County/Photo by Lin Daquan

The Ancient Town of Taining is in Taining County on the southern foot of Wuyi Shan. It is a well-preserved Ming Dynasty residential community in the Jiangnan area of China.

As for establishing a relationship with local aboriginal peoples, the immigrants wisely chose intermarriage. When their descendants traced the origins of their ancestors, they were often still proud of their native places in the north. By that time, immigrants from northern China had completely changed the bloodline structure and cultural identity of the Min people.

Whether you were an official, army man, aristocrat, or a powerful person, whether you were a peasant, criminal, Taoist, or monk, whether you were from Henan, Jiangxi, or Zhejiang, you became a new Fujianese, sharing the same identity.

Fujian began to accelerate its development. The Fujianese fired bricks and tiles and built various types of residential buildings, including *tulou*. Thousands of villages emerged from the wilderness, and the villages expanded and eventually became towns; they expanded again into counties; the counties expanded and became medium-sized cities. Fuzhou and Quanzhou both became famous throughout the country at this stage.

At this time, the high mountains and fragmented terrain still affected the daily life of the new Fujianese. They had a distinct Zhongyuan accent of the Tang and Song dynasties, but they had evolved independently in their small circles, developing more dialects. As a result, even the residents who were separated only by a single mountain or a river might not be able to communicate with each other. This created many culturally isolated islands with distinct traditions.

They had developed their own traditional operas. In addition to the five major genres of traditional operas such as the Min opera, there were more than 20 minor genres of traditional operas. They worshiped as many as 1,000 different kinds of deities and totems, including the snake, frog and horse, as well as Lao Tzu, the founder of Taoism. They built various temples in the mountains. Folk festivals here were also dazzling. For example, the dragon boat race in Sanxi Village of Changle will last for several hours and will not reach its climax until the evening. People call this the "Dragon Boat Night Cruise." In the dragon dances popular in Gutian Town, Liancheng County, the dragon's body will have hundreds of knots and a length of more than 500 meters. A dragon dance often requires hundreds of people to participate. It was locally called the "Dragon Parade."

The new Fujianese were committed to building roads and bridges, water facilities, terraced fields, villages, and towns, and developed a rich variety of languages and cultural customs across the province.

However, if Fujian had stopped its development here, it would still be just an ordinary province. Fujian had even more ambitious dreams.

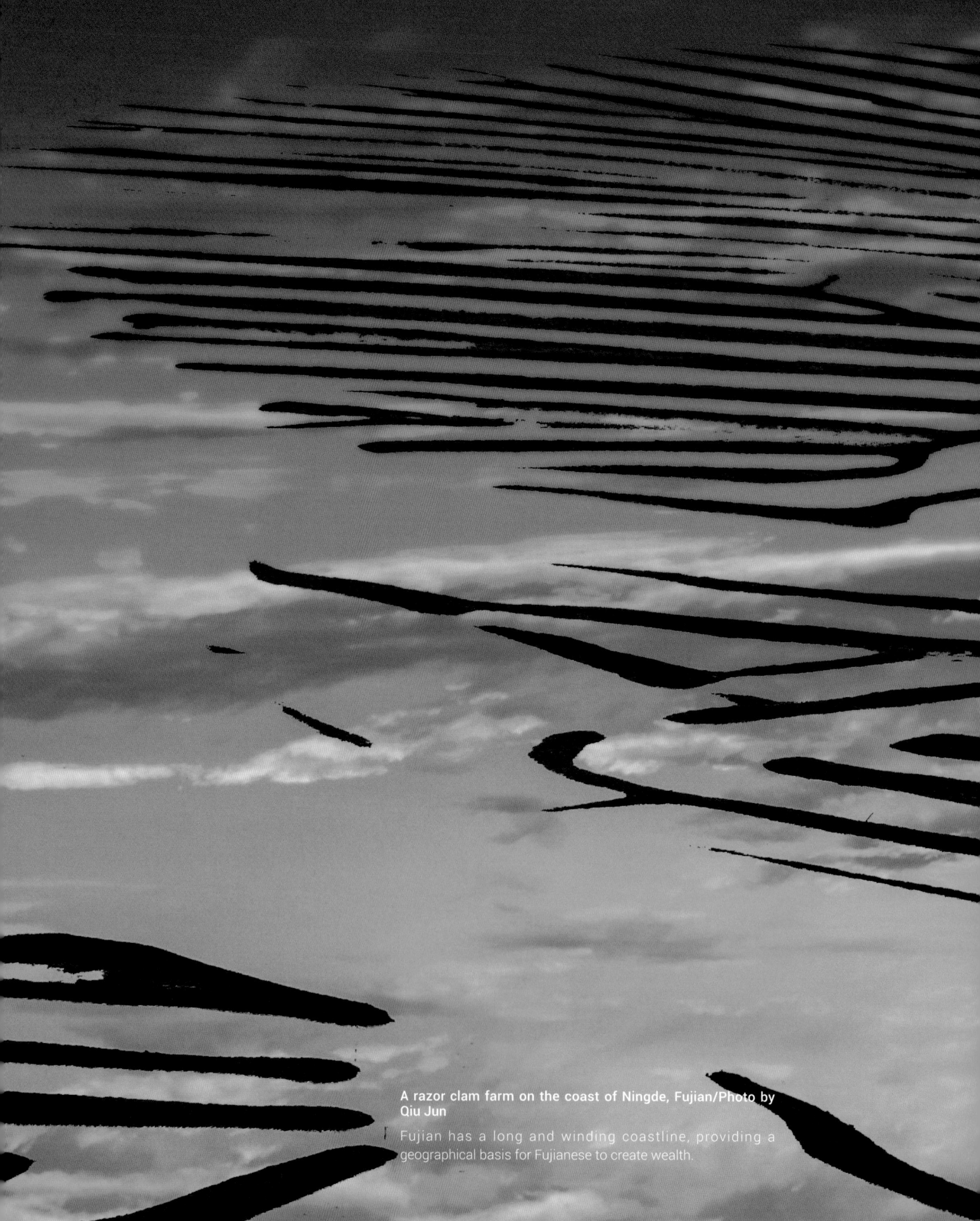

A razor clam farm on the coast of Ningde, Fujian/Photo by Qiu Jun

Fujian has a long and winding coastline, providing a geographical basis for Fujianese to create wealth.

4 Sea Ranch

Fujian's dream lies within the ocean.

The straight-line distance between the north and south coastlines of Fujian is only 500 kilometers, but due to the coast's twists and turns, the length of the province's coastline is 3,752 kilometers, the second-longest in the country.

Fujian has more than 1,400 islands. Dayushan Dao (Dayushan Island) in Ningde is a small island with scenery like the vast grasslands to the north of the Great Wall. There are also two lakes that are surrounded by peaks on the island. Dongshan Dao (Dongshan Island), located in Zhangzhou, is the second-largest island in Fujian. There are many colorful reefs around the island. When the sun rises, the view is particularly gorgeous.

The long coastline and numerous islands have enabled the Fujianese to make use of marine resources starting very early in their history. Some of the fishing villages they established have a history dating back thousands of years. They use the sea as their field, picking razor clams, collecting oysters, drying kelp, and catching fish fry. Local fishermen either sail out to fish on the sea or comb the tidal flats for crabs, and the scene of their busy work is like an abstract painting. More importantly, the ocean provides a channel for trade with the world. As the saying goes:

> *The land ends at the edge of the city, and the clouds on the sea come from the island.*
> —Han Wo, *Visiting the Pagoda of the South Shenguang Temple,*
> also known as *Visiting the South Taiceng Temple*

Fujianese built the best sea-going ships, which could carry more than 600 tons of cargo and more than 500 people each. An ordinary Fujian woman has been deified as the most powerful protector on the sea in Chinese mythology. She is Mazu. Under her protection, seagoing ships set off from Quanzhou and carried Chinese porcelain and tea to every corner of the world.

> Beiqi Village, Ningde, Fujian/Photo by Lyu Wei
This picture shows the scene of fishermen working on the beach.

Quanzhou/Photo by Wang Shimin
This picture shows the street view of the Licheng District in Quanzhou, with the Chaotian Gate at the center.

Gulangyu Islet/Photo by Chen Yanbin
Gulangyu, also known as Kulangsu, is located to the southwest off the coast of Xiamen. It is famous for its exotic architecture of various styles. The building in the middle of the picture is the Xiamen Marine Garden Hotel.

In less than three centuries, from the Tang Dynasty to the Yuan Dynasty, the prosperity of Quanzhou first surpassed Ningbo in the Northern Song Dynasty and then surpassed Guangzhou at the end of the Southern Song Dynasty. In the Yuan Dynasty, it became one of the world's most famous ports. The Italian explorer Marco Polo described Quanzhou of the Yuan Dynasty like this:

> *Many merchants gather here, the goods pile up like mountains, and the prosperity of business is beyond imagination.*

The prosperous maritime trade stimulated the industries of inland Fujian. Many people specialized in producing porcelain, textiles and other products for export. The most representative example of this was Wuyi rock tea. This kind of tea was exported in large quantities, and at one time it accounted for 1/3 of the country's total tea exports. This prompted Wuyi Shan to open countless tea gardens and formed a unique landscape. Tea farmers in Yongfu Town, Zhangping also planted the oriental cherry in their tea gardens, forming a unique tea-fruit farming pattern.

Fujian merchants not only exported their products but also imported many aspects of overseas cultures into the country. Southern Fujian merchants liked the Spanish red brick buildings which they had seen in the Philippines. They would rather overstep the ritual customs of the feudal system just for the pleasure of building bright red brick houses in their hometowns. In modern times, such absorption of exotic cultures has made the famous Gulangyu acquire its present appearance. This small island of only 1.78 square kilometers has many types of architecture, and it could even be called a World Architecture Museum.

Religion was also prospering in Fujian. Buddhism, Taoism, Christianity, Manichaeism, and Islam all had many followers in Fujian. During the Song and Yuan dynasties, Arab businessmen who believed in Islam gathered in Quanzhou and formed a group of considerable size.

At the same time, Fujian was also the birthplace for many talented people. In the Song Dynasty, there were more than 7,000 Jinshi (a successful candidate in the highest imperial examinations) in Fujian, and as many as 50 officials served as prime ministers in the imperial court.

In addition, many Fujianese have emigrated overseas, forming China's largest overseas Chinese business community. According to statistics, the number of people in this group exceeds 10 million.

The maritime trade was developed, the inland economy was booming, the culture was blooming, and its talented pioneers had spread all over the world. The great changes in Fujian were described like this:

> *Ouyue, which was dangerous and remote in the past, is now the most prosperous place in the southeast.*
> —Quoted from Wang Xiangzhi's *Yu Di Ji Sheng*

In 2024, Fujian's per capita GDP ranked 8th in China, and it is among the provinces currently seeing some of the fastest economic growth.

All of this is closely related to the pioneers in the history of Fujian, who overcame barriers and fought for their survival and dreams.

They were pioneers, adventurers, and explorers. They created a new world with their hard work and wisdom.

A beach at Xiaohao Village, Sansha Town, Xiapu County, Fujian/Photo by Qiu Jun

The urban aesthetics of Qingdao surpassed most other cities in China when it was first established. During the century that followed, although it regressed or stagnated, it immediately resumed its journey and started a new chapter. With many twists and turns, its development can be described as a condensed history of the evolution of Chinese urban aesthetics.

3.4 Qingdao:
A History of Urban Aesthetics

If you were living in the late Qing Dynasty or the Republic of China period, you would be shocked by the frequent rise and fall experienced by many Chinese cities. Even those with a history of thousands of years might decline almost overnight in response to the great changes during these times. Traditional industrial and commercial cities such as Xi'an, Zhenjiang, and Jiujiang suffered from an influx of imported goods, causing all domestic industries to be in decline. Huai'an, Jiading, and Yangzhou, which were crowded with boats and noted for commercial prosperity in the past, all experienced a dramatic decline due to the siltation of Jinghang Yunhe and could not recover after the setback. Suzhou, Nanchang, and Kaifeng were almost razed to the ground by years of war and natural disasters.

In accordance with the ebb and flow of traditional metropolises, emerging cities began to appear in large numbers in modern China. Under the strong demand of the industrial age, the mining industry led to the rise of Tangshan, Pingxiang, and Fushun. The increasingly important railways soon pushed Shijiazhuang, Zhengzhou, and Harbin to become seats of provincial capitals. Under the strong influence of the Western colonists, Shanghai, Tianjin, and Qingdao became new economic and cultural centers.

At the same time, people's views on urban construction were also changing. Scientific planning and intentional control of the overall style of the city began to draw public attention. We call this "urban aesthetics."

In this regard, Qingdao, one of the youngest cities in China, was particularly praised worldwide. In the first half of the twentieth century there were many scholars living in Qingdao, such as Cai Yuanpei, Shen Congwen, Ba Jin, Wen Yiduo, Yu Dafu and Lao She. They all admired and spoke highly of the city.

More than that, Liang Shiqiu regarded Qingdao as a paradise:

> *I have not been to heaven... Although I have not been to many places, I have traveled more than a dozen provinces from Liaodong in the north to Baiyue in the south. I think Qingdao should be the place where people linger and cannot bear to leave.*
>
> –Liang Shiqiu, *Recalling Qingdao*

Today, in addition to the two municipalities directly under the Central Government—Beijing and Tianjin, Qingdao is not only a city with great economic strength in northern China. It is also a popular tourist destination that draws people from around the country. Many people have an inexplicable affection for and fascination with Qingdao.

Why does Qingdao, which has much fewer historical legacies than many other cities, enjoy such a high reputation?

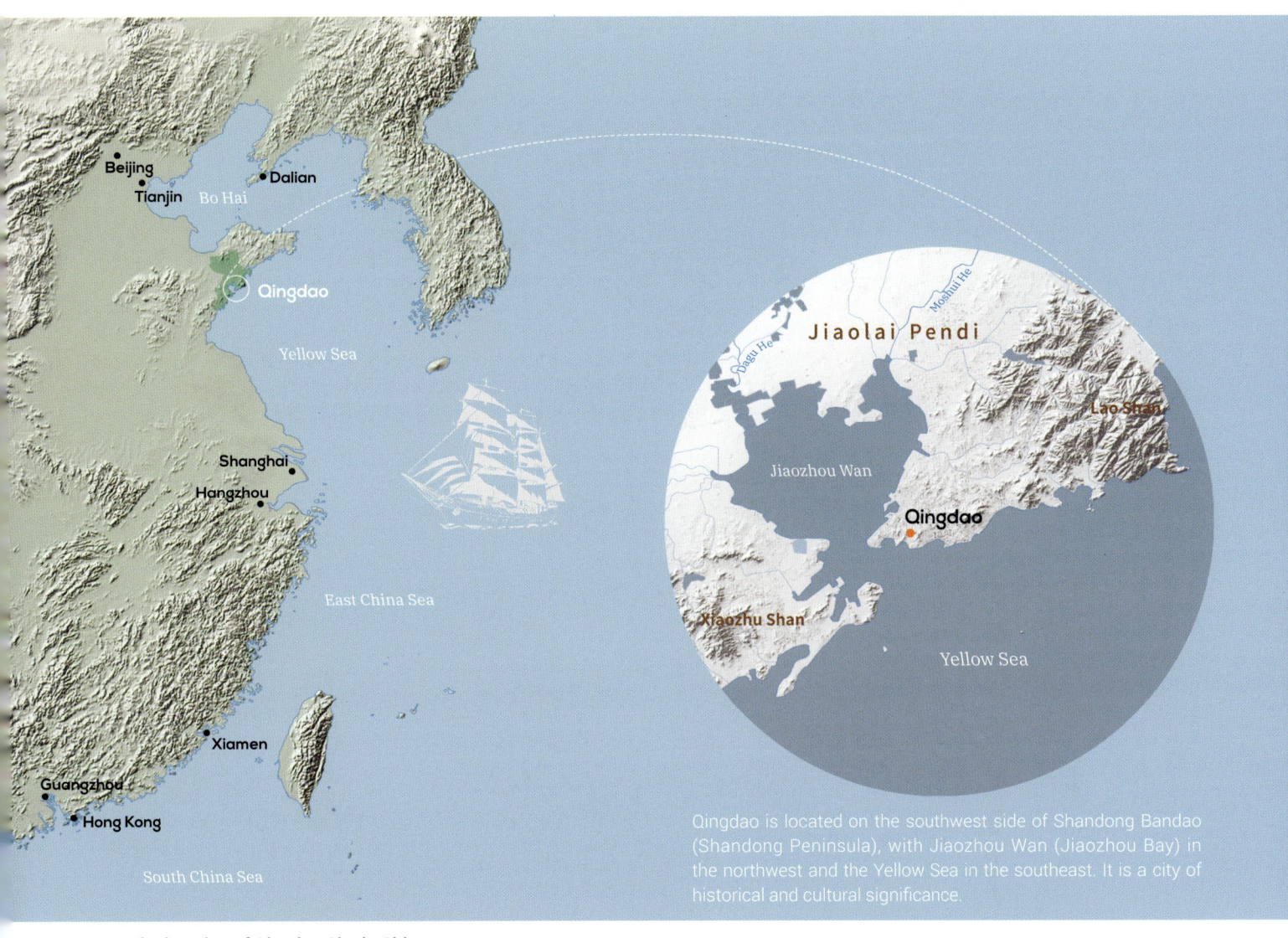

Qingdao is located on the southwest side of Shandong Bandao (Shandong Peninsula), with Jiaozhou Wan (Jiaozhou Bay) in the northwest and the Yellow Sea in the southeast. It is a city of historical and cultural significance.

▲ The location of Qingdao City in China

From the perspective of urban aesthetics, the Institute for Planets will discuss how Qingdao developed. In fact, Qingdao's urban aesthetics surpassed those of most other cities that emerged in the same period in China as Qingdao was first being built. In the hundred years following its birth, although development may have stopped or regressed at times, the city always opened a new chapter shortly afterwards. These ups and downs epitomize the evolution of urban aesthetics in China.

1 The Prototype of Qingdao

Qingdao is located at the southwestern end of Shandong Bandao (Shandong Peninsula), bordered by Daze Shan (Daze Mountains) in the north, the Yellow Sea in the south, and Jiaolai Pendi (Jiaolai Basin) which spreads from east to west across the middle of the peninsula.

Where the land and the sea meet, Lao Shan (Mount Laoshan), Dazhu Shan (Dazhu Mountain), Xiaozhu Shan (Xiaozhu Mountain), and Tiejue Shan (Tiejue Mountain), tower aloft one after another, surrounding and protecting Jiaozhou Wan (Jiaozhou Bay). The highest peak of Lao Shan reaches 1,132 meters above sea level, which makes it the highest mountain on the coastline of China's mainland. The mountains protrude into the sea and the sea murmurs at the foot of the mountains. When there is a fog, the landscapes are like a Chinese ink painting. Where the mountains and the sea are connected, there are reefs and rocks. As the stormy waves hit the shore, the fine sand whispers with tenderness like water.

Far from the coast, many islands are covered with lush vegetation and are isolated from the rest of the world. In addition, Qingdao has a rugged coastline with bays and capes, and there are as many as 49 bays of varied sizes. The geography makes Qingdao a good natural port of significant economic and military value.

In ancient times, the people of Qingdao considered the sea as their home and made a living through fishing. By the Qing Dynasty, hundreds of villages had been formed, with tens of thousands of residents in total.

In 1892, the Qing Empire decided to make coastal Qingdao (then known as "Jiao'ao") a naval defense base and began to improve its fortifications. Streets of different widths and more than 60 shops appeared. As an emerging city, Qingdao had officially stepped onto the stage of history.

At that time, however, people did not realize Qingdao's great potential. It was merely regarded as a military base and people still lacked a true understanding of how to get the most out of its urban capacity.

‹ **Zhanqiao Pier in Qingdao/Photo by Wang Gang**
The trestle bridge, built in 1892, is the first artificial pier in modern Qingdao.

A fishing village at the foot of Lao Shan/Photo by Chai Dicheng
This picture shows Huangshan Village located at the eastern foot of Lao Shan.

2 The First Upgrade

The man who discovered Qingdao's potential was the famous German traveler and geographer Ferdinand von Richthofen, also known for inventing the term "Silkroad." He had made several trips to China and knew the country very well. After his explorations, he tried his best to propose to the German government that they occupy Qingdao:

> *A railway network extending to North China can be built here... If you want to develop the power of the Far East, you must occupy Jiaozhou Bay.*
> *—Quoted from* A Commentary on the Activities of Foreign "Explorers" in China in the Late Qing Dynasty *by Guo Shuanglin.*

By the end of the 19th century, Germany—although it had missed out on the golden age when the great powers divided the world—began to establish itself as a world power. Its economic growth rate far exceeded that of traditional powers such as Britain and France. Therefore, they had ambition and a great desire to prove to the world, by building a "model colony," that Germany could also surpass those old empires in managing colonies.

Qingdao was the best choice for this "model colony." It had excellent geographical conditions, Germany did not need to share it with other powers like Shanghai, and the city did not already have too much existing urban infrastructure like Tianjin. Qingdao was like a piece of blank paper, allowing the Germans to build a colony according to their own blueprint. On November 14, 1897, the German navy sent troops to occupy Qingdao. The preindustrial, waning Qing Empire was forced to concede the area to Germany.

The colonists were full of ambition, and a "model city" was about to emerge. They were not eager to carry out large-scale urban construction immediately, so they first conducted a thorough land survey. After the

> **The former Kiautschou Governor's Hall and its surrounding buildings/Photo by Lu Hui**

The southern half of the central square building (in the left half of the picture) is the former Kiautschou Governor's Hall, and the northern half (in the right half of the picture) is a new building built after 1949 in the same style. The six roads around the square on the left can be seen from this aerial photo.

completion of the first urban planning in Qingdao's history, construction then began in full swing.

Colonists forcibly drove out the local residents and tore down their houses. The local residents were discriminated and forced to live in a different area from the colonists. The administrative center of the entire city radiated out from around the Kiautschou Governor's Hall. Right in front was an open square, and six radial roads met in the square, highlighting the central position of the Governor's Hall, which was built on the hillside of Guanhai Shan (Guanhai Mountain). The four-story building stands 20 meters high, and it has a gross area of 7,500 square meters.

The building featured a modern steel structure, using steel shipped from Germany by Krupp. The facade was constructed with polished granite ashlars that could be seen everywhere in Qingdao. The entire building is solemn and majestic.

To ensure the quality of construction, the colonial government hired architects and professional technical workers from Germany. The building materials, machinery, and equipment that could not be produced locally were shipped directly from Germany. The Governor of Jiao'ao visited the construction site personally after getting off work, and he even climbed onto the scaffolding to check the quality of the construction project, allowing no errors at all. Detailed regulations regarding all administrative, religious and residential buildings were made through legislative means:

> *The height of a house shall not exceed 18 meters, with no higher than three floors. The area occupied by the building shall be less than 6/10 of that of the homestead. The distance between two adjacent buildings shall be three meters, or four meters when there are windows.*
> —Legal document "Land Purchase Regulations" during the German colonial rule

⌄ The former Kiautschou Governor's Hall/Photo by Chen Xi

This picture shows the former Kiautschou Governor's Hall. The street in front of it is Yishui Road of Shinan District, Qingdao. The building was designed by the German architect Friedrich Mahlke between 1901 and 1902 based on the style of European public buildings in the 19th century, and it was constructed in 1903. The main building was completed in 1905 and was opened in the spring of 1906 as the Jiao'ao Governor's Palace. Today, this is the office of Qingdao Municipal People's Congress Standing Committee and Qingdao Municipal Committee of the Chinese People's Political Consultative Conference.

One of the regulations had a more pronounced impact on Qingdao. It mandated that the shapes of buildings could not be repeated. This regulation directly caused buildings of various styles and types to be built in Qingdao.

For example, the 30-meter-high Governor's Hall with floor areas exceeding 4,000 square meters was one of the most luxurious buildings in Qingdao under German colonial rule. Its architectural style was a combination of neo-Roman and Jugendstil. The large-area open verandah with pillars and the orderly arrangement of granite finishing made this building extremely vivid. Viewed from different angles, the building accentuates different landscapes.

The Evangelische Kirche built in 1910 has a clock tower with a striking shape. The clock tower renders the entire area into a space with a strong sense of European style, imbuing a great amount of charm that changes its feel in different seasons and when viewed from various angles.

Other representative historical buildings of various shapes in Qingdao included the Jiaozhou Post Office, Seaside Hotel, Barbershop on Prince Henry Road, Anna Villa, and more.

In addition to the pursuit of fine architectural details, the Germans also attached great importance to the city's landscaping. To this end, a special "Forest Service Office" was established, and they spared no effort to introduce tree species such as the oriental plane tree, locust tree, and ginkgo biloba. Qingdao was known as a green city throughout the country at that time, and even cities like Shanghai and Beijing sent representatives here to learn from its landscaping expertise. Green plants were also interspersed between the buildings and on both sides of the roads. An old saying described Qingdao as a city with "red tiles, green trees, blue sky, and blue sea." Qingdao, in this regard, was unique among all the cities in China.

∧ The Evangelische Kirche/Photo by Zhang Xiao

The Protestant Church in the Jugendstil style is a building that sets off the landscapes along several nearby streets such as Yishui Road and Longshan Road.

∨ Qingdao Post and Telecommunications Museum/Photo by Wang Kai

This is the former site of the German Empire Post Office in Jiao'ao. The intersection in the picture is the crossroads of Guangxi Road and Anhui Road. The post office was originally constructed from 1900 to 1901 and was the seat of the German postal agency in Qingdao under German colonial rule. It is now the Qingdao Post and Telecommunications Museum.

Kiautschou Governor's Hall / Photo by Wang Kai

Standing atop Xinhao Shan (Signal Hill), we can see that the building is surrounded by various tree species.

As there were mountainous areas and hills in the urban area of Qingdao, the architecture was built according to the terrain. The contours of the building complexes were undulating and staggered, forming impressive landscapes.

In general, the construction of Qingdao by the Germans laid the foundation for the city's urban layout and style during the modern time. This was the origin of Qingdao's urban aesthetics.

At that time, Qingdao was no longer an ordinary small fishing village or military fortress, but a city with distinctive characteristics. The economic development of the city was equally impressive. The Qingdao Port, built with the world's most advanced technology and concepts at the time, had been hailed as "the largest port in the Far East" since its completion. It surpassed Hong Kong and Shanghai in many aspects, and the Germans' goal of building a "model colony" was initially realized.

However, the "good time" did not last long. After the Germans ruled Qingdao for 17 years, World War I broke out. In 1914, Japanese troops occupied the city after Japan's declaration of war on Germany. The Japanese colonists adopted an approach to rule Qingdao completely different from that of the Germans. They focused more on the rapid expansion and short-sighted plundering, including moving tens of thousands of Japanese nationals to Qingdao to fully control Qingdao's industrial, commercial, and financial sectors. Although the size of Qingdao's urban area during this period tripled compared to the period of the German occupation, such expansion remained disorderly and spontaneous, without a long-term planning. The quality of architecture in this period also declined significantly. Overall, it was a big step backward.

The days of stagnation and decline were long. The second improvement of Qingdao's urban aesthetics would not come until more than 10 years later.

> A panoramic view of the old district of Qingdao/Photo by Zhang Xiao

The photo was taken at Fada Building, Zhongshan Road, Qingdao. Observing the old district of Qingdao from here, you can see distinctive buildings against the mountains, with red tiles and green trees complementing each other.

3 The Second Upgrade

After the end of World War I, slogans such as "we would rather fight to death to recover Qingdao" resounded throughout the country during the May 4th Movement. Although the Beiyang government recovered Qingdao in 1922, in the following years, the warlords kept fighting with each other in China, and the Chinese people lived in misery. In the chaos, Qingdao's urban construction plummeted. People at the time commented on Qingdao's architecture in the 1920s:

> *The Chinese buildings in recent years... have adopted the principle of excessive perfectionism in terms of material selection and construction. They are not as strong and neat as those built by the Germans.*
>
> —Qingdao Choreography, *Gazetteer of Jiao'ao*

It was not until 1931 that the admiral of the Chinese naval troops stationed in Qingdao, Shen Honglie, was appointed as mayor of Qingdao that the city gradually moved away from the war, and the situation stabilized.

The second upgrade of Qingdao's urban aesthetics began. This time it was completely dominated by the Chinese.

First, the Qingdao municipal government improved regulations on urban construction. It set up an urban engineering design committee to focus on improving the quality of the city buildings. There was even a building construction aesthetic committee responsible for stopping buildings that did not conform to Qingdao's overall style and rewarding excellent designs.

The well-known Badaguan, or the Eight Great Passes, reached its peak during this period. It was dominated by two-and-three-story mansions with exquisite designs. The place was cordial and quiet, just like a tranquil village hidden in the hustle and bustle of the city.

∧ A mansion in the Badaguan area/Photo by Wang Kai

The photo was taken at the entrance of No.1 Branch Road of Zhengyangguan. Zhengyangguan (literally, Zhengyang Pass) was one of the Eight Great Passes. The road radiates to five directions here. The building in the picture is a Nordic country-style mansion at No. 22 Shaoguan Road.

∨ Autumn scenery at Zhanshan 3rd Road/Photo by Zhang Xiao

The Zhanshan Street is in the east of Shinan District, Qingdao, Shandong. It is named after Zhan Shan (Zhanshan Mountain) in the north. The vegetation on both sides of the road has become a great landscape.

Secondly, the Qingdao municipal government optimized the road landscapes through greening and some special designs, making many roads in Qingdao quite charming.

The most classic was the use of "opposite scenery," a method of Chinese ancient garden design, that is, to appreciate one landscape from another, and the two sights facing each other will produce a wonderful visual feast.

We can take St. Michael's Cathedral built in 1934 as an example. This is a 56-meter-tall building with twin towers, which is striking in Qingdao's city proper. Against the streetscape, the cathedral towering at the end of the road looks particularly magnificent and beautiful. In this case, the architecture is highlighted and looks more impressive. People can look up at the spires of the cathedral's twin towers hidden in lush trees or overlook them from the top of a mountain in the heart of the city.

1 | 2

1 St. Michael's Cathedral/Photo by Zhang Xiao

St. Michael's Cathedral is a Catholic church that stands at the top of a hill at the intersection of Zhejiang Road and Dexian Road. In addition to its beautifully decorated facade, it is also the opposite scenery of Zhejiang Road and Feicheng Road. The picture was taken on Feicheng Road.

2 St. Michael's Cathedral/Photo by Li Wenbo

The photo was taken on Zhejiang Road. Looking at St. Michael's Cathedral from here, you could see the spires of its twin towers and the trees on both sides of the road setting off each other.

Finally, unlike the periods under the German and Japanese colonial rules, the Qingdao municipal government under the Chinese rule paid more attention to the balanced development of urban and rural areas and the transformation of slums on the fringes of the city. With unified planning and layout, each courtyard was equipped with faucets and public toilets to meet people's basic needs.

A kind of residential building that originated in the period of the German occupation—Li Yuan, or Li courtyard—was constructed on a large scale during the period. This type of architecture combined the styles of European townhouses and Chinese quadrangle dwellings. It could accommodate more people in a limited building area. The residents included ordinary staff, lower-level officers, workers, and small traders. In 1932, Qingdao had 506 Li courtyards, accommodating 10,669 households. Today we can appreciate the geometric beauty of this type of residence more clearly with the help of aerial photography technology. We just do not know how many "Qingdao Dreams" were hidden in this kind of small patios back then.

In 1935, the Qingdao municipal government unveiled the first blueprint for the city's development drafted by Chinese planners based on the remarkable urban construction achievements it had made, which even included a planned railway linking Qingdao and Europe via Xinjiang. It was an ambitious project.

However, before the blueprint was implemented, the Japanese invaders caused Qingdao's development to stagnate again. The third upgrade of Qingdao's urban aesthetics didn't arrive until decades later.

‹ Li courtyards after snow/Photo by Lu Hui

Li courtyard is a kind of unique residential building in Qingdao. According to Essentials of Qingdao, it is "a combination of Chinese and Western architectural styles." Its buildings are constructed along the streets, which are connected to form a courtyard in the center. Most of these buildings have two to three stories. The 1st floor is mostly for commercial use, and the second floor and above are residential buildings.

4 The Third Upgrade

After the end of the Chinese People's War of Resistance against Japanese Aggression, Qingdao experienced the War of Liberation and tortuous exploration in the early days of the People's Republic of China. Some buildings were destroyed and the city's architectural style changed drastically. For example, under the influence of Soviet architectural theory, many halls and sanatoriums featuring "thick beams and columns" appeared between 1950 and 1960. In the early stage of the reform and opening up, destruction and disharmony intensified in the blind worship of skyscrapers. The most typical example is the Donghai Grand Hotel built in 1990. It stands upright on the bay and spoils the scenery.

Real changes have occurred in recent years. The ability of human beings to transform natural and geographical conditions has been enhanced rapidly. We can reclaim land from the sea, remove mountains, and fill valleys. The cityscape of Qingdao has completely gone out of the previous development context and has taken on a brand-new look. The city is no longer all about red tiles and green trees, but tall buildings that are distributed compactly and densely.

1 | 2

1 The coastline of Qingdao/Photo by Lu Hui

The red building in the middle is Qingdao's iconic sculpture "Wind of May" in memory of the May Fourth Movement of 1919.

2 The old and new views of Qingdao City/Photo by Lu Hui

From the former German governor's residence in the foreground to the courtyard buildings in the middle ground and then to modern skyscrapers in the background, this picture gathers buildings of various styles from different historical periods in Qingdao.

Unlike other cities full of skyscrapers, Qingdao's characteristics are still quite different. Its coastlines are extremely beautiful with large and small bays successively and continuously in endless succession. The urban buildings and the sea are interspersed, and the coastal buildings are overlapped layer by layer according to the terrain, creating a unique landscape.

On the land, the rigidity of the dense high-rise buildings is neutralized by towering peaks, which helps Qingdao maintain a wild vibe with its concrete jungle.

At night, the city lights are bright, piercing through the mist, and the scene is even more magnificent. When the fog is thick, the entire city will be completely shrouded, and only some scaffoldings will emerge above the mist, revealing the heated and fast-changing urban construction on the ground. While the new district of the city rises rapidly, the distinctive old district has not vanished. The two contrasting facets of Qingdao co-exist in great harmony.

Whether Qingdao will retain red tiles, green trees, blue sky, and blue sea in the future may be determined by our generation, because the time for the third upgrade of Qingdao's urban aesthetics has come.

If there is a place in China that boasts all the good things people long for, it is undoubtedly Jiangnan. Numerous poems and literary works depict Jiangnan as paradise on earth with its excellent climate, pleasant scenery, great prosperity and the tender affection one can feel coming from this place. The region represents the ultimate yearning for a better life that fills Chinese people's hearts.

3.5 Jiangnan:
A Great Feast of River, Lake, and Sea

The map of Jiangnan

As a term, the regions that belong to Jiangnan may be interpreted differently depending on the context. This article selects the core areas that best represent Jiangnan, namely the lower reaches of Chang Jiang and Qiantang Jiang as well as Taihu Pingyuan (Taihu Plain).

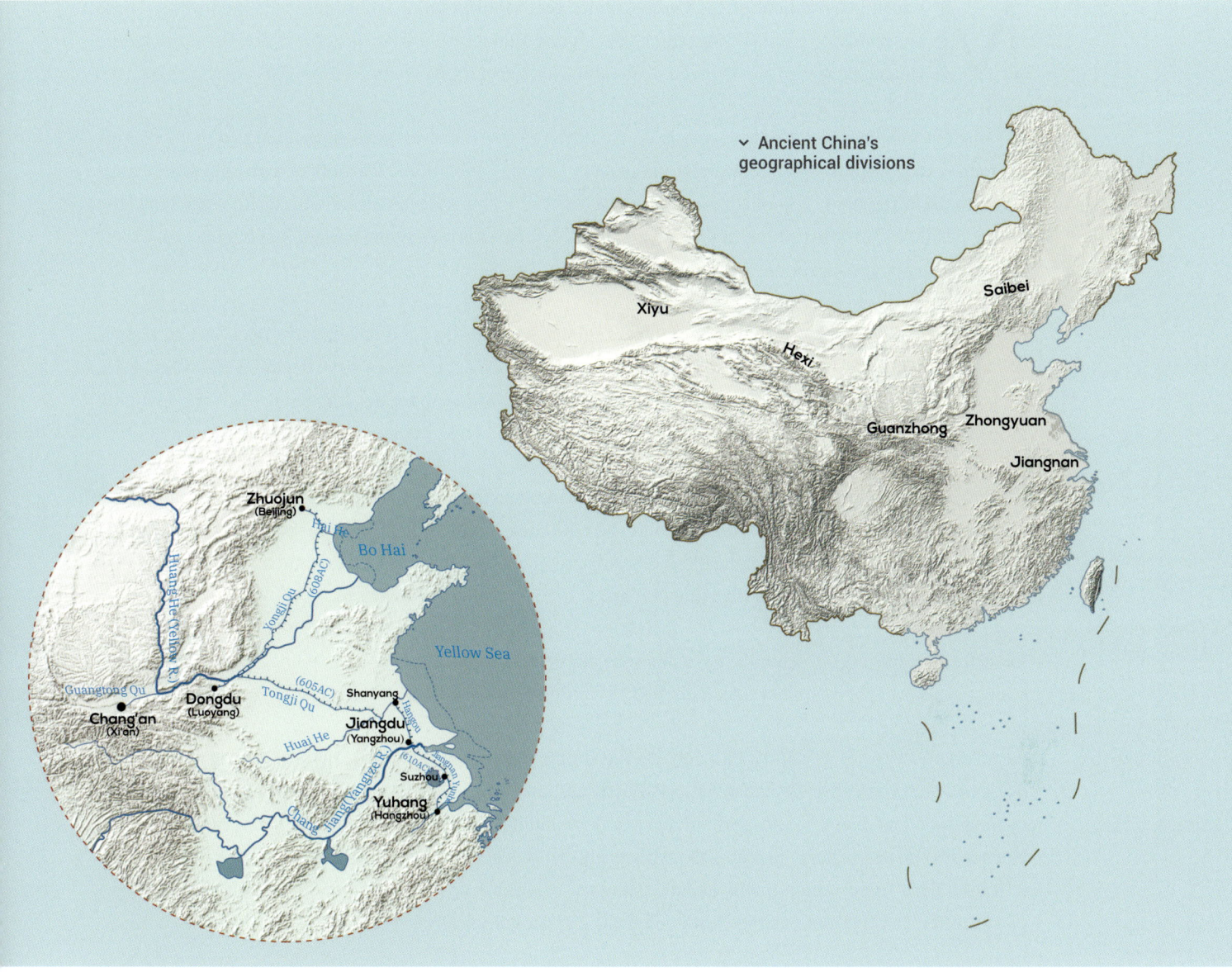

▲ Jinghang Yunhe during the Sui and Tang dynasties

From 605 to 610, Emperor Yang of the Sui Dynasty recruited millions of laborers to build Jinghang Yunhe, which was intended to supply Luoyang. This canal linked Hangzhou in the south and Beijing in the north. For the first time, the five major water systems of Qiantang Jiang, Chang Jiang, Huai He, Huang He, and Hai He were connected, representing the peak of canal excavation in China. After the collapse of the Sui Dynasty, the Tang Dynasty continued to use and dredge Jinghang Yunhe. The continued use of this waterway led it to be referred to as the "Sui-Tang Grand Canal."

Modern geographers often divide China's geographical units according to its landforms. There are plateaus, such as Qingzang Gaoyuan and Huangtu Gaoyuan, and there are plains, including Huabei Pingyuan and Dongbei Pingyuan (Northeast China Plain).

The ancient people who inhabited what is now modern China, however, gave geographical regions charming names that were based on cultural homogeneity and the topographic features of a given region. Jiangnan ("South of the River"), Saibei ("North of the Great Wall"), Zhongyuan, Guanzhong ("Within the Wall," the Weihe Basin), Hexi ("West of the Yellow River"), and Xiyu (Western Regions, today's Xinjiang) are all examples of this naming convention.

However, the old names of some geographical regions, such as Xiyu and Saibei, have been lost to history and are consequently no longer used by modern people. Some of the regions have declined and faded away, such as Zhongyuan and Guanzhong. After the highs and lows that have accompanied a history spanning thousands of years, only Jiangnan remains a place that most Chinese people yearn for to this very day.

Here, "Jiangnan" doesn't refer to all areas south of Chang Jiang in a strict geographical sense, but rather it is a blend of cultural and geographical concepts. Its core areas include the lower reaches of Chang Jiang and Qiantang Jiang as well as Taihu Pendi (Taihu Basin) that is nestled in between. The total area is about 80,000 square kilometers, which is less than one percent of the country's total land area.

Nevertheless, this region seems to have amassed all the things that Chinese people imagine to be beautiful. Many places over the years have been dubbed as "Little Jiangnan."

For example, as early as 1,400 years ago, during the Northern and Southern Dynasties, Ningxia Pingyuan (Ningxia Plain) was called "Jiangnan in northwestern China." Today, our geographical horizons have been extremely broadened, and we possess a deeper understanding of the diversity of China's natural and cultural landscapes. However, many people still respectively call Nyingchi in the Xizang Autonomous Region and Yili in the Xinjiang Uygur Autonomous Region "Jiangnan of Xizang" and "Jiangnan of Saiwai," although the two places differ sharply from Jiangnan both culturally and geographically.

Why do the Chinese like Jiangnan so much? Why has their preference remained as strong as it was a thousand years ago?

In fact, unlike other regions, the rise of Jiangnan is not some one-off achievement. Rather, over the past thousand years, especially five major cities in the region have taken turns to push Jiangnan to the peak of economy and culture. These five cities are closely related to the neighboring rivers, lakes, and seas. Thus, the region can be called a great feast of river, lake, and sea.

The Xitang Ancient Town/Photo by Zhao Gaoxiang
The Xitang Ancient Town, located in Jiashan, Zhejiang, was once a bustling commercial hub south of Chang Jiang.

1 The Era of Chang Jiang

The Chang Jiang era came first.

At the end of the Western Jin Dynasty, many Western Jin imperial clans and gentry moved south following the Upheaval of the Eight Princes and the Rebellion of Yongjia Reign. Nanjing, which was the beneficiary of the natural feature that is Chang Jiang, became the best choice for the revival of the Jin Dynasty.

Chang Jiang rushes past Nanjing to the north and to the west and could block attacks from aggressors coming down from the north. In addition, Zhong Shan (Zhongshan Mountain), the Stone City, Jinhua Shan, Jilong Shan (Mount Jilong), and other mountainous areas lie in front of Nanjing. The city was also surrounded by rivers and lakes such as Xuanwu Hu (Xuanwu Lake) and Qinhuai He (Qinhuai River). The mountains, rivers and lakes therefore constituted a natural barrier for the forces within Jiangnan. Zhuge Liang once wrote about the geographical advantages of Nanjing:

> *Zhongshan Mountain winds like a dragon, and the Stone City resembles a crouching tiger. This is an ideal abode for the emperor*
>
> —Zhang Bo, *Records of Wu*

The confluence of Wai Qinhuai He (Outer Qinhuai River) and Chang Jiang/ Photo by Fang Fei
On the left of the picture are Wai Qinhuai He in downtown Nanjing, and on the right is Chang Jiang.

In 317, Sima Rui, the prince of Langya, ascended the throne in Nanjing, becoming the first emperor of the Eastern Jin Dynasty (317-420). Since then, successive dynasties in the Southern Dynasties Period made Nanjing their capital city. Hence, Nanjing is dubbed the "Capital of the Six Dynasties."

In this context, Nanjing rapidly rose to prominence.

The Han people who fled to the south brought culture and technology from Zhongyuan to Nanjing, and a large swaths of wasteland was reclaimed as farmland. This boosted grain production and promoted population growth.

With the natural benefits provided by Chang Jiang, Qinhuai He, and other river systems, Nanjing became a gathering place for a burgeoning population and the wealth of Jiangnan. The wharfs often berthed thousands of merchant ships from both home and abroad. Six dynasties claimed Nanjing as their capital over the years, bringing Jiangnan to a stage of large-scale development for the first time. An old description of the city says, "Jinling (Nanjing) has millions of households and is the capital city of six dynasties." Wu Jingzi, a Chinese scholar and writer, wrote in his *Unofficial History of the Scholars*:

> *(Nanjing's) servants who deliver the food and its bartenders have the temperament of six dynasties.*

In addition, the years of wars and chaos following the end of the Eastern Han Dynasty led to the flourishing of Buddhism. Many temples were erected in the Jiangnan area with Nanjing as the center thanks to a strong push from the ruling class of the Southern Dynasties. Du Mu, a poet of the Tang Dynasty, once wrote:

> *More than 480 ancient temples of the Southern Dynasties remain to this day. Countless pavilions are shrouded in mist and rain.*
>
> —Du Mu, *The Spring of Jiangnan*

After the Northern and Southern Dynasties, the Sui Dynasty unified China and re-established its capital in the north. Since then, Nanjing has never been able to hold its position as a capital city for a long period, and the era of Chang Jiang with Nanjing as the center came to an end.

> Nei Qinhuai He (Inner Qinhuai River)/Photo by Fang Fei

During the Six Dynasties, both sides of Nei Qinhuai He were bustling residential areas and commercial districts.

Jiming Temple/Photo by Chen Guoxi

The Jiming Temple is located at the eastern foot of Jilong Shan (Jilong Mountain), Xuanwu District, Nanjing. It is a renowned Buddhist temple in Nanjing. The original construction time is debatable, but the current building was rebuilt in 1980.

2 The Era of Jinghang Yunhe

When Yang Guang, the talented and resourceful Emperor Yang of the Sui Dynasty, noticed how the empire's economic center was shifting southward, he considered making the construction of a link between the north and south to bridge the gap a top priority. With that, an unprecedented super project was launched—the construction of Jinghang Yunhe.

That project propelled Jiangnan into its second historical period, the Era of Jinghang Yunhe.

From 605 to 610, the Sui Dynasty dug and dredged the Tongji Channel, Han Conduit, Yongji Channel, and the Jiangnan Canal, which collectively formed Jinghang Yunhe with a length of more than 2,000 kilometers. With the construction of this canal, the five major river systems of Hai He (Haihe River), Huang He, Chang Jiang, and Qiantang Jiang were connected. The town of Yangzhou, located on the northern border of Jiangnan, became the hub for north-south transportation.

The Jiangnan area was densely covered with rivers, lakes, and water networks. The construction of Jinghang Yunhe connected these natural rivers into a complete water transport network that linked villages and towns. As a result, money, food, and products in Jiangnan could be transported via Jinghang Yunhe to Yangzhou on the north bank of Chang Jiang, where they could then be transferred to every corner of the country. Talent from the north likewise travelled straight to Jiangnan via Yangzhou. The area of Yangzhou teemed with merchants and shops. It gradually became the economic and cultural center of the country.

Yangzhou took to the stage.

The government of the Tang Dynasty, which followed the Sui Dynasty, carried on with the dredging of Jinghang Yunhe, and Yangzhou's economy and culture continued to prosper. The poem "Downstream to Yangzhou amid Misty April Flowers," was widely circulated among the literati and poets at that time.

‹ **Shou Xi Hu (Slender West Lake)/Photo by Wu Cixin**

The picture shows the Fishing Platform of Shou Xi Hu. Peach blossoms, lake water, pavilions, and willows set each other off. Everything is dreamlike.

After the An-Shi Rebellion during the Tang Dynasty, people from the north once again moved south en masse, and the already prosperous Jiangnan was particularly attractive to these people in need of a new home. Stimulated by the influx of new population, the development of Chang'an and the city of Luoyang, became one of the richest in the world. People would say, "Yangzhou first and Yizhou second." served as an official in Yangzhou, wrote many poems about the richness, prosperity, romance, and passion of Yangzhou.

The poet Zhang Hu even wrote that "one should only die in Yangzhou."

However, the once prosperous city of Yangzhou was destroyed during the endless wars in the late Tang Dynasty, and the Era of Jinghang Yunhe with Yangzhou as its central business hub ended.

The Yangzhou section of Jinghang Yunhe/Photo by Yang Kui
The picture shows Dashui Wan (Dashui Bay) of the Ancient Canal in Yangzhou, which is now a sports and leisure park.

The tide of Qiantang Jiang/Photo by Pan Jincao

Qiantang Jiang in Zhejiang eventually flows into the East China Sea. Its trumpet-shaped estuary is large outside and small inside. When the surging seawater enters the estuary, it will accumulate and become higher and higher, forming a tidal bore.

3 The Era of Qiantang Jiang

During the Song Dynasty, China's economic center of gravity continued to move south, and the center of Jiangnan also began to shift from Chang Jiang in the same direction.

Another big river took the mantel of central geographical feature from Chang Jiang, and Jiangnan consequently entered the third historical period—the Era of Qiantang Jiang.

Qiantang Jiang originates in Anhui, and its Hangzhou section flows in a zigzag, hence the name "Zhe Jiang," "Zhi Jiang," which in Chinese means the bending river. It connected Ningbo and Shaoxing through the Eastern Zhejiang Canal yet also intersected with the southernmost end of Jinghang Yunhe, bringing the towns of eastern Zhejiang into Jinghang Yunhe's river system. Hangzhou was one of the hubs within this network. Boasting convenient transportation, Hangzhou gradually became a cargo distribution center on both sides of Qiantang Jiang. During the Wuyue Kingdom (907–978), which was one of the kingdoms in the period of "Five Dynasties and Ten Kingdoms (907–960)," it was described like this:

> *The boats converge in lines so long that one cannot see both ends.*
> *—Tao Yue, Supplement to the History of the Five Dynasties–A Pair of Qi and Ying*

After the Jingkang Incident, an invasion against the Song Dynasty that lasted from 1125 to 1127, the invading Jin army turned Nanjing and Yangzhou into cities right on the front lines. Because Hangzhou was far away from Chang Jiang and was supplied with water transportation from Qiantang Jiang, it began to draw the attention of the imperial court of what would become the Southern Song Dynasty. In 1138, Emperor Gaozong of Song, who once fled to the sea, ultimately decided to make Hangzhou the capital.

Thus, Hangzhou rose.

Many Zhongyuan scholars went south with the imperial court of the Song Dynasty. Someone wrote, "people from everywhere gathered in Zhejiang, a hundred times more than normal." Excessive population pressure once again accelerated the cultivation of Jiangnan, and the emperor himself also began to join the effort to encourage agricultural development. Jiangnan in the Era of Qiantang Jiang began to surpass the north in terms of its economy and culture thanks to the sustained economic development and growing population. Ancient Chinese scholars once wrote about the reversal of the North-South situation thus:

> *Many scholars in the south travel in groups. Northern visitors are scarce, seemingly like fainting stars... The generals and political leaders are mostly from Jiangsu, Zhejiang, Fujian, and Sichuan.*
> —Volume 3142 of the incomplete *Yongle Encyclopedia* and *The First Letter to Emperor Xiaozong* written by Chen Liang of the Song Dynasty

Hangzhou quickly became the most prosperous city in China. Substantial numbers of people, chariots, and horses gathered here, a city that brimmed with vitality.

The proverb from *Wu Jun Zhi (Gazetteer of Wu Prefecture)*, written by Fan Chengda of the Song Dynasty praised the area: "The beauty of Jiangnan is on par with heaven." Such statements reflect how Hangzhou surpassed other cities to become the ideal place in the eyes of Chinese literati.

The most talented governors of the city built water conservancy projects and constructed roads and bridges around a lake spanning several square kilometers west of Hangzhou. After several generations of continuous construction, Xi Hu, the most famous lake for urban sightseeing in China, was finally created. As a poem reads:

> *If you compare Xi Hu to the famed beauty of the woman Xi Shi, both light and heavy makeups are both very suitable.*
> —Su Shi, *Drinking on Xi Hu and Admiring the First Sunny and Later Rainy Views*

However, in the late Southern Song Dynasty, the Mongol Empire invaded from north, and finally seized Hangzhou in 1276, resulting in the destruction of this capital. The city no longer enjoyed a lofty status, and the Era of Qiantang Jiang with Hangzhou as its center concluded.

> Xi Hu of Hangzhou/Photo by Xiao Yisan
>
> Navigating the mirror-like Xi Hu feels like floating in the air. The picturesque Xi Hu is an important reason behind the literati's preference for Hangzhou.

^ Tai Hu/Photo by Zhao Yongqing

Tai Hu is one of the five largest freshwater lakes in China and the largest lake in Jiangsu.

4 The Era of Tai Hu

The fall of Hangzhou would not stop Jiangnan's rise. During the Ming and Qing dynasties, a certain lake began to exert its strength on Jiangnan after the rivers. This ushered in Jiangnan's fourth historical period—the Era of Tai Hu.

Tai Hu is located in the heart of Jiangnan and covers an area of about 2,400 square kilometers, which is 20 percent larger than the area of Shenzhen. It is one of the five largest freshwater lakes in China. The surrounding rivers and lakes, large and small, connect to Tai Hu. The vastness of this lake seems to sweep away the delicacy of Jiangnan's little bridges and flowing water. It is truly enormous.

Suzhou, the hinterland of Taihu Pendi, with its rich products, convenient transportation, and dense population, began to embark on a journey of urban development that relied on no political factors. The growth of this city was based on handicraft industry and commerce.

Suzhou rose.

After the Song and Yuan dynasties, the cultivation of mulberry and cotton became increasingly popular in Jiangnan. Thanks to the region's transportation advantages, silk and cotton could be transported to towns and cities quickly, and after rough processing, they were sold throughout the country. The fact that the economic gains stemming from these goods were far higher than grain production further stimulated their expansion. In the Ming and Qing dynasties, Jiangnan, with Suzhou as its core, ranked first in the country in the production of silk and cotton, and merchants from everywhere gathered in Suzhou. During the reign of Emperor Qianlong of the Qing Dynasty, almost every household in the eastern area of Suzhou engaged in the silk weaving industry. There were no less than 10,000 textile machines and 300-400 dyeing workshops in the city.

Craftsmen even began to copy Western glasses and kaleidoscopes. Other fields such as food processing, ready-to-wear clothes, daily necessities, paper printing, the processing of jewelry, jade, and iron were also divided into different categories and became increasingly specialized.

> Shantang Street, Suzhou/Photo by Lu Wen

Shantang Street is now a pedestrian street in Gusu District, Suzhou. In the 9th century, when Bai Juyi served as the governor of Suzhou, he excavated Shangtang He (Shantang River) from Huqiu in the west to Changmen in the east. The road, which was built to the north of the river, was called Shantang Street. Since then, Shantang Street has long been a famous commercial street in Suzhou.

The prosperity of Suzhou also led to the rapid development of the surrounding cities and towns. For example, the town of Zhenze in Wujiang was just a small village with only a few dozen residents during the Yuan Dynasty. By the end of the Ming Dynasty (around 1644), it had developed into a large town with a population of 50,000. The famous towns of Zhouzhuang and Tongli both boomed during the Ming and Qing dynasties. As a result, Jiangnan became a region where numerous towns and cities shined like stars surrounding a brilliant moon.

After growing wealthy, people in Jiangnan began to pursue a refined material life. Scholar-officials built private gardens of various sizes, and Jiangnan approximated the ideal example of the Chinese "poetic dwelling."

The refinement of material life in the region was accompanied by cultural enrichment. A culture of femininity in Jiangnan reached its peak in the Era of Tai Hu. Even several female poets, such as Liu Rushi, Xu Can, He Shuangqing, Chen Duansheng, and Shen Shanbao, appeared on the literary stage, and people began to have the impression that Jiangnan had "many talented women." These women contributed significantly to Jiangnan's image of "tenderness" in the country, and there was almost no place that could match Jiangnan nationwide.

⌄ **The Humble Administrator's Garden/Photo by Zhao Yongqing**
The Humble Administrator's Garden is located at 178 Northeast Street, Suzhou. It is a representative work of Jiangnan's classical gardens. It was built in the early 16th century. In the picture, the Beisi Pagoda can be seen in the distance. Bringing in the landscape from outside the courtyard's walls to be viewed within the courtyard was a common landscaping technique in classical garden architecture.

^ A corner of the Humble Administrator's Garden/Photo by Zhao Yongqing

Richness, refinement, and talented women were three labels that defined and brought Jiangnan into its heyday during the Era of Tai Hu. In the minds of Chinese people, Jiangnan became a "land of wealth and elegance."

However, the Opium War and the Taiping Rebellion in the late Qing Dynasty ended the Era of Tai Hu in Jiangnan. Most of the city of Suzhou was burned down by Taiping Rebels. The history books recorded:

> The burned down houses were all prosperous places in the past... but now they are nothing more than debris.
>
> —Wu Dacheng, *Diary of Court Historian Wu Qingqing*

5 The Era of the Sea

The last era of Jiangnan was linked to the East China Sea.

Jiangnan entered a new historical period—the Era of the Sea.

The East China Sea is the final destination of the Chang Jiang and Qiantang Jiang systems. Shanghai, located at the mouth of the sea, was the dominating force of the entire river system when maritime civilization arrived. After the signing of the Nanjing Treaty in 1842, Shanghai became one of five treaty ports.

Shanghai rose.

Most people are familiar with what happened next. The Changjiang Delta with Shanghai as the crown jewel became the most dynamic region in modern China.

Over many years, Jiangnan rose to prominence with different cities taking the center stage. In the Era of Chang Jiang, there was Nanjing, and Yangzhou underwent a meteoric rise during the Era of Jinghang Yunhe. The Era of Qiantang Jiang featured Hangzhou as a central area. Suzhou became a bustling commercial center during the Era of Tai Hu, and finally we come to the Era of the Sea with Shanghai as the core. Jiangnan has weathered disasters. These moments of ill fortune, however, facilitated the rise of new cities in different eras, helped the entire region to regenerate and brought infinite possibilities to Chinese civilization. It is not surprising that thousands of years later Chinese people still long for Jiangnan.

‹ **Lujiazui, Shanghai/Photo Lyu Wei**

At night, Lujiazui shines as a prosperous and modern area. It is China's most influential financial center.

Aerial photo of Huangpu Jiang (Huangpu River) and the buildings/Photo by Yuan Bo

What Is China?

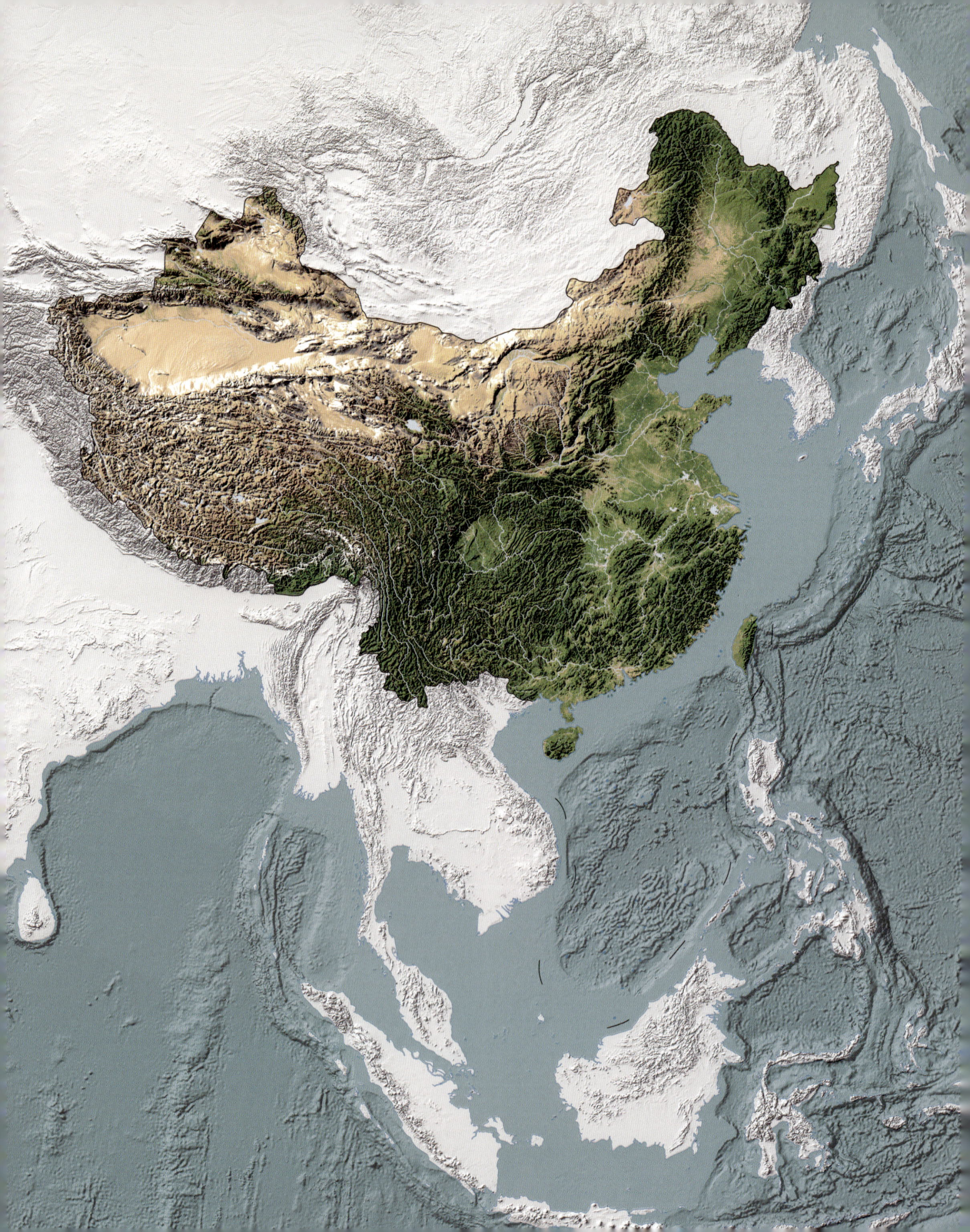

1 Vast Land

Some 65 million years ago, the Indian and Eurasian Plates began to collide and squeeze together. The Qingzang Gaoyuan was violently lifted up. Its elevation rose to more than 4,000 meters, and the atmospheric circulation in eastern Eurasia began to undergo major changes.

The circulation in the west and the dry and cold winter monsoon that had prevailed here were blocked by the Qingzang Gaoyuan and instead gathered inland toward the northwest. The southern Indian Ocean summer monsoon carried huge water vapor that surged northward. After hitting the towering Himalayas, it had to stagnate to the south of the mountains. In winter, the dry and cold airflow gathered, and during the summer, the warm, humid airflow could not enter the area. From Xinjiang to Nei Mongol, from Gansu to Ningxia, the entire northwest of China grew arid, with deserts such as Takelamagan and Kumtag expanding through the region.

Abundant sands and dusts were rolled up by the strong northwest wind, which carried it to eastern Gansu, Shaanxi, and Shanxi. After tens of millions of years of accumulation, Huangtu Gaoyuan was born, with an average thickness of 50 to 80 meters.

In contrast, eastern China benefited greatly from the geological change. After the uplift of Qingzang Gaoyuan, the East Asian monsoon gained more strength. Every summer, it carried massive amounts of water vapor westward and northward, going deep into the hinterland of China. The eastern region, especially Jiangnan, became warmer and humid with this increased precipitation. This is how the so-called "Misty and Rainy Jiangnan" came into being.

The Alpine Region of Qinghai-Xizang, the Northwestern Arid and Semi-arid Region, and Eastern Monsoon Region together constitute China's basic physical geography.

‹ **The map of China**

China is located on the eastern edge of the Eurasian continent, and the overall terrain presents a three-step ladder pattern with the west at a high elevation and the east low. This topographic feature profoundly impacted on China's natural landscape, history, and civilization.

This is a vast land with a kaleidoscope of topography and landforms: from land to ocean, from mountains to valleys, from volcanoes to glaciers, from small streams to large rivers, and from deserts to lakes. Coupled with an extremely wide span of longitude and latitude, China is rich in the diversity of its flora and fauna. We can take plants as an example. Among the 225,000 species of plants in the world, there are 30,000 species in China. In eastern China some 8,000 years ago, large animals such as crocodiles, rhinos, and elephants were widely distributed. Who knows, if you could travel through time and space, you might even encounter a wild panda in Beijing.

Three natural regions, diverse topography, and rich biological resources, these constitute China's earliest form. The larger-scale landscape shaping will be completed by the humans living on this land.

As the famous American geographer George B. Cressey said:

> *The most significant element in the Chinese landscape is thus not the soil, plants, or climate, but the people.*
>
> —Quoted from *Chinese Environmental History*

Desert-like sand dunes in Shannan/Photo by Li Heng

These desert-like sand dunes are aeolian deposits developed on the basis of fluvial sediments in the river valley of Yarlung Zangbo Jiang in Zhanang County, Shannan, Xizang.

Kumtag Shamo (Kumtag Desert)/Photo by Liu Chen
Kumtag Shamo is located at the junction of Xinjiang and Gansu, between Dunhuang and Lop Nur.

Forest and Grassland in Künes Town, Xinjiang/Photo by Xu Guibin

The Künes Forest and Grassland are located in Hejing County, Bayingolin Mongol Autonomous Prefecture, Xinjiang. It is on the upper reaches of Künes He (Künes River) at an altitude of 1,600 to 2,400 meters. From the aerial perspective in the picture, the *picea schrenkiana* are clustered like countless arrows pointing skyward.

Kenting Coast/Photo by Lu Yukun

Kenting is located on Hengchun Bandao (Hengchun Peninsula) of Pingtung County, Taiwan, China, covering the southernmost area of the island of Taiwan along the Bashi Channel. It is surrounded by the sea on three sides, the Pacific Ocean to the east, the Taiwan Strait to the west, and the Bashi Channel to the south.

2 Using Resources

Some 40,000 to 60,000 years ago, *Homo sapiens* came to this land. With their arrival, a development full of power and wisdom was about to kick off.

They cleared the wilds and destroyed the primeval forest. They expanded everywhere and attempted to conquer the rivers. To become the masters of this fertile land, they needed to learn to survive in the wild, defeat fierce, wild animals, and at the same time defeat their fellow human competitors. The key to success was mastering resources.

Ten thousand years ago, the land in the middle and lower reaches of Chang Jiang and both sides of Zhu Jiang (Zhujiang River) were covered by large forests and swamps. The wild rice, which was the first important resource that the ancients of China were about to master, grew around them. One of these ancient explorers first noticed the special features of this herbaceous plant. After the flood brought by the monsoon receded, he sowed the rice seeds into the mudflat. The seeds would germinate within a month, and the rice would be fully harvested a few months after that. Although we do not know this person's name, there is no

doubt that he is the first farmer in Chinese history.

More people began to imitate his innovative agricultural technique. For the first time, a large area of man-made landscapes, namely rice fields, appeared in prehistoric China. Some years later, it would spread all over what is now southern China.

^ Rice harvesting/Photo by Zhang Dianwen

This picture was taken in Jiangxiang Township, Nanchang County, Nanchang. The harvester was reaping rice.

< Xixi Wetland, Hangzhou/Photo by Pan Jincao

This picture shows the Xixi Wetland in Hangzhou, which is one of many wetland landscapes in the south.

Unlike the rainy south, the climate of the north is relatively dry, and low grasslands represent the main landscape here. There was no wild rice growing here, but there were other kinds of plant—millet, including pale yellow millet and bronzing millet. These crops could self-pollinate and were easy to hybridize with other varieties. These characteristics made them highly adaptable to different environments. The distribution range of wild millet was wider than that of rice, stretching up and down China. Almost at the same time as the origin of rice in the south, Chinese ancestors in the north also successfully planted millet. The fields where millet was planted expanded rapidly. Millet was the most important food source in the north for thousands of years.

Two agricultural models spread in China: southern rice and northern millet cultivation. Regardless of how these two models would compete in the future, they both brought a new feature to the landscape, villages. To take care of the crops on the fields, farmers settled nearby and gathered, thus forming villages.

1 2 3

1 Villages and terraces in Danzhai County, Guizhou/Photo by Yao Chaohui

2 Farmland of Huabei Pingyuan/Photo by Jiao Xiaoxiang

The photo was taken by Huai He in Xi County, Xinyang, Henan. In the early days, Huabei Pingyuan was the main planting area of millet in China, which has now been replaced by other crops such as wheat and corn.

3 Nalati Caoyuan (Nalati Grassland), Xinjiang/Photo by Li Heng

This picture looks like a primordial savanna landscape in northern China. The photo was taken in the Nalati Caoyuan in Xinjiang. It is for reference only and is not the northern part of China mentioned in the article.

During the Xia Dynasty in 2000 BC, there might have been 1,000 villages in China. By the Eastern Han Dynasty, 60 million people were living in villages. Villages and farmland became the most important aspects of China's landscape at that time.

As the population grew and people gathered, villages evolved into cities. From ancient times to the 17th century, China built a total of 4,478 large and small cities. Despite wars, demolitions, and the burning down of buildings, a small number of ancient cities have survived, becoming rare remnants of ancient architecture in modern China.

These ancient cities established friendly relations with surrounding villages from the very beginning. The excrement produced by urban residents would be collected by special personnel at night, sent to a nearby village, and then scattered into the fields by farmers. The people called it "night soil." This not only reduced pollution to cities and rivers but also supplied farmlands with necessary nutrients. In return, villages, now equipped with sufficient fertilizer, would provide cities with more abundant and better-quality agricultural products.

Large-scale production in villages and cities spurred the Chinese people's intense demand for wood, another important resource. In ancient China, timber-frame buildings were convenient as their materials could be easily obtained and the buildings themselves could be constructed rapidly. With the addition of bricks, stones, and other materials, these structures could become places for living, leisure, and worship. As a result, many forests were destroyed, and wooden-framed buildings appeared in various forms. All kinds of architecture, from ordinary residences to imperial palaces, including those exquisite pavilions and even the Fujian *tulou*, which was mainly made of sand and soil, featured a mixture of earth, brick, and wood inside.

Chinese ancients liked to combine a variety of single timber-frame buildings to form a magnificent building complex. This is the most significant feature of ancient Chinese architecture. Among all well preserved pieces of architecture in China, none surpasses the Forbidden City in Beijing. More than 980 palaces and houses with different functions form this super architecture complex with an area of 725,000 square meters.

^ Langzhong Ancient Town, Sichuan/Photo by Jiang Xi

Not all cities were formed out of villages. Some could have been formed in many other ways. This picture shows Langzhong, an ancient town in Sichuan, and the green pavilion in the picture is Huaguang Pavilion.

v Liedechong, Guangzhou/Photo by Chen Chong

This picture shows Liedechong in Guangzhou, where dragon boat races are traditionally held during the Dragon Boat Festival.

Chili pepper being dried in Yanqi Hui Autonomous County, Xinjiang/Photo by Wang Wei

3 The Power of the Chinese

The new landscapes that have been brought to us by resources such as rice, millet, and wood are already very amazing. However, when they all add up, they cannot compare to the energy of another resource–people.

Since social classes emerged in human society, in the ruling class perspective, men were like some kind of usable resources or materials, just like woods to the wooden houses.

In 221 BC, the First Emperor of the Qin Dynasty unified the six states, giving birth to a powerful centralized government. The following rulers of China would demonstrate a great level of ease when mobilizing huge bases of manpower and material resources. They assumed personal command in magnificent capital cities, used Confucianism to unify their empires and constantly initiated unprecedented super projects. Tens of thousands to hundreds of thousands of people were mobilized to build large-scale water conservancy projects. There were 300,000 people mobilized to build the Great Wall and 700,000 people for building the emperor's tomb. More manpower was mobilized to build roads across the country, and millions of people were mobilized to build canals...

Overall, the centralization of power brought a relatively stable political environment to China, and the population began to increase substantially. Ge Jianxiong, a historical geographer, pointed out that China's population had exceeded 100 million during the Northern Song Dynasty. The large population also brought with it a greater power to transform the earth.

˅ Hefangkou Great Wall/Photo by Yang Dong

The Hefangkou Great Wall, located in Beijing's Huairou District, is an important pass of the Ming Dynasty Great Wall.

∧ **Western Xia mausoleums/Photo by Liu Supei**

The number of people who built the mausoleums of the emperors in the past dynasties varied, but most of them were large in scale. This picture shows the Western Xia mausoleums, which occupy an area of some 50 square kilometers.

More rice varieties with better quality were introduced into China, such as Champa rice. Iron farm tools that were smelted in mass quantity made it easier for people to chop down trees and clear wasteland. In addition, the rulers of the past dynasties all vigorously expanded agriculture, and the areas for rice cultivation subsequently grew larger. This aggressive promotion of agriculture led to almost the entire south being cultivated into rice fields. Places that were not easy to cultivate eventually were transformed through the highly creative invention of terraces.

Millet in the north lost its former glory during this agricultural revolution. Wheat, a crop initially foreign to China, became the most important crop; Corn, sweet potatoes, and potatoes introduced from the Americas enjoyed strong popularity for a time. The landscape created by crops not native still has an impact on Chinese soil today. For example, lavender, a crop with great ornamental value, has become a beloved plant to many people.

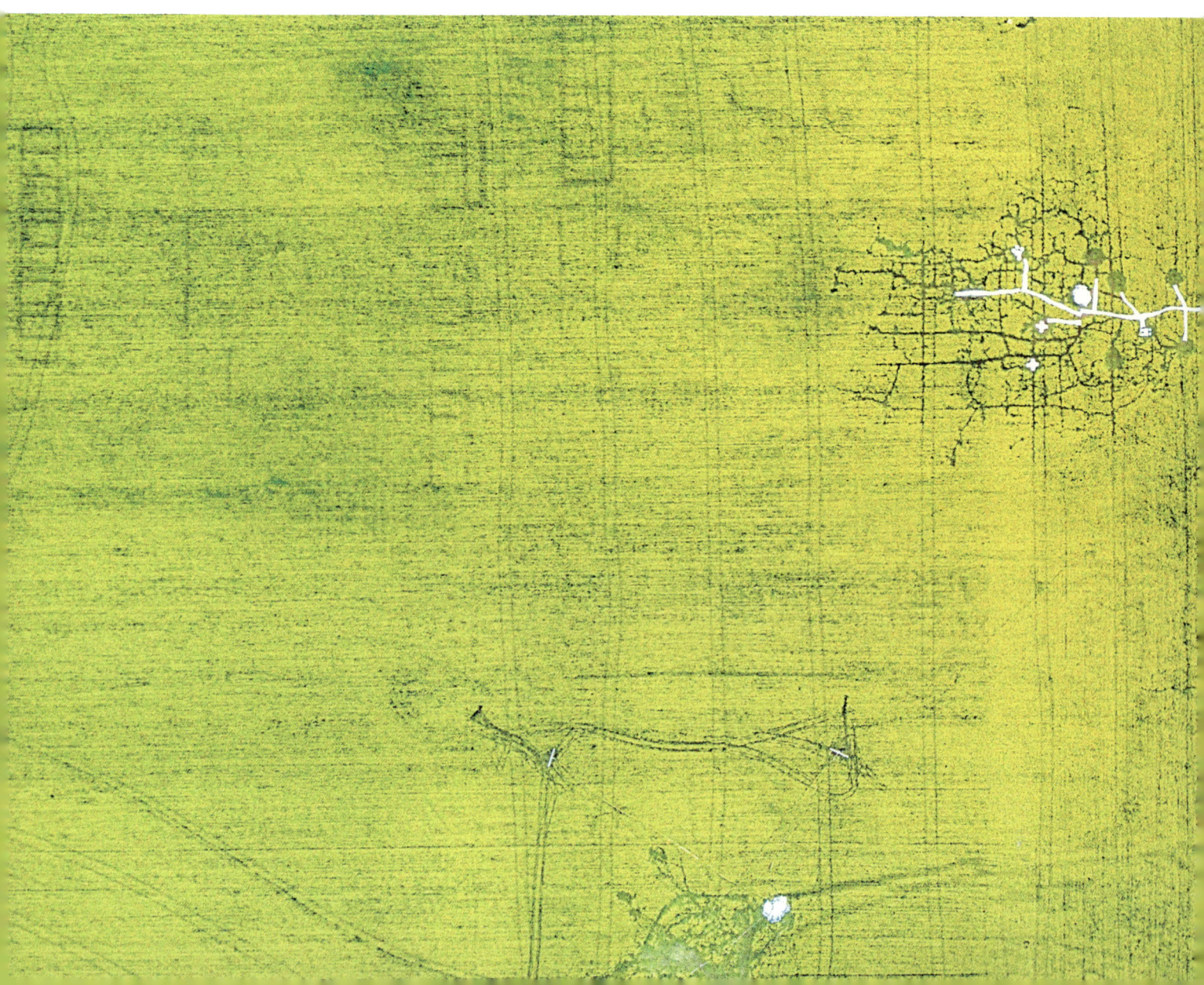

The growth of the livestock industry was equally impressive. As early as Shang Dynasty people recorded the consumption of cattle on oracle bones at offering ceremonies. There were 9 instances recording the consumption of 100 cows at one single ceremony, three inscriptions recorded the use of 300 cows, and some even recorded the sacrifice of 500 and 1,000 cows at one ceremony. Other meats, such as pork and mutton, also entered the daily diet of the ancient Chinese.

⌄ **A flowering field of rapeseed in Menyuan Hui Autonomous County/Photo by Liu Chen**

Rapeseed is an important economic crop. If cultivated on a grand scale, it is of great ornamental value. In recent years, Huangling in Wuyuan, Jiangxi, Hanzhong Pendi (Hanzhong Basin), Luoping Pingyuan (Luoping Plain) in Yunnan, and Menyuan Hui Autonomous County in Qinghai have all become popular places for viewing and admiring rapeseed flowers.

A flock of sheep on Bashang Caoyuan (Bashang Grassland)/Photo by Chen Hua

Bashang Caoyuan is in northwest Hebei and bordering areas of Inner Mongolia, elevation of 1,500 to 2,000 meters. It is a temperate savanna.

In addition to strong centralization, the mobilization of human resources by religion should not be underestimated. People chiseled mountains and cracked rocks to build giant buddhas. Almost all famous mountains and rivers in eastern China, no matter whether their altitudes are 1,000 meters, 2,000 meters, or 3,000 meters, are dotted with monasteries and temples. In the alpine Qingzang Gaoyuan, religious buildings and activities have made a significant impact on the surface landscape.

In Sêrtar County, Garzê Tibetan Autonomous Prefecture, Sichuan, believers spontaneously built tens of thousands of red houses, forming a stunning landscape. Western missionaries who came from afar were equally pious. During the hundred years after the Opium War, various churches quickly spread throughout China's urban and rural areas.

1 | 2

1 Sêrtar Buddhist Institute/Photo by Aaron Liu

The Sêrtar Buddhist Institute, formally named the Sêrtar Larung Five Science Buddhist Academy, is located in Sêrtar County, Garzê Tibetan Autonomous Prefecture, Sichuan. It was officially founded in the 1980s and then quickly became a world-renowned Tibetan Buddhist academy.

2 Emei Jin Ding (Golden Summit of Mount Emei)/Photo by Jiang Xi

Emei Jin Ding is at an elevation of 3,079 meters. There is a cliff on one side of Jin Ding that is referred to as the "Cliff of Sacrifice."

4 Modern China

In 1840, the colonists knocked on the door of China, and modern industry and commerce gradually spread across China. In 1978, the policies for reform and opening-up slowly lifted the curtain. Brand-new modern technology, a freer market, and the government's tremendous ability to mobilize have made this period the most critical time for the Chinese to alter surface landscapes.

We mine minerals, set up factories, build docks, and export products to the world.

We manage the land, build mechanized farmland, and constantly establish new construction sites. A variety of brand-new buildings have emerged. Shopping malls, theaters, art centers, office buildings, memorials, museums, stadiums, and residential buildings that may be sparse or dense finally combine into super cities.

We try to utilize the resources of the ocean, place wind turbines on the sea, create dense waterways, and develop new islands.

We build high-speed rail networks and roads that stretch out in all four directions, we cross the ocean and desert, and establish a kingdom of automobiles.

‹ A factory in Shanghai/Photo by Lyu Wei

Li Shutong Memorial in Pinghu, Zhejiang/Photo by Ye Yi

Wide and Narrow Lanes/Photo by Ye Qing
The Wide and Narrow Lanes are located near Changshun Street, Chengdu, Sichuan. It consists of the Wide Lane, the Narrow Lane, and the Jing Lane arranged in parallel. It is a relatively large-scale ancient street in Chengdu from the Qing Dynasty, and it is now a famous commercial street.

Buildings in Hong Kong/Photo by Qiu Huo

A desert highway across Qaidam Pendi/Photo by Xu Guibin

Zhengzhou East High-speed EMU Depot/Photo by Jiao Xiaoxiang

Nansha Harbor Area, Guangzhou/Photo by Lin Yuxian

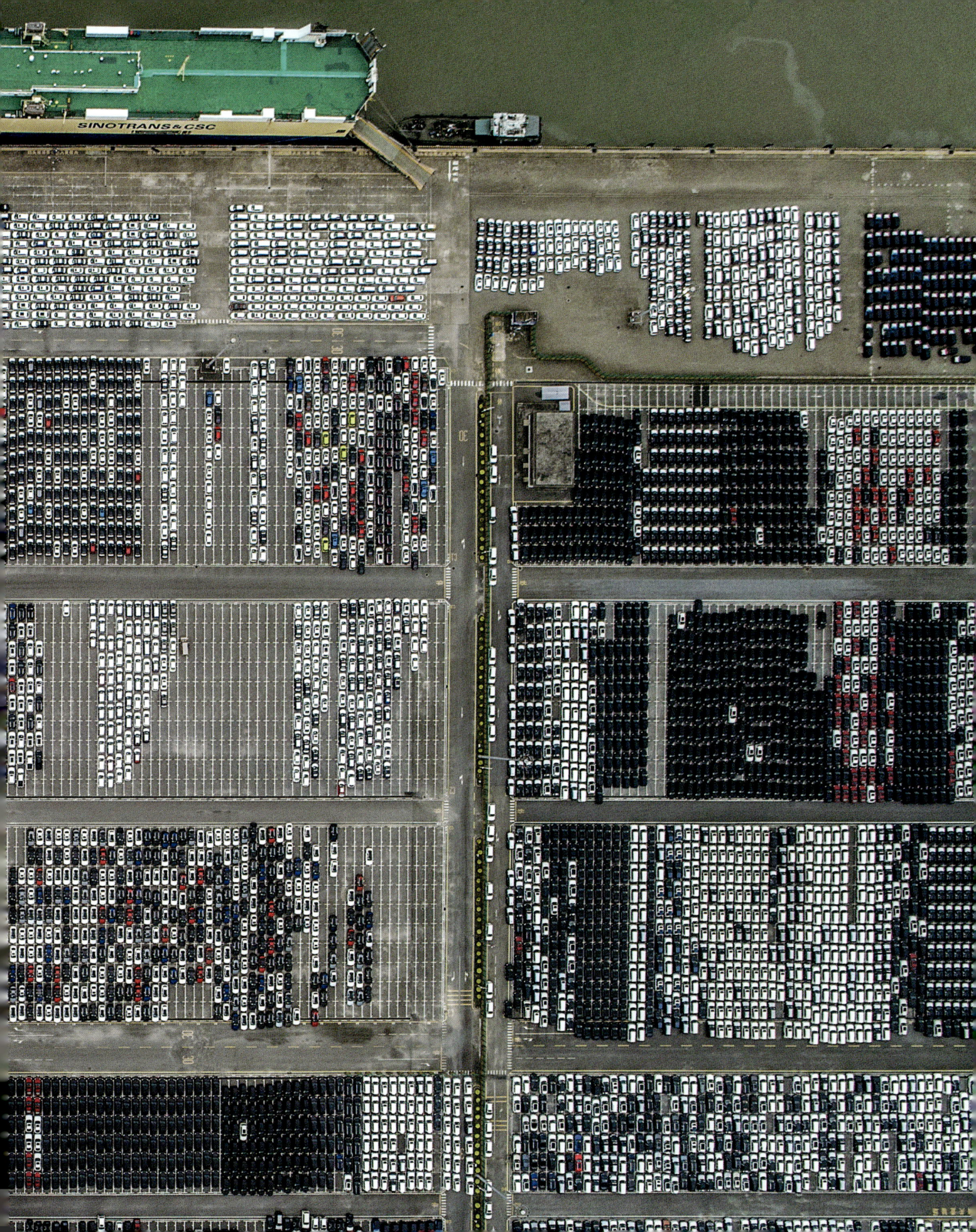

Jiaozhou Wan Bridge/Photo by Meng Tao

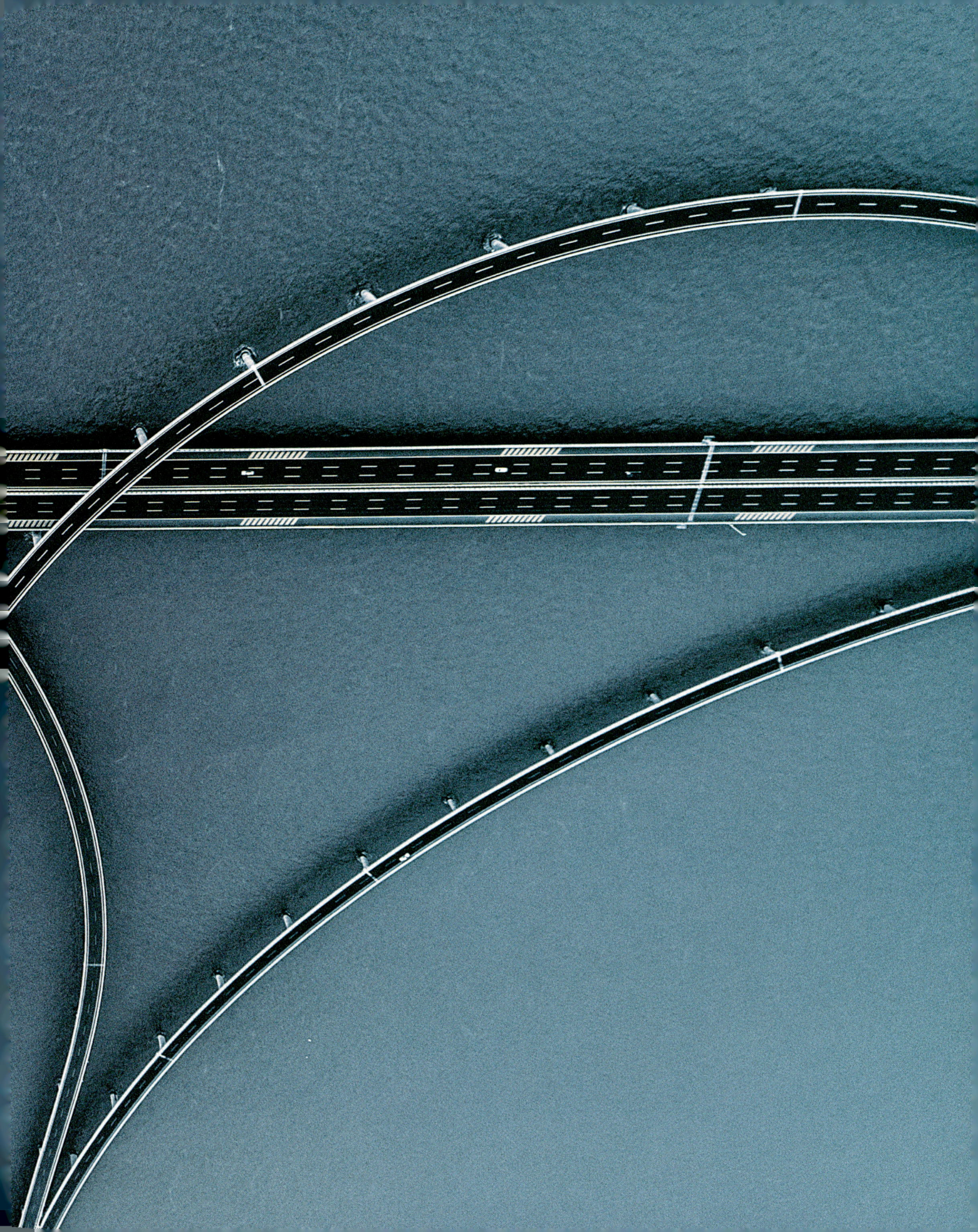

Dragon Boat Race at Liedeyong, Guangzhou/Photo by Chen Chong

This is China, a place that awakens the sleeping mountains and changes the appearance of rivers. It is an ancient land, yet the power of youth is everywhere.

In the beginning,
there was no China in the world.
Relying on the resources of
nature, the Chinese created China.

References

Where Does China Come From?

1. Zheng Du, Yao Tandong. *Uplifting of Tibetan Plateau with Its Environmental Effects* [M]. Beijing: Science Press, 2004.

2. Shi Yafeng, Li Jijun, Li Bingyuan. *Tibetan Plateau Uplift during Late Cenozoic and Environment Changes* [M]. Guangzhou: Guangdong Science & Technology Press, 1998, 1:463.

3. Zheng Du. *The Formation Environment and Development of the Qinghai-Tibet Plateau* [M]. Shijiazhuang: Hebei Science and Technology Press, 2003.

4. The Scientific Expedition Team of CAS to the Qinghai-Xizang Plateau, *Geomorphology of Xizang* [M]. Beijing: Science Press, 1983.

5. Shi Yafeng, Huang Maohuan, Ren Binghui. *Introduction of Glaciers in China* [M]. Beijing: Science Press, 1988:8.

6. Li Bingyuan. The Scope of the Qinghai-Tibet Plateau [J]. *Geographical Research*, 1987(3):57-64.

7. Zhang Yili, Li Bingyuan, Zheng Du. On the Scope and Area of the Qinghai-Tibet Plateau [J]. *Geographical Research*, 2002, 21(1):1-8.

8. Yao Tandong, Chen Fahu, Cui Peng, et al. Special Topic: Progress in Comprehensive Scientific Research on the Qinghai-Tibet Plateau—From Tibetan Plateau to Third Pole and Pan-Third Pole [J]. *Bulletin of Chinese Academy of Sciences*, 2017(9).

9. Deng Tao, Wang Xiaoming, Li Qiang, et al. Tibetan Plateau: From Paradise of Tropical Animals and Plants to Cradle of Ice Age Mammalian Fauna [J]. *Bulletin of Chinese Academy of Sciences*, 2017, 32(9):959-966.

10. Ding Lin, Li Zhenyu, Song Peiping. Core Fragments of Tibetan Plateau from Gondwanaland United in Northern HemisphereQin [J]. *Bulletin of Chinese Academy of Sciences*, 2017, 32(9):945-950.

11. Cui Peng, Jia Yang, Su Fenghuan, et al. Natural Hazards in Tibetan Plateau and Key Issue for Feature Research [J]. *Bulletin of Chinese Academy of Sciences*, 2017, 32(9):985-992.

12. Yao Tandong, Piao Shilong, Shen Miaogen, et al. Chained Impacts on Modern Environment of Interaction between Westerlies and Indian Monsoon on Tibetan Plateau [J]. *Bulletin of Chinese Academy of Sciences*, 2017, 32(9):976-984.

13. Deng Tao. Mammalian Evolution Related to the Tibetan Plateau Uplift [J]. *Chinese Journal of Nature*, 2013, 35(3):193-199.

14. Wu Guoxiong, Duan Anmin, Liu Yimin, et al. Recent Advances in the Study on the Dynamics of the Asian Summer Monsoon Onset [J]. *Chinese Journal of Atmospheric Sciences*, 2013, 37(2):211-228.

15. Wu Guoxiong, Liu Yimin, Bao Qing, et al. Review of the Impact of the Tibetan Plateau Sensible Heat Driven Air-pump on the Asian Summer Monsoon [J]. *Chinese Journal of Atmospheric Sciences*, 2018(3):488-504.

16. Wu Guoxiong, Liu Xin, Zhang Qiong, et al. Progresses in the Study of the Climate Impacts of the Elevated Heating Over the Tibetan Plateau [J]. *Climatic and Environmental Research*, 2002, 7(2):184-201.

17. Zhang Kexin, Wang Guocan, Hong Hanlie, et al. The Study of the Genozoic Uplift in the Tibetan Plateau: A Review [J]. *Geological Bulletin*, 2013, 32(1):1-18.

18. Liu Xiaohui, Xu Qiang, Ding Lin. Differential Surface Uplift: Cenozoic Paleoelevation History of the Tibetan Plateau [J]. *Scientia Sinica (Terrae)*, 2017(1).

19. Xu Zhiqin, Yang Jingsui, Hou Zengqian, et al. The Progress in the Study of Continental Dynamics of the Tibetan Plateau [J]. *Geology in China*, 2016, 43(1):1-42.

20. Ding Lin, Zhong Dalai. The Tectonic Evolution of the Eastern Himalaya Syntaxis Since the Collision of the Indian and Eurasian Plates [J]. *Chinese Journal of Geology*, 2013, 48(2):317-333.

21. Ma Lihua. *Brilliant Rays of Qinghai-Tibet* [M]. Beijing: Beijing October Literature and Art Publishing House, 2018: 03.

22. Du Xiurong, Tang Jianjun. *China Administrative Map* [M]. Beijing: SinoMaps Press, 2011: 01.

23. Zhu Dagang, et al. *Remote Sensing Survey and Research on the Ecological and Geological Environment of Rivers and Lakes in the Qinghai-Tibet Plateau* [M]. Beijing: Geological Publishing House, 2007.

24. Liu Shiyin, Yao Xiaojun, Guo Wanqin, et al. The Contemporary Glaciers in China Based on the Second Chinese Glacier Inventory [J]. *Acta Geographica Sinica*, 2015, 70(1):3-16.

1.1 Hoh Xil: China's Greatest Wilderness

1. Hoh Xil Comprehensive Scientific Expedition Team. *An Integrated Scientific Survey to Hoh Xil* [M]. Shanghai: Shanghai Scientific & Technical Publishers, 1994.

2. Li Bingyuan, Li Mingsen, Fan Yunqi, et al. *The Dust-Laden Past in the Uninhabited Area of Northern Tibet The First Comprehensive Scientific Investigation Record of Qiangtang* [M]. Beijing: Xueyuan Publishing House, 2009.

3. Li Jingsheng, Chen Xuxia. *Walk into Hoh Xil* [M]. Nanning: Guangxi People's Publishing House, 2005.

4. Zheng Du. *Physical Geography of Karakoram-Kunlun Mountain Region* [M]. Beijing: Science Press, 1999.

5. Li Bingyuan, Hoh Xil Comprehensive Scientific Expedition Team. *Physical Environment of Hoh Xil Region, Qinghai* [M]. Beijing: Science Press, 1996.

6. Li Jianghai. *Geology and Geomorphology of Hoh Xil and Its Formation and Evolution* [M]. Beijing: Science Press, 2017.

7. Hu Dongsheng. Investigation and Study on Lake Resources in Kekexili Region [J]. *Arid Land Geography*, 1992(3):50-58.

8. Huang Rongfu. The Cushion Plant In The Hoh Xil Area of Qinghai [J]. *Bulletin of Botany*, 1994(2):130-137.

9. Hu Dongsheng. Lake Evolution in the Hoh Xil Region [J]. *Arid Land Geography (Chinese Edition)*, 1995(1):60-67.

10. George B. Schaller, Kang Aili. *Wildlife of the Tibetan Steppe* [M]. Shanghai: East China Normal University Press, 2003.

11. Wen Cheng, Hu Ruocheng, Gu Yiyun, et al. Spatial Definition of the Biodiversity Value of the Hoh Xil World Heritage Site in Qinghai [J]. *Research on Heritages and Preservation*, 2017(7):1-6.

12. Guo Ke. Vegetation of Qinghai Hoh Xil Region [J]. *Chinese Journal of Plant Ecology*, 2012, 17(2).

13. Lian Xinming, Li Xiaoxiao, Yan Peishi, et al. Behavioural Time Budgets and Diurnal Rhythms of the Female Tibetan Gazelles in the Kekexili National Nature Reserve [J]. *Acta Ecologica Sinica*, 2012, 32(3):663-670.

14. Mayan, Gerili. The Research Status of Tibetan antelope [J]. *Chinese High Altitude Medicine and Biology*, 2017, 38(3):206-212.

15. Kong Fei. *The Adaptability of Tibetan Antelope to the Qinghai-Tibet Railway Wild Animal Passage and the Behavioral Study When Crossing the Passage* [D]. Xi'an: Northwest University, 2009.

16. Wu Sugong, Feng Zuojian. *The Biology and Human Physiology in the Hoh Xil Region* [M]. Beijing: Science Press, 1996, 12.

17. Li Bingyuan, Li Mingsen, Fan Yunqi, et al. *The Dust-Laden Past in the Uninhabited Area of Northern Tibet The First Comprehensive Scientific Investigation Record of Qiangtang* [M]. Beijing: Xueyuan Publishing House, 2009: 01.

18. Yao Xiaojun, Liu Shiyin, Li Long, et al. Spatial-temporal Variations of Lake Area in Hoh Xil Region in the Past 40 Years [J]. *Acta Geographica Sinica*, 2013, 68(7):886-896.

19. Xu Aichun, et al. *Biodiversity in the Kekexili Region* [M]. Beijing: Scientific and Technical Documentation Press, 2014.

1.2 Ngari: The Civilization of the Wildness

1. Chen Qingying, Gao Shufen. *A Complete History of Tibet* [M]. Zhengzhou: Zhongzhou Ancient Book Publishing House, 2003.

2. Tibet Autonomous Region Local Chronicles Compilation Committee. *Ngari Prefecture Chronicles* [M]. Beijing: China Tibetology Publishing House, 2009.

3. Huo Wei. Archaeology Outlines Ali's Civilization [J]. *Chinese Social Sciences Today*, 2013: 489.

4. Guge Cirenjiabu. *Legend Ngari Prefecture* [M]. Beijing: China Tibetology Publishing House, 2014.

5. Jin Shubo. *Coming from Shang Shung* [M]. Lhasa: Tibet People's Publishing House, 2012.

6. Hou Lifeng, Liu Jianbing. Formation Conditions and Evolution Process of the Landform of Zanda Earth pillars in Tibet [J]. *Western Mining Engineering*, 2017, 29(2):65-68.

7. Suolangwangdui, Li Yongxian, et al. *Records of Cultural Relics of Ngari Region* [M]. Lhasa: The Tibet People's Publishing House, 1993.

8. Ma Lihua. *Documentary of Ma Lihua's Journey through Tibet: Go West to Ngari* [M]. Beijing: China Tibetology Publishing House, 2007.

9. Zhu Dagang, Meng Xiangang, Shao Zhaogang, et al. Features of Pliocene-Lower Pleistocene Sedimentary Facies and Tectonic Evolution in the Zanda Basin, Ngari Area, Tibet [J]. *Chinese Journal of Geomechanics*, 2004, 10(3):245-252.

10. Zhu Dagang, et al. *Remote Sensing Survey and Research on the Ecological and Geological Environment of Rivers and Lakes in the Qinghai-Tibet Plateau* [M]. Beijing: Geological Publishing House, 2007.

11. Guge Cirenjiabu. *History of Ngari* [M]. Lhasa: The Tibet People's Publishing House, 2003: 03.

12. Tibet Architectural Survey and Design Institute. *Architectural Ruins of the Kingdom of Guge* [M]. Beijing: China Architecture & Building Press, 2011: 8.

13. Tsering Dawa, Tone Bleie. Historical Migration of Ngari Region [J]. *Journal of Tibet University*, 2017(3):204.

14. Tsering Thar. Beliefs in Mount Kailash and Its Surrounding Ancient Culture [J]. *Chinese Tibetology*, 1996(1):67-79.

15. Tongmei. Beliefs in Mount Kailash and Its Characteristics from the Perspective of Tibetan-Indian Culture—Memorial of the Year of the Horse of Gangdis Mountain Worship [J]. *China Tibetology*, 2015(3):357-366.

16. Huang Bo. Remarks on the Dissemination and Dispute of the Various Sects of Tibetan Buddhism in Ngari Prefecture in Guge Period [J]. *Journal of Sichuan Normal University (Social Sciences Edition)*, 2012, 39(1):161-167.

17. Huo Wei, Zhang Changhong, Lyu Hongliang. Archaeological Investigation and Study of Buddhist Remains in the Kazi River Valley in the Xiangquan River Basin of Ngari, Tibet [J]. *Acta Archaeologica Sinica*, 2009(4):547-577.

18. Du Xiurong, Tang Jianjun. *China Administrative Map* [M]. Beijing: SinoMaps Press, 2011: 01.

19. Mi Desheng, Xie Zichu. *Catalog of Chinese Glaciers: Ganges River System, Indian River System* [M]. Xi'an: Xi'an Maps Publishing House, 2002.

1.3 Hengduan Shan: A Mountain Range with the Most Breathtaking Scenery in China

1. Li Bingyuan. Discussion on the Scope of the Hengduan Mountains [J]. *Mountain Research*, 1987(2):74-82.

2. Li Bingyuan. Geomorphological Regionalization of the Hengduan Mountainous Region [J]. *Mountain Research*, 1989(1):13-20.

3. Zhang Lihan, et al. *Chinese Mountains and Rivers* [M]. Qingdao: Qingdao Publishing House, 2005.

4. The Qinghai-Tibet Plateau Comprehensive Scientific Expedition Team of the Chinese Academy of Sciences. *Natural Geography of the Hengduan Area* [M]. Beijing: Science Press, 1997.

5. Lyu Ruren, Li Deji. *Surface Process and Geological Structure Foundation of the Qinghai-Tibet Plateau* [M]. Chengdu: Sichuan Science and Technology Press, 2015.

6. Shi Shuo. *The Tibetan-Yi Corridor·The Origin of Civilization and People* [M]. Chengdu: Sichuan People's Publishing House, 2009.

7. Chen Fubin. The Origin of the "Hengduan Mountains" Name [J]. *Mountain Research*,1984,2(1):31-35.

8. Chinese Academy of Sciences Qinghai-Tibet Plateau Comprehensive Scientific Expedition Team. *The Hengduan*

Mountains Special Collection 2 of Qinghai-Tibet Plateau Research* [M]. Beijing: Beijing Science and Technology Press, 1986.

9. Chen Fubin, Chen Ronghua. *A Textual Research On The Item "Hengduan Mountain Range"* [M]. Chengdu: Chengdu Cartographic Publishing House, 1992: 1-12.

10. Song Mingkun. Investigation of Hengduan Mountain Glacier [J]. *Journal of Glaciology and Geocryology*, 1985,7(1):98.

11. Long Yongcheng, Ke Ruige, Zhong Tai, et al. Status and Conservation Strategy of the Yunnan Snub-nosed Monkey [J]. *Biodiversity*, 1996, 04(3):145-152.

12. Li Zongsheng, He Yuanqing, Wang Shijin, et al. Changes of Some Monsoonal Temperate Glaciers in Hengduan Mountains Region during 1900-2007 [J]. *Acta Geographica Sinica*, 2009, 64(11):1319-1330.

13. Xu Zhiqin, Yang Jingsui, Hou Zengqian, et al. The Progress in the Study of Continental Dynamics of the Tibetan Plateau [J]. *Geology in China*, 2016, 43(1):1-42.

14. Fan Pengfei, Shi Lin, Ma Changyong, et al. Ten years of Searching for Gibbons. The Discovery and Naming of the Skywalker Hoolock Gibbon [J]. *Nature History*, 2017(8):50-53.

15. Zheng Hongbo, Wei Xiaochun, Wang Ping, et al. Geological Evolution of the Yangtze Jiang (in Chinese) [J]. *SCIENTIA SINICA Terrae*, 2017(4):385-393.

1.4 Jiuzhaigou: Destruction and Creation

1. Deng Guiping. *Study of Tourism Geosciences Landscape Formation and Protection of Jiuzhaigou World Natural Heritage Site* [D]. Chengdu: Chengdu University of Technology, 2011.

2. Zhang Ruiying, He Zhengwei. Formation and Development Trend of Jiuzhaigou Scenic Spot, Sichuan Province [J]. *The Chinese Journal of Geological Hazard and Control*, 2007(1):54-58.

3. Yan Hao, Liu Zaihua, Deng Zeping, Sun Hailong, Zhang Jinliu. Origin of the Tufa at Jiuzhaigou Scenic Spot in Sichuan [J]. *Carsologica Sinica*, 2013, 32(1):15-22.

4. Zhou Rongjun, Pu Xiaohong, He Yulin, et al. Recent Activity of Minjiang Fault Zone, Uplift of Minshan Blook and Their Relationship with Seismicity of Sichuan [J]. *Seismology and Geology*, 2000, 22(3):285-294.

5. Zhou Xulun, Liu Minsheng. Travertine Dissolution and Formation of Lake Waterfall Landscape in the Jiuzhai Valley [J]. *Acta Geologica Sichuan*, 2012, 32(3):333-338.

6. Li Yongxin, Tian Youping, Li Yin. Tufa Algae and Biological Karstification at Huanglong, Sichuan [J]. *Carsologica Sinica*, 2011, 30(1):86-92.

7. Chen Pan, Tang Ya, Qiao Xue, et al. Environmental Change Revealed by Lake Sedimentation in Jiuzhaigou National Reserve, Sichuan, China [J]. Journal of Mountain Science [J]. *Mountain Research*, 2011(5):534-542.

8. Tang Wenqing, Liu Yuping, Chen Zhiliang, et al. The Preliminary Study of the Tectonic Activities Along the Boundary Faults Around the Minshan Uplift, Western Sichuan [J]. *Sedimentary Geology and Tethyan Geology*, 2004, 24(4):31-34.

9. Guo Jianqiang. On Protection of Travertine Landscape in the Jiuzhai Valley and Huanglong Scenic Spots [J]. *Acta*

Geologica Sichuan, 2005, 25(1):23-26.

10. Zhou Xulun. The Changhai Lake in the Jiuzhaigou Scenic Area of Sichuan is Not a Glacial Barrier Lake but a Collapsed Barrier Lake [J]. Geological Bulletin of China, 2009(7):970-978.

11. Zhang Ruiying, He Zhengwei. Analysis and Evaluation of Landscape Formation and Evolution Trend in Jiuzhaigou, Sichuan [J]. The Chinese Journal of Geological Hazard and Control, 2007,18(1):54-58.

1.5 Siguniang Shan: A Song of Ice and Rock

1. Jon Krakauer. *Into Thin Air* [M]. Zhang Hongmei, Translated. Beijing: China Renmin University Press, 2010.

2. Dai Zongming. *Uplift of the Late Cenozoic in the Mount Siguniang Area in the Eastern Part of the Qinghai-Tibet Plateau* [D]. Chengdu: Chengdu University of Technology, 2012.

3. Liu Shuzhen, Chai Zongxin, Chen Jiliang. Preliminary Investigation on Glaciation in Siguniang Mountainous Region of Wenchuan County in Sichuan Province [J]. *Journal of Glaciology and Geocryology*, 1986(1): 72-82.

4. Cao Jun. Geomorphic Features of the Mount Siguniang Scenic Area in Sichuan [J]. *Acta Geologica Sichuan*, 2004(4):237-240.

5. Zheng Yuanchang, Gao Shenghuai, Zhong Xianghao. Soil In Siguniang Mountainous Region and Its Vertical Distribution [J]. *Mountain Research*, 1988(4):227-234.

6. Mick Fowler. *On Thin Ice: 12 Adventures on the Precipice of Mick Fowler* [M]. Huang Jiyun, Translated. Beijing: Posts & Telecom Press, 2015.

7. Peng Dong, Xie Yunxi, Wu Shutong, et al. The Last Glacial Stage Gravel Sediments and Ice Wedge Features of Siguniang Mountains on the Southeast Margin of Qinghai-Tibet Plateau, China [J]. *Journal of Chengdu University of Technology (Sciences & Technology Edition)*, 2006, 33(5):491-496.

8. Dai Zongming, Sun Chuanmin, Zhang Kuanzhong, et al. Geochemistry and U-Pb Dating of Zircons From the Four-Girl Mountain Plutons in the Eastern Margin of Tibetan Plateau [J]. *Geological Science and Technology Information*, 2011, 30(4):1-14.

9. Peng Dong, Guo Jianqiang, Lu Zhiming. Application of Regional Geochemistry and Geophysical Data in Ecological Environment Assessment of Mount Siguniang Area [J]. *Computer Techniques for Geophysical and Geochemical Exploration*, 2001, 23(3):244-249.

10. Peng Dong, Guo Jianqiang, Zhu Lixue. Special Geological Relics in Mount Siguniang Area—Exotic Vegetation under the Background of Special Elements [J]. *Computer Techniques for Geophysical and Geochemical Exploration*, 2002, 24(3):263-267+272.

11. Cao Jun, Luo Zhongyun, Deng Zejin. Discussion on the Cause of Fish-free Condition in Changpinggou, Mount Siguniang, Sichuan [J]. *Acta Geologica Sichuan*, 2004(3):155-158.

12. Zhang Kuanzhong, Li Zhenjiang, Huang Cheng. Granite Emplacement and Mountain Uplift of Mount Siguniang [J]. *Acta Geologica Sichuan*, 2009, 29(S2):99-102.

13. Dai Zongming, et al. U-Pb Dating of Zircons from the Four-Girl Mountain Pluton in the Songpan-Garzê Terrane,

and the Relationship Between the Pluton and the Wenchuan Ms 8.0 Earthquakei of 2008 [J]. *Geology in China*, 2011, 38(3):623-636.

14. Zhang Qidong, Xie Qiang, Yang Han, et al. Study on Water-holding Capacity of Minjiang River Abies Fir Litter and Soil in Mount Siguniang National Nature Reserve [J]. *Sichuan Environment*, 2013, 32(2):42-45.

2.1 Ili: A Corner of the Far West of China

1. Mansur Sabit. *Xinjiang Geography* [M]. Beijing: Beijing Normal University Press, 2012.

2. Lai Hongbo. *Yili History and Geography Collection* [M]. Urumqi: Xinjiang People's Publishing House, 2005.

3. He Ling. *The Silk Road: Ili Studies* [M]. Urumqi: Xinjiang People's Publishing House, 2010.

4. Hu Ruji. *Physical Geography of the Tianshan Mountains in China* [M]. Beijing: China Environmental Science Press, 2004.

5. Wu Xiaocheng. Ili in the Eyes of Foreigners A Hundred Years Ago [J]. *Journal of Yili Normal University (Social Sciences Edition)*, 2011(4):37-43.

6. Luan Mingfu, Wang Fang, Xiong Heigang. Spatio-temporal Distribution of Cultural Sites and Geographic Backgrounds in the Ili River Valley [J]. *Arid Land Geography*, 2017, 40(1): 211-221.

7. Binghua. *Collected Works of Archaeological and Historical Studies of the Western Regions* [M]. Beijing: Renmin University of China Press, 2008.

8. Wu Yiqun. On the Emergence of the Yili City System in the Qing Dynasty [J]. *Journal of Xinjiang University (Philosophy·Humanities and Social Sciences Edition)*, 2009, 37(3):62-68.

9. Tong Keli. Summary of Yili Data and Research [J]. *Journal of Yili Normal University (Social Sciences Edition)*, 2005(1):28-32.

10. Lai Hongbo. On the Development of Multi-Ethnic Immigration in Yili in the Qing Dynasty and Its Historical Significance [J]. *Journal of Yili Normal University (Social Sciences and Chinese Edition)*, 2010(4):33-42.

11. Li Yuanbin. Nation, Country, and Ethnicity: An Interpretation of Uyghurs in Ili in Qing Dynasty from the Perspective of Historical Anthropology (1760-1860) [J]. *Journal of Xinjiang University (Philosophy·Humanities and Social Sciences Edition)*, 2014,42(3):61-67.

2.2 Lop Nur: The Rise and Fall of Loulan during Five Thousand Years

1. Xia Xuncheng. *Lop Nur in China* [M]. Beijing: Science Press, 2007.

2. Lin Meicun. *Looking for the Loulan Kingdom (Illustrated)* [M]. Beijing: Peking University Press, 2009.

3. Wang Binghua. *Experience Archaeology Series·Suspense of Loulan·Jing Jue* [M]. Hangzhou: Zhejiang Literature & Art Publishing House, 2012.

4. A. Herrmann. *Series of Expedition to the Western Regions: Loulan* [M]. Yao Kekun, Translated. Urumqi: Xinjiang

People's Publishing House, 2013.

5. Idilis Abdurensule, Li Wenying. The Great Archaeological Discovery in Search of the Disappeared Civilization-Xiaohe [J]. *Popular Archaeology*, 2014(4):24-32.

6. Hou Can. Brief Report on Investigation and Trial Excavation of Loulan Ancient City Site [J]. *Cultural Relics*, 1988(7):1-22+98.

7. Huang Shengzhang. On the Issue of Loulan City, the First Capital of Loulan Kingdom, and LE City [J]. *Cultural Relics*, 1996(8):62-72.

8. Idris Abdurusul, Liu Guorui, Li Wenying. The Excavation Report of Xiaohe Cemetery [J]. *Frontier Archaeological Research*, 2004(1):338-398.

9. Idilis, et al. Brief Report on the Excavation at Xinjang Lop Nur Xiaohe Cemetery in 2003 [J]. *Cultural Relics*, 2007(10):4-42.

10. Idilis, Liu Guorui, Yi Li, et al. Archaeological Investigation of Xiaohe River Basin in Lop Nur Area [J]. *Frontier Archaeological Research*, 2008(1):371-407.

11. Wang Fubao, Ma Chunmei, Xia Xuncheng, et al. Environmental Evolution in Lop Nur Since Late Pleistocene and Its Response to the Global Chinese [J]. *Quaternary Studies*, 2008, 28 (1):150-153.

12. Fan Zili, Xu Hailiang, Zhang Qingqing, et al. Changes of Tarim River and Evolution of Lop Nur [J]. *Quaternary Research*, 2009, 29 (2):232-240.

13. Song Xiaomei. Lop Nur Area's Environmental Variation during the Different Historical Periods [J]. *Arid Land Geography*, 2009, 32(1):107-111.

14. Lyu Houyuan, Xia Xuncheng, Liu Jiaqi, et al. A Preliminary Study of Chronology for a Newly Discovered Ancient City and Five Archaeological Sites in Lop Nur, China [J]. *Chinese Science Bulletin*, 2010, 55(3):237-245.

15. Li Chunxiang. *The Molecular Genetics Studies on Xiaohe Ancient Remains* [D]. Changchun: Jilin University, 2010.

16. Dong Li. *The Sedimentary Characteristics and Cause Analysis of Yardangs in Lop Nur* [D]. Urumqi: Xinjiang Normal University, 2013.

2.3 Gansu: The More Diverse, the More Beautiful

1. Chinese Vegetation Editorial Committee. *Chinese Vegetation* [M]. Beijing: Science Press, 1980.

2. Chen Ying, Gao Hong. *History and Culture of Gansu* [M]. Lanzhou: Gansu Culture Publishing House, 2011.

3. Shi Zongzheng, Qin Binfeng. *The Hexi Corridor, Gansu I* [M]. Shenyang: Liaoning University Publishing House, 2015.

4. Wang Jin, Wu Xiaojun, Li Chunfang, et al. *General History of Gansu·Contemporary Volume* [M]. Lanzhou: Gansu People's Publishing House, 2013.

5. Zhu Zhongxi. *General History of Gansu·Pre-Qin Volume* [M]. Lanzhou: Gansu People's Publishing House, 2009: 08.

6. Wang Shoukuan. *General History of Gansu·Qin and Han Dynasties* [M]. Lanzhou: Gansu People's Publishing

House, 2009: 08.

7. Zhao Xiangqun. *General History of Gansu·The Wei, Jin and Southern and Northern Dynasties* [M]. Lanzhou: Gansu People's Publishing House, 2009: 08.

8. Yin Weixian, Yang Fuxue, Wei Mingkong. *General History of Gansu·Sui and Tang Five Dynasties Volume* [M]. Lanzhou: Gansu People's Publishing House, 2009: 08.

9. Liu Jianli. *General History of Gansu·Song, Xia, Jin and Yuan Volume* [M]. Lanzhou: Gansu People's Publishing House, 2009: 08.

10. Wu Mu. *General History of Gansu·Ming and Qing Dynasties* [M]. Lanzhou: Gansu People's Publishing House, 2009: 08.

11. Zheng Du. *General Introduction to Chinese Physical Geography* [M]. Beijing: Science Press, 2015.

12. You Lianyuan, Yang Jingchun. *Geomorphology of China* [M]. Beijing: Science Press, 2013.

2.4 Xi'an: Rich and Affluent for a Thousand Years

1. Huang Liuzhu. *General History of Xi'an* [M]. Xi'an: Shaanxi People's Publishing House, 2016.

2. Zhu Shiguang. *Historical Changes and Development of Xi'an* [M]. Xi'an: Xi'an Publishing House, 2003.

3. He Congrong. T*he Ancient Capital of Xi'an* [M]. Beijing: Tsinghua University Press, 2012.

4. Tatsuhiko Seo. *Urban Planning in Chang'an* [M]. Gao Bingbing, Translated. Xi'an: Sanqin Publishing House, 2012.

5. Ishida Kannosuke. *The Spring of Chang'an* [M]. Qian Wanyue, Translated. Beijing: Tsinghua University Press, 2015.

6. Xue Aihua. Edward Hetzel Schafer. *The Golden Peaches of Samarkand: A Study of T'ang Exotics* [M]. Wu Yugui, Translated. Beijing: Social Sciences Academic Press, 2016.

7. Wu Hongqi. *Xi'an Historical Geography Research* [M]. Xi'an: Xi'an Maps Publishing House, 2006:07.

8. Niu Zhigong. On the Issue of Dynasties in the Establishment of the Capital of Xi'an [J]. *Journal of Shaanxi Normal University (Philosophy and Social Sciences Edition)*, 1994(1):114-118.

9. Meng Qingren. The Origin of Qinling Mountains [J]. SCIENTIA SINICA Terrae, 2017(4):34-42.

2.5 Chengdu: Three Thousand Years of Vibrant Traditional Lifestyles

1. General History of Chengdu Compilation Committee. *General History of Chengdu* [M]. Chengdu: Sichuan People's Publishing House, 2011.

2. Editorial Department of Fifty Years of Chengdu. *Fifty Years of Chengdu 1949-1999* [M]. Beijing: China Statistics Press, 1999.

3. Dai Bin. *Chengdu: Reality and Future* [M]. Chengdu: Southwest Jiaotong University Press, 2006.

4. Li Yanli. *Research on the Protection and Utilization Mode of Historic Buildings and Blocks in the Central Urban*

Area of Chengdu City [D]. Chengdu: Southwest Jiaotong University, 2005.

5. Zeng Zhizhong, You Deyan. *Old Chengdu in the View of Educated People* [M]. Chengdu: Sichuan Literature & Art Publishing House, 1999.

6. Xu Shiyu, Zhang Jing, Shen Congle. Go to Chengdu! [J]. *China Business News Weekly*, 2016: 23.

7. Sun Xiaofen. *Immigration in the Early Qing Dynasty Fills in Sichuan—Where Did the Ancestors of Sichuanese Come From* [M]. Chengdu: Sichuan University Press, 1997: 02.

8. He Yimin. *Chinese Urban History* [M]. Chengdu: Sichuan University Press, 1994: 08.

9. Huang Ming, Ma Chunmei, Zhu Cheng. Progress of the Mid-Late Holocene Environmental Archaeology in Chengdu Plain [J]. *Journal of Palaeogeography*, 2017, 19(6):1087-1098.

10. Kong Jun, Zhou Rongjun. The Division of Longmen Mountain and Chengdu Seismic Tectonic Area [J]. *Technology for Earthquake Disaster Prevention*, 2014, 9(1):64-73.

11. Fu Hong, Luo Qian. Analysis of Guild Hall Culture and Immigrant Society—Talking from Guild Hall Building in Luodai Town, Chengdu [J]. *Journal of Southwest Minzu University (Humanities and Social Sciences Edition)*, 2004, 25(4):382-385.

2.6 Fanjing Mountain: A Paradise in the Secular World

1. The Management Office of Fanjing Mountain National Nature Reserve, Guizhou Forestry Department. *Fanjing Mountain Research* [M]. Guiyang: Guizhou People's Publishing House, 1990.

2. Editorial Committee for Scientific Expeditions to Fanjing Mountain in Guizhou. *Scientific Expeditions to Fanjing Mountain in Guizhou* [M]. Beijing: China Environmental Science Press, 1987.

3. Yang Yeqin, et al. *Fanjing Mountain Research: The Wild Ecology of Yunnan Snub-nosed Monkey* [M]. Guiyang: Guizhou Science and Technology Publishing House, 2002.

4. Wang Min, Dai Chuangu, Chen Jianshu, et al. Neoproterozoic Geochronologic Framework of Magmatism in Fanjingshan Area and Its Tectonic Implications [J]. *Geology in China*, 2016, 43(3): 843-856.

5. Wang Ziqiang, Gao Linzhi, Ding Xiaozhong, et al. Tectonic Environment and Evolution Characteristics of the Formation of Metamorphic Basement of "Jiangnan Orogen" [J]. *Geological Review*, 2012, 58(3): 401-443.

6. Li Bosheng, Long Fuyun. The Only Person in the World to Re-recognize the Value of Fanjing Mountain [J]. *Man and the Biosphere*, 2015(3): 6-17.

7. Lyu Yina. *Global Comparative Analysis of the Ecological Environment Evolution of Fanjing Mountain and Its Value of World Heritage* [D]. Guiyang: Guizhou Normal University, 2017.

8. Wu Renxia. *Global Comparative Analysis on Ecosystem Diversity and World Heritage Value in Fanjingshan* [D]. Guiyang: Guizhou Normal University, 2017.

9. Wu Renxia, Xiong Kangning, Rong Li. Characteristics of Spermatophyte Flora of Fanjing Mountain and Its Phytogeographical Significance [J]. *Guihaia*, 2017(10):1348-1354.

10. Zhong Youping, Shu Guoyong, Yan Lihua. Analysis of the Influence of Fanjing Mountain on Local Climate [J]. *Guizhou Meteorology*, 2011, 35(6):25-28.

11. Dai Chuangu, Chen Jianshu, Lu Dingbiao, et al. Wuling Orogeny in Eastern Guizhou and Its Adjacent Regions and Its Geological Significance [J]. *Journal of Geomechanics*, 2010,16(1).

12. Wang Ziqiang, Gao Linzhi, Ding Xiaozhong, et al. Tectonic Environment of the Metamorphosed Basement in the Jiangnan Orogen and Its Evolutional Features [J]. *Geological Review*, 2012(3):401-413.

13. Xiong Yuanxin, Yang Chuandong. *Fanjing Mountain National Nature Reserve, Common Herb Seed Plant Map* [M]. Guiyang: Guizhou Science and Technology Publishing House, 2009: 11.

14. Yang Yeqin, Chen Zhijun. A Brief History of the Ecology of Fanjing Mountain [J]. *Man and the Biosphere*, 2015: 03.

3.1 Henan: Mountain, Water, and Contributions to China

1. Cheng Youwei, Wang Tianjiang. *General History of Henan* [M]. Zhengzhou: Henan People's Publishing House, 2005.

2. Henan Provincial Bureau of Geology and Mineral Resources. *People's Republic of China Ministry of Geology and Mineral Resources Geological Memoirs* [M]. Beijing: Geological Publishing House, 1989.

3. Zou Yilin, Zhang Xiugui, Wang Shouchun. *Chinese Historical and Physical Geography* [M]. Beijing: Science Press, 2013.

4. Zhang Lansheng. *Paleogeography of China* [M]. Beijing: Science Press, 2012.

5. Ren Chongyue. *A Brief History of Central Plains Immigration* [M]. Zhengzhou: Henan People's Publishing House, 2006.

6. Meng Qingren. The Origin of the Qinling Mountains [J]. *SCIENTIA SINICA Terrae*, 2017(4):34-42.

7. Meng Yuanku, Wang Xinwen, Chen Jie. Geological Evidence of the Cenozoic Tectonic Uplifting in Taihang Mountains-Apatite Fission Track Evidence from Well Qincan 1 [J]. *Journal of the Guilin University of Technology*, 2015, 35 (1): 15-28.

8. Cao Xianzhi, Li Sanzhong, Liu Xin, et al. The Intraplate Morphotectonic Inversion along the Eastern Taihang Mountain Fault Zone,North China and Its Mechanism [J]. *Earth Science Frontiers*, 2013, 20(4):88-103.

9. Li Yongwen. *Henan Geography* [M]. Beijing: Beijing Normal University Press, 2010: 04.

10. Jiang Laili, Wu Weiping, et al. Extension after Collision in the Northern Part of the Dabie Mountains—Thrust Nappe Structure [J]. *Chinese Science Bulletin*, 2003(14):1557-1563.

11. Lin Wei, Wang Qingchen, et al. Different Deformation Stages of the Dabieshan Mountains and UHP Rocks Exhumation Mechanism [J]. *Acta Geologica Sinica*, 2003(1):44-54+147.

3.2 Zhejiang: A Province of Invincible Productivity

1. Jin Pusen. *General History of Zhejiang* [M]. Hangzhou: Zhejiang People's Publishing House, 2005.

2. Zhu Lidong. *Concise Zhejiang Geography Course* [M]. Wuhan: Wuhan University Press, 2012.

3. Zhejiang Overview Compilation Committee. *Overview of Zhejiang* [M]. Hangzhou: Zhejiang People's Publishing House, 2011.

4. The Party History Research Office of Zhejiang Provincial Committee of the Communist Party of China, Contemporary Zhejiang Research Institute. *Urban Development of Contemporary Zhejiang (3 volumes)* [M]. Beijing: Contemporary China Publishing House, 2012.

5. The Party History Research Office of Zhejiang Provincial Committee of the Communist Party of China. *Overview of Contemporary Zhejiang* [M]. Beijing: Contemporary China Publishing House, 2012.

6. Editorial Board of Chinese Ocean Culture. *China Ocean Culture·Zhejiang Volume* [M]. Beijing: China Ocean Press, 2016.

7. Wu Xiaobo. *Forty Years of Turmoil: Chinese Enterprises 1978-2018 (All Three Volumes)* [M]. Beijing: CITIC Press, 2017.

8. Chen Qiaoyi, et al. *Geography of Zhejiang Province* [M]. Hangzhou: Zhejiang Education Publishing House, 1985: 09.

9. Ye Wei. *Geography of Zhejiang* [M]. Beijing: Beijing Normal University Press, 2013: 08.

10. Yin Zekai. *Research on the Coastal Defense Settlement System in the Ming Dynasty* [D]. Tianjin: Tianjin University, 2015.

11. Chinese Ocean Culture Editorial Board. *China Ocean Culture·Zhejiang Volume* [M]. Beijing: China Ocean Press, 2016: 07.

3.3 Fujian: The Legend of Pioneers

1. Xu Xiaowang. *General History of Fujian* [M]. Fuzhou: Fujian People's Publishing House, 2006.

2. Fujian Provincial Local Chronicles Compilation Committee. *Fujian Provincial Chronicles·Geography Chronicles* [M]. Beijing: Local Records Publishing House, 2001.

3. Ge Jianxiong. *Chinese Population History* [M]. Shanghai: Fudan University Press, 2005.

4. Ge Jianxiong, et al. *History of Chinese Immigration* [M]. Fuzhou: Fujian People's Publishing House, 1997.

5. Ge Jianxiong. Critical Study of the Facts on the History of Early Immigration in Fujian [J]. *Fudan Journal: Social Sciences Edition*, 1995(3):165-171.

6. Lin Guoping, et al. *History of Fujian Immigration* [M]. Beijing: Local Records Publishing House, 2005.

7. Zhao Zhaobing. *Geography of Fujian Province* [M]. Fuzhou: Fujian People's Publishing House, 1993: 12.

8. Liu Xitao. *Research on Fujian Historical Geography* [M]. Fuzhou: Fujian Education Press, 2017: 07.

9. Lin Kaiming. *Fujian Shipping History (Ancient and Modern Part)* [M]. Beijing: China Communications Press, 1994: 01.

10. Liao Dake. *Fujian Overseas Traffic History* [M]. Fuzhou: Fujian People's Publishing House, 2002: 10.

11. Liang Erping. *The Maritime Silk Road in 2000 Years* [M]. Shanghai: Shanghai Jiaotong University Press, 2016: 11.

3.4 Qingdao: A History of Urban Aesthetics

1. Liu Min. *Value Evaluation as well as Cultural and Ecological Protection and Renewal of Qingdao as A Famous Historical and Cultural City* [D]. Chongqing: Chongqing University, 2004.

2. Li Dongquan, Xu Feipeng. Three Leaps in the History of Qingdao's Urban Development—Also on the Relationship Between Urban Planning and Urban Development [J]. *Urban Planning Forum*, 2003(1): 37-44+95.

3. Chen Li. *Research on Qingdao Architecture in the German Lease Period* [D]. Tianjin: Tianjin University, 2007.

4. Ma Ke. *Research on the Evolution of Qingdao's Urban Planning Thoughts Since the German Occupation Period (1897-1949)* [D]. Xi'an: Xi'an University of Architecture and Technology, 2009.

5. Li Cai. *Research on the History of Qingdao Modern Urban Planning* [D]. Wuhan: Wuhan University of Technology, 2005.

6. Li Baihao, Li Cai. A Study on the History of Modern Urban Planning in Qingdao (1891-1949) [J]. *Urban Planning Forum*, 2005(6):81-86.

7. Li Dongquan. Historical Study and Revelation on the Relationship between Urban Planning and Urban Development of Qingdao in Modern Times [J]. *Journal of Chinese Historical Geography*, 2007, 22(2):125-136.

8. Tan Wenjing. Research on the Characteristics of Qingdao Urban Planning Ideas During the German Occupation [J]. *Science & Technology Information*, 2009(21):164-165.

9. Li Dongquan. *Qingdao Urban Planning and Urban Development Research (1897-1937)* [M]. Beijing: China Architecture & Building Press, 2012.

10. Sheng Lifang, Liang Weifang, Wang Dan, et al. Analysis on Impact of Marine Meteorology Condition on One Advection Sea Fog in Qingdao [J]. *Journal of Ocean University of China (Natural Sciences Edition)*, 2010(6):1-10.

11. Chen Daijun. The Characteristics of Qingdao Urban Planning During the German Occupation [J]. *Science & Technology Vision*, 2012(28):325-326.

12. Qingdao City History and Chronicles Office. *Natural Geography Chronicles of Qingdao City Chronicles · Meteorology Chronicles* [M]. Beijing: Xinhua Publishing House, 1997: 08.

3.5 Jiangnan: A Great Feast of River, Lake, and Sea

1. Hu Xiaoming. On the Four Essentials of Jiangnan Identity [J]. *Journal of East China Normal University (Humanities and Social Sciences Edition)*, 2012, 44(5): 58-64+154.

2. Ge Jianxiong. *History of China's Population Development* [M]. Fuzhou: Fujian People's Publishing House, 1991.

3. Hu Axiang, Li Tianshi, Lu Haiming. *The Six Dynasties·The General History of Nanjing* [M]. Nanjing: Nanjing Press, 2009.

4. Lin Zhengqiu. *Ancient City History of Hangzhou* [M]. Hangzhou: Zhejiang People's Publishing House, 2011.

5. Linda Johnson. *Cities of Jiangnan in Late Imperial China* [M]. Cheng Yinong, Translated. Shanghai: Shanghai People's Publishing House, 2005.

6. Li Bozhong. *Early Industrialization in Jiangnan (1550-1850) (Revised Edition)* [M]. Beijing: China Renmin University Press, 2010.

7. Lai Ping. A Review of Jiankang as the Capital of the Eastern Jin and Southern Dynasties [J]. 2006, 22(2):21-525.

8. Xu Maoming. The Historical Connotation of Jiangnan and Regional Changes [J]. *Historical Review*, 2002(3):52-56.

9. Zhang Huanzhou, Wang Bo. A study of Ancient Town in Jiangnan from the Commonness and Value—Six Ancient Towns in Taihu River Basin [J]. *Journal of Zhejiang University (Science Edition)*, 2007, 34(6):696-701.

10. Qin Dongmei. A Brief Introduction to the Development of Jiangdong Agriculture in the Six Dynasties [J]. *Ancient and Modern Agriculture*, 1998(3):1-9.

11. Gao Yuan. The Influence of the Emergence of Capitalism in the Ming and Qing Dynasties on the Style of Suzhou City [J]. *Beauty and Times (Part)*, 2013(3):74.

12. Chen Ying. The Spatial Awareness and Aesthetics of Suzhou Gardens [J]. *Chinese Garden*, 1994(4):14-15.

13. Suzhou National Architectural Society. *Records of Suzhou Classical Garden Construction* [M]. Beijing: China Architecture & Building Press, 2003.

14. Zhang Huiru. *Research on the Interactive Relationship Between the Water Environment and Urban Development of Hangzhou in the Southern Song Dynasty* [D]. Xi'an: Shaanxi Normal University, 2007.

15. Chen Bixian. *History of the Grand Canal in China* [M]. Beijing: Zhonghua Book Company, 2001.

What Is China?

1. Zheng Du. *Chinese Natural Geography Monographs Series: General Introduction to Chinese Natural Geography* [M]. Beijing: Science Press, 2015.

2. Zou Yilin, Zhang Xiugui, Wang Shouchun. *Chinese Historical and Physical Geography* [M]. Beijing: Science Press, 2013.

3. Hark Elvin. *The Retreat of the Elephants: An Environmental History of China* [M]. Mei Xueqin, Mao Lixia, Wang Yushan, Translated. Nanjing: Jiangsu People's Publishing House, 2014.

4. Ma Libo. Robert B. Marks. *China: An Environmental History* [M]. Guan Yongqiang, Gao Lijie, Translated. Beijing: China Renmin University Press, 2015.

5. Pan Guxi. *Chinese Architecture History (5th Edition)* [M]. Beijing: China Architecture & Building Press, 2004.

6. Xue Fengxuan. *The Evolution of Chinese Cities and Their Civilization* [M]. Beijing: World Publishing Corporation Beijing Publishing Company, 2015.

7. Ge Jianxiong. *Chinese Population History* [M]. Shanghai: Fudan University Press, 2005.

8. Ge Jianxiong. *History of China's Population Development* [M]. Fuzhou: Fujian People's Publishing House, 1991.

9. Patricia Buckley Ebrey. *The Cambridge Illustrated History of China* [M]. Zhao Shiyu, et al, Translated. Jinan: Shandong Pictorial Publishing House, 2001.

10. Joseph Needham. *Science and Civilization in China* [M]. Translation Team of History of Science and Technology in China, Translated. Beijing: Science Press, 2003.

11. Bi Jianheng. *An Overview of the History of Science and Technology in China* [M]. Chengdu: Sichuan Academy of Social Sciences Press, 1985.

12. Jin Qiupeng. *Figures in the History of Science and Technology in China* [M]. Beijing: Science Press, 1998.

13. Yan Wanying, Yin Yinghua. *History of Chinese Agricultural Development* [M]. Tianjin: Tianjin Science and Technology Press, 1992.

14. Du Shiran. *History of Chinese Science and Technology·General History Volume* [M]. Beijing: Science Press, 2003.

15. Zhuang Linde, Zhang Jingxiang. *History of Urban Development and Construction in China* [M]. Nanjing: Southeast University Press, 2002: 08.

Glossary in *Pinyin* and English

Ansha/Shoal, Reef
Arxan/Hot spring
Bandao/Peninsula (Pen.)
Bei/North
Bulag/Spring
Caoyuan/Grassland
Chi/Lake (L.)
Chuan/River (R.)
Co/Lake (L.)
Da/Greater, Grand
Daban/Ridge, Pass
Dalai/Sea, Lake
Dao/Island (L.)
Dian/Shallow lake
Ding/Peak, Top
Dong/East
Feng/Peak, Mount
Fenhongqu/Flood diversion arca
Gang/Harbour, Port
Gaoyuan/Plateau (PlL.)
Gobi/Gobi, Semidesert
Gol/River (R.)
Gonglu/Highway
Gou/Gully
Gou/River (R.), Ditch
Guan/Pass
Hai/Sca
Haixia/Strait(Str.), Channel (Chan.)
He/River (R.)
Hegu/River Valley
Hou/Back
Hu/Lake (L.)

Hudag/Well
Jiang/River (R.)
Jiao/Reef
Jie/Street (St.), Avenue (A.)
Jing/Well
Kou/Mouth
Liedao/lslands (Is.)
Ling/Mountains(Mts.), Ridge
Linqu/Forest region
Lu/Road (Rd.)
Moron/River
Muchang/Pasture
Nan/South
Nei/Inner
Nongchang/Farm
Nur/Lake (L.)
Pao/Lake (L.)
Pendi/Basin (Bsn.)
Pingyuan/Plain (Pln.)
Po/Lake (L.)
Pubu/Waterfall
Qi/Banner (B.)
Qian/Front
Qiao/Bridge
Qiuling/Hills
Qu/Irrigation canal
Qu/River (R.)
Quan/Spring
Qundao/Islands (Is.)
Qunjiao/Reefs
Shadi/Sandy land, Desert
Shamo/Desert (Des.)

Shan/Mountain(Mt.), Mountains (Mts.)
Shandi/Mountain land
Shang/Upper
Shankou/Pass
Shanmai/Mountains (Mts.)
Shi/City
Shui/River (R.)
Shuidao/Channel (Chan.)
Shuiku/Reservoir (Res.)
Tag/Mountain
Tan/Beach
Tan/Pool
Ul/Mountain
Wai/Outer
Wan/Gulf (G.), Bay
Xi/West
Xia/Lower
Xi/Stream, Brook
Xia/Gorge,Valley
Xian/County (Co.)
Xueshan/Snowberg
Yan/Rock, Crag
Yanhu/Salt lake
You/Right
Yu/lsland (I.)
Yunhe/Canal
Zangbo/River
Zhaoze/Swamp, Marsh
Zhong/Central, Middle
Zuo/Left
Zoulang/Corridor

HI, I'M CHINA

by

Institute for Planets and The China Society on Tibetan Plateau

First English Edition 2025

By China Pictorial Press Co., Ltd.

CHINA INTERNATIONAL COMMUNICATIONS GROUP

Copyright © China Pictorial Press Co., Ltd.

All rights reserved.

No part of this publication may be reproduced, stored in a retrieval system, or transmitted in any form or by any means, electronic, mechanical, photocopying, recording, or otherwise, without the prior written permission of China Pictorial Press Co., Ltd., except for the inclusion of brief quotations in an acknowledged review.

Address: 33 Chegongzhuang Xilu, Haidian District, Beijing, 100048, China

ISBN 978-7-5146-2126-6